Lip Reading

Maureen Lipman

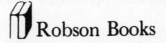

Robson Books

First published in Great Britain in 1999 by Robson Books,
10 Blenheim Court, Brewery Road, London N7 9NT

A member of the Chrysalis Group plc

British Library Cataloguing in Publication Data
A catalogue record for this title is available from the British
Library

ISBN 1–86105–289–8

Typeset by FSH Ltd., London
Printed and bound in Great Britain by Butler & Tanner Ltd.,
London and Frome

Lip Reading

I dedicate this book to Zelma, Mr Crockard, Mr Bradford, Graham Douglas and the memory of Margaret Beth Corey who went from freak to *frummer* and left early to sort out the Lord

Contents

Contents

Persona Non Gratis

Jack: Husband, writer, lover, pal. A man whose idea of a good night out is staying in. Ogden Nash got it right:
> He tells you when you've got on too
> much lipstick
> And helps you with your girdle when your
> hips stick.

Amy: Daughter and soulmate. Writer and ditherer. Orange hair. Aged 25 or 10, depending on amount of responsibility demanded.

Adam: Son, Classics graduate, Cambridge. Aged 23. He's put me under oath not to mention him again.

Zelma: Mother, ageless. She's put me under oath to mention her as much as possible.

Anastasia Lipman: Niece. Two law degrees, bilingual, my dresser for *Oklahoma!*

Jacquie: Secretary, assistant, factotum mensch. (Without her this book would be scrawled on the back of 14,000 envelopes.)

Carmela: Housekeeper, assistant, factotum, green-fingered mensch.

Tony Porter: The finest reflexologist in the Western Hemisphere. From my feet to your ears.

Hugh Jackman: Adorable Aussie actor, played Curly in *Oklahoma!* – stayed one night chez Rosenthal in order to catch dawn Luton flight. Maureen, Zelma and Amy all up to see him off at 4.30 a.m. in mascara and blusher.

Starter

My cigarette packet kindly informs me that it will kill me if I consume its contents. My nightdress tells me what will happen to my skin (my largest organ) if I combust in it. Peanuts may asphyxiate me, eggs will clog up my passages, steak will make me moo, sugar will rot my teeth, fluoride will prevent them rotting but slowly poison the rest of me.

If I ride a bicycle without a mask I'll be polluted, if I swim in the sea I'll be covered in effluence, if I sunbathe I will look healthy but actually will be suffering from melanoma and prematurely aged skin. If I exercise I will live for a long time but arthritic joints will render me immobile. If I cook in aluminium pans I will lose my marbles, if acid rain hits my tongue it may burn through it. Margarine contains sump oil, butter will sit on my heart. I must eat fibre in order to excrete but not cereal because it may have been genetically interfered with. Carrots will make my hair see in the dark, spinach will enable me to tear up telephone books. I should drink my own urine and juice my own pomegranites and organic food is worth the extra and tomatoes and chocolate are acidic and kippers come back at you and wheat blows you up and as for milk – here's what the label said on a piece of Tesco's Brie de Meaux: 'Made using unpasteurised milk which will contain naturally occurring bacteria. These may be harmful to the health of pregnant women, children, the elderly and anyone with a low resistance to infection. People in these groups should not eat this product.' This was a warning on a piece of cheese! And *I* bought it!

What can I do that is danger free? Well, I suppose I can pick up a book – not too heavy, it may drop on my foot – and read.

I have no greater pleasure in life than reading. It is the ultimate trip. I read, I'm afraid, whilst eating breakfast, dinner and watching

1

television. I read in the loo. A fact I'm reminded of every time I visit a bookshop and immediately need the loo. I have three books on the go, and though I find plays more difficult to read, I usually have a couple of must-reads there as well.

I have, alas, reached the stage where I can read a book until three-quarters of the way through before realising I've already read it. I read quickly, because if I don't, I'll have forgotten by the middle who the characters were in the beginning.

I read *The Week, The Big Issue, Good Housekeeping,* the *Telegraph,* the *Guardian* on holiday, the Sundays, the *Jewish Chronicle* and the *Hampstead and Highgate Express.* I read until 1.30 in the morning. I would have hours more in my day if I trod on my spectacles.

A real guilt trip is to go to bed in the afternoon with a new Carol Shields or an old George Eliot. This easily obtainable pipe-dream is completely out of my reach. I'll never do it. I'd feel easier in my mind if the book was a lover. In my dreams.

So for you who will read *Lip Reading* in 24 hours, and for you who will read one chapter every time you visit the bathroom, and for you who've bought it for your mother (who loved the commercials) and are just sneaking a look before you wrap it, and for you who will order it from the library because they have no intention of stocking it and for you who will unwrap it on your birthday and say, 'Oh, *not* the new Anita Brookner then?' and for first-time readers and faithful readers and bath-time readers and flight-time readers and recovery-ward readers, I just want to say, 'There are other things in life besides bloody reading!'

This product is guaranteed free from artificial insinuations and contains no sweeteners for critics or flavour of the month enhancers. Store in a warm, dry place and consume within three years of opening. To open, grasp bottom right hand corner firmly, lift, turn and enjoy contents. If you are not entirely satisfied with this product please keep it to yourself.

Main Course

Part I

Author Lines Empty Nest

Festive Run-Down

The approach of the festive season makes me think of one thing only. I don't mean turkey or presents or Chanukah candles or what do I buy the man who doesn't want anything?

I really mean my plans – my perfect arrangements – and how badly I will screw them up. For I'm a cock-eyed idealist. I do want a soft blend of ritual traditionalism with friends and family. I do want old friends to get on with new friends and my kids to be at home rather than at their friends' houses and people to pop in and gas coal log effect fires to crackle and not to have to use my formidable acting skills when unwrapping that necklace. (I'm one of the few people I know who really would like a bedjacket and a couple of satsumas.)

Late last summer, when the sun was beating down in a way I associate with Bridlington and a bucket of tiddlers, I tried to organise a 'do' – a nice picnic on Hampstead Heath. The idea was that my son Adam and his girlfriend, her sister and my daughter Amy and husband Jack and I and anyone else who had a plastic plate should turn up at Kenwood House on the Heath (or as Amy used unforgettably to call it, Hampstead Underneath).

'We could just have it in the garden,' said Jack, always slow to rally round a charred chicken leg in an uncomfortable neck of the woods. 'Save shlepping all that . . . stuff . . .'

'No. That's not the point. We have to go somewhere, then the phone won't ring all the time. The kids will talk to us and so will their friends. We'll discuss issues.' His pained face was beginning to get up my nose. 'It'll be lovely.'

Being a mixture of sloth and spendthrift, I spent an obscene amount of money in the delicatessen (instead of buttering and egging a sliced white loaf like my mother would have done, pressing hard down on each sandwich with the heel of her hand) on artichokes in brine, chicken kebabs, curried this, pesto'd that, and bottles of sparkly stuffs inundated with ginsengy bits to make you frisky at two quid a gulp.

Amy and I packed the food into boxes, put rugs and sheets into bags and stacked the coolbox with wine and ice while Jack peered gloomily at the darkening skies and Adam chose the music. We set off in two cars to pick up their friends. As we left the house, Amy caught sight of her brother and said, 'He's got my Frisbee!'

'So?' I said. 'What's wrong with that? We'll have a game.'

'Yes, but he didn't ask me. It's mine.'

'You cannot be serious! I mean . . .'

'Well! He should have asked me, that's all. Neil and I play with that Frisbee!'

She could have been serious, she could have been joking. With my age and experience I should have plumped for the latter. Instead, settling into an ancient agenda, I lost my rag completely and we began to banshee each other.

'And it's *my* coolbox!' I yelled. 'And *my* rug and *my* bottle opener, for God's sake!' She, by now, was quite calm and accused me (correctly) of overreacting.

By the time we reached the Heath we were both 'on simmer'. 'I'll drop you off and you can have the bloody picnic without me,' I muttered. She suggested in mature fashion that it just might look better all round if we pretended it had never happened.

She got out with the bags. As I reversed the car, I caught sight of her blithely telling all and sundry about the row.

Later, she told me she had seriously thought that I was going to run her over. She said I looked like a Mafia hitman. I felt like hiring one. Instead, we walked grimly on to the Heath where we laid out our rugs and filled our plates and glasses with selections of picnic fare.

'Who hasn't got potato salad?' I cried, dolloping out stuff from plastic containers on to individual plates. The atmosphere improved and I smiled rather smugly at Jack. 'See. It can be done.'

Quite suddenly, instead of eight, we were nine. A large, brown-clad man stood beside us and informed us, pleasantly but with regret, that the gates closed in ten minutes, so would we move on. We were frozen in mid-spoon.

'Gates?' I said incredulously. 'This is Hampstead Heath! It covers 791 acres! What bloody gates?'

Once again I was in the wrong. We were still within the perimeter of Kenwood House and would need to walk much further to reach public property.

Have you ever tried replacing eight individual portions of potato salad, eight half-eaten kebabs, eight half-drunk Sauvignons and a sliced loaf into their respective receptacles whilst packing rugs, reboxing a cream gâteau, cursing bureaucracy and avoiding your husband's gaze? Well, don't. Trust me, it's enough that one of us has done it, for all of mankind.

Biblically, we trudged across the tundra in search of fresh watering holes as night fell and the Heath emptied of all but the most intrepid joggers. By the time we recamped the food was in clumps and Jack was sitting on a bench apart from us. When he wasn't enquiring who said what, he was up and down like an Austrian blind, asking anyone who passed us the shortest way back to the main road.

Whichever way we took, it was the longest. Like a travelling production of *The Inn of the Sixth Happiness*, we trudged on towards the glorious sound of traffic on tarmac. Not speaking to each other and apparently carrying more than we'd started out with, we fetched up a mile from where we'd parked. There were no taxis and finally all eight of us plus luggage clambered on to a pay-as-you-enter bus – two stops only.

So when it crosses my mind to barbecue a turkey for fifteen on Christmas Eve or make Swedish meatballs for twenty on Boxing Day or do songsheets with specially written words to see the New Year in – will somebody please remind me that the best-laid plans of mice and Maureen are the ones which entail booking a B&B in Barbados. For two.

Broody

I've taken to smiling gormlessly at prams as they go past me in the park. Even empty prams. The cafés I frequent with girlfriends when I've walked enough mileage to earn my cappuccino are full of tiny quilted Georges and Olivias and Megans who engage me in badinage across the table-tops and turn me from a dignified bespectacled matron with imperceptible pewter roots into a barmy, burbling grandma who's taken leave of her senses.

'Helloooo!' I gurgle. 'Helloooo! Who's a gorgeous beautiful chap?' and, just to confirm the to *her* parents my insanity, add, 'Aren't you? Adorable! Yes, you are! Yes, you are!'

The thing is they nearly always respond, which can't be said to be true of all the strangers I accost in cafés. Like my mother before me, babies seem to find my antics amusing. I remember being hugely embarrassed when my mother would start singing 'When You Wish Upon A Star' to miniature people whose life span could be measured in hours. 'Mother, do you *have* to?' I would mutter. Similarly, my daughter, in her mid-twenties, gets positively fretful when I start my baby-wooing antics. 'You like them better than you do me,' she's been known to mutter, only half-jokingly. My remonstrations sound unconvincing even to my ears. What can I say? 'But, darling, they just see me – they don't see through me.'

The truth is babies are the perfect audience. Given that they are not hungry, thirsty, exhausted or bored, they will laugh at you, even if you're about as funny as Ann Widdecombe, and you don't have to use your most sophisticated material.

Take Max, for example. Max was 'baby Molly' in a TV film I was in. Called out on a draughty location at some unholy hour in an echoing college hall in Bushey, he behaved like a prince from dawn till dusk (and I don't mean a real prince – he didn't clench his gums, put one hand behind his back or bag a single 'grice' not once – I mean a real proper fictional prince with manners and tights and a happy ending). Max was a 'sweetpea' baby with a plump pixie face and a temperament so sunny he bronzed you just to look at him. He was only a few months old and showed no objections to being dressed up in a pink dress and frothy tights and bounced about from one pair of luvvie hands to another while people screamed 'Turnover! Sound running – action!' seven or eight times at a stretch. What's more, he was a fantastic mimic! Whatever gobbledegook I tried on him, he did it right back. I smacked my lips and said 'Boo!' He smacked his and said 'Boo!' I cackled – he cackled. I blew a raspberry, he blew two. It was one of the most rewarding episodes of my entire life. We had total rapport, infant and thespian. If that child doesn't win a Baby BAFTA and a year's supply of Rose-Hip Syrup, then my name is not an anagram of 'pure animal men' and William Hague is an hairy man.

Then again, another occasion found me lunching alfresco in St John's Wood where I wittingly became nanny/security guard to baby Sam, whose parents were lunching at a table opposite. Baby Sam was a kind of Swampy of the infant world. Having learned to crawl, he was damned if he was going to remain sedentary in the company of a Fisher Price dog in three primary colours when there was DIRT and FILTH and TRAFFIC just a few metres down the pavement. My dears, my pine nuts and pesto with goats cheese on rocket salad barely grazed my lips – the child was an escapologist and the parents seemed content to trust him to have the good sense to return to his table after taking a turn around the pavements.

Not so me. I was on the edge of my seat with my thighs in the sprint position throughout the whole meal and though I waited till the last possible second before his head seemed to me to be heading firmly for the concrete, I couldn't help hurtling forward at least three or four times to retrieve him. His parents were very nice about it in that they didn't actually get cross with me for saving Sam's young life on a fairly regular basis. They implied that Sam was a bit of a character and his dad whirled him round his head a few times to prove it was true. Fair enough, Sam really did seem to enjoy defying gravity and death, but I had to be taken home and put to bed with a copy of *Miffy the Rabbit* and a 4" x 6" snap of my godchildren.

It seems the merest flash since Jack and I were gingerly bringing home our own babies from the maternity wards. We were terrified of every bump in the road, every overtaking car – of bathing them, of burping them, of spending an evening away from them. It's hard to believe those bundles are the same looming masses of popping hormones who are now prone to pat us on the head and say, 'Don't wait up. We're just going out to get rat-arsed.'

Possibly now that my brood has trashed the nest, the answer leads me clearly in the direction of a lead. Not one in the West End with billing on the left but one which extends outwards with a small sturdy canine on the other end. I only just resisted a divine beagle puppy the other week – Amy said he looked like an animated sock – but I realised just in time that it wasn't fair to Jack to have two of us to look after when the show is over.

So. I've watered my fuchsias and patted potted petunia plugs into a grow bag. They're all blooming. Everybody seems to be managing fine without me. As Les Dawson used to say, 'Me dad used to breed ferrets, until he realised they could do it perfectly well on their own.'

The Parting of Names

As we speak, someone tired, sweaty and fulfilled, let's say an Emma, is naming her 45-minute-old baby, Jack. 'It's a real man's name,' she is saying mistily, and, 'I don't know why we thought of it – it just was always going to be Jack if it was a boy.'

'They're calling him Jack,' her mother, Heather, is saying down the phone to her friend, Bernice. 'Jack Albert...Yes, well, it's modern. You know, the young people nowadays, they like all the old-fangled names...Well, of course – I know – but that was five years ago! Five years ago *everyone* was calling them Dominic!'

And so it goes on. A generation of Maisies and Alfreds, rejecting the names of peers and parents, spawn a generation of Brendas and Bobs from whom issue a plethora of Sheilas and Geoffreys, who in turn beget Samanthas and Tristrams, whose trousers are bursting to produce Maisies and Alfreds.

Each of us believes we are being utterly original. Each of us is wrong, a fact only proven on day one at school when, child so carefully named after Louisa May Alcott's most precious of characters, shares her coat hooks with Amy D, Amy S, Amy H-G and Amy Polyandropulous.

Which is not to say that I would extol the originality of the ex-Mrs Geldof. Peaches Fifi Trixibelle Rosenthal would never have been high on my list, nor would I have embarrassed my progeny any more than I already have by labelling her 'Rose' 'China' or 'Second-Hand'. I mean, the child wants to be identifiable but not so's the entire class keels over every time the register is read out. They want to know the derivation of their name, but not if it's a hallucinogenic drug their parents were on or a high-pitched sound their father always made during foreplay.

As always, fashion has a great deal to answer for in that, on the

11

whole, fashion suits the original wearer, and by the time it has filtered down to bargain basement, it fits and suits no-one, least of all the buyer.

Fashion also dictates linguistics and you'd be hard pressed to find anyone answering to the name of the nineteenth century's most popular nomenclature. Oh, no. Very few Fannys at your modern comprehensives these days. That ended for ever, I suppose, the day Johnny Craddock, husband of the famous TV chef Fanny, said, live on camera, '...and I hope all your tarts come up like Fanny's.'

People don't change their names co much as they did earlier in the century to avoid being classified. As a child I knew well that Danny Kaye was David Kaminski, Tony Curtis was Bernie Schwartz and Issur Danielovitch Demske changed to Isidore Demsky before finally calling himself Kirk Douglas. I knew this because at home we were quietly proud of it, even though it meant a kind of betrayal. Our guys were losing to win. Or was it the other way round? Meryl Streep hasn't been held back by a name which, according to Barry Humphries, sounds like a gynaecological complaint, nor Uma Thurman by one which sounds like a storage heater.

Just think of the explanation required one day for all those Kylies and Stings and Hayleys, for heaven's sake! 'Well, it doesn't mean anything, darling – it's from Hayley Mills. Well, she's an actress and her mother named her after her own maiden name. No, she was a writer, actually...Oh, shut up and be thankful I didn't call you Sigourney like your father wanted...'

I am Maureen because my Uncle Louis liked the film star Maureen O'Hara. Fine. The fact that a small sallow baby born in Hull was unlikely to grow up into a flame-haired temptress with flashing green eyes and a cleavage the size of Galway was neither here nor there. Maureen I became. Or *Marine* on the other side of the Atlantic. Also no-one in our house could foresee that since my father's name was Maurice I would be constantly called, with mounting frustration, 'Mauri-Morry-Maureen!'

I longed for a heroine's name. With a 'y' on the end. 'Vicky at St Clair's', 'Nicky, New Girl', 'Ginny Saves St Kilda's'. Somehow, 'Maureen Pulls It Off' sounds more like I got a great bargain in the sales.

My class of '65 was full of Paulines and Valeries and Marilyns and Janets and Susans and Lindas. These post-war names gave us a sell-by date as clear as the one on a Sainsbury's corner yoghurt. And they are just about to make a comeback, it seems to me, in my role as Witch of the North, so watch this space. Or better still, the birth lists at the back of *The Times* and the *Telegraph*. The circle perpetuates.

When my friend Sally became pregnant, her partner Manuel declared, 'If it is a man baby, we call him Manuel, and if it is a woman baby, we call him Manuela,' which certainly solves the *Pan Book of Boys' Names* and the *Pan Book of Girls' Names* nightly saga.

God, if I had a 5p and a marzipan fruit-cake for every thumb mark on those two tattered paperbacks, I'd be a richer and fatter woman.

It seems to me that Henrietta, Geraldine, Edwina and, unkindest of all, Nigella, emerged in direct response to parental expectation of a MALE child. Never mind thinking of something suitable for a small bundle of femininity – just stick an 'ella' on the end. Or an 'ina' or an 'etta'. You don't agree? Then why doesn't it work the other way round? Show me a Fionaron or an Emmatom for every Samantha and Georgina and I'll show you a chauvinistic society in no hurry to advance. Then there are the mysterious 'unisex' ones, rather like the hairdressers which call themselves by that term, but are clearly barber shops with a Wella concession. These include Evelyn, Sydney, Hilary, Jocelyn and, in the US, Marion, the original first name of the aggressively macho John Wayne. I guess it toughened you up, rather like the message in that great song, 'A Boy Named Sue'.

The big trick is to call your baby by a proper name, either biblical, Shakespearean or of historical origin. It may look momentarily dull on a plastic wristband next to cots of squalling Amber Jades but they won't half thank you for it when they are Uncle David and Auntie Rachel instead of Auntie Kimberley and Uncle Keanu.

Having said this, of course, I should steer clear of Romeo, Bottom or Shylock, because it's awfully hard to be identified with a lover, an ass or a money-lender when you weigh six pounds and the only thing you've ever seen is a nipple.

Likewise, diminutives. You can rant on all you like about how your child is going to be Richard not Dick and Alexander not Alex and Beverley not Bev, but when the little guy with the big name gets to big school, his larger mates will call him what they jolly well please, and frankly you should thank your lucky stars it's Dick and not Dick'ead.

As I write, there are hundreds of tiny continents packing their tuck-boxes into their satchels as I write. Little India's mum is picking up little China and little Savanna in the Cherokee, then later it all gets a bit more suburban back at little Chelsea's birthday sleep over, with Paris, Florence and Roma hurrying to the same destination. No sign of a truculent Grimsby or a pugnacious Pontefract yet, but I wouldn't hold your breath. Spicing up the trend for naming by atlas are baby Brooklyn Beckham and Phoenix Chi – it's lucky the girls weren't touring in Middle Wallop when the earth moved with such consequence.

'What's the most famous fact about Winston Churchill?' goes the joke. Answer: 'He was the last white man to be called Winston.' Interesting, though, isn't it? After the war the British threw out the man and his name, wanting no reminders of the years of deprivation, in spite of the victory. But to those coming into the country, the new life and the victory were personified by the man. Not too many Maggies and Johns around but watch out for a millennium crop of seven-pound unisex Blairs.

Finally, here's something which has always puzzled me about calendar names. They only apply to the summer months. I know that most conception is done in the winter months when the night draws in and expectations rise, but is that the only reason why April, May, June, Julie and Augusta book their places in the school register and October, December and February don't? And wherefore Dawn and not Dusk?

As a kid I often amused myself by drawing cartoons of girls called Marian Haste, Jacqueline Hyde, Edna Clouds and, favourite of all, Sheila Blige. Recently, on Radio 4's *Home Truths*, I heard the story of a 21st son, desperately named Finisher Coronation Kingshill. Apparently there was a 22nd child. For those of you old enough to remember the term, wouldn't Johnny have been appropriate?

Cambridge Blues

I found myself in Cambridge – seat of learning, cradle of academia, world centre for spy recruitment and supplier of satirists to the sixties – filming Jack's BBC play, at that time titled *Eskimo Day*, subject to the author finding something he liked better, which he did roughly twice a day. It was about Cambridge candidates going for their interviews. Actually, it was about parents 'letting go' of their kids. You might say there were parallels in my life.

We'd been filming for a week and the sun was shining down heartlessly on the stone portals of historic Queens' College, the birds were singing on the ancient spires and the punts were punting smoothly along the glassy Cam river . . . This was not good news for the cast and crew of 'Nice Here Inuit' or whatever they were calling it that day.

Then it rained. All day long. Great sad, dreary, endless shards of rain fell on filmmakers and actors as we huddled together in damp clumps. Anoraks balanced on the shoulders of our real anoraks, which we couldn't get wet, large umbrellas were held high by weak-wristed wardrobe assistants, and acting shoes were held in hands until the last minute to replace wet loafers. David Ross and I played the working-class parents of Neil (Ben Sandiford) and over and over the three of us walked the 25 yards up to the approach to Queens' College with suitable trepidation on our faces.

Camera operator:	'Sorry, we'll have to go again – water spots on the lens.'
Sound operator:	'One more time, please – there was a plane.'
1st Assistant:	'First positions, please, last time now. Very good, actors! Passers-by, would you *please* not look at the camera!'

'Does anyone want to see anything before we go again?' shouts the 1st Assistant. 'Yes,' chunters one of the largest riggers. 'Me muvver!'

It is very rare for 'one more time' to be called because an *actor* is dissatisfied. We know our place in the pecking order. First in the lunch queue – last in the decision-making process. Rest of the time, keep your head down. That's OK. Gives us more gossiping time.

The prop men hosed down the streets with industrial pipes, to make the ground match up with previously filmed rainsodden ground, and the passers-by looked mystified as gallons of water poured out for reasons to which they were not privy.

The best part of working away from home is *not* working. A day off is a heady mixture of irresponsibility, mischief and idleness. David Ross and I, being inveterate shoppers, ignored the medieval splendours on offer for the entirely evil pleasures of Marks & Spencer. Several shirts and jackets later, guilt entirely assuaged by token socks for our other halves, we shared a plate-sized amaretto cake for brunch and headed off for the cinema. There were only five people watching *While You Were Sleeping* that day and two of them were us. I began to snuffle ten minutes into this Cinderella saga and soaked David's hanky to a pulp. He just sniffed, and pretended not to.

A damp couple of hours later, we left. It was 3.55pm and I couldn't help noticing that *The Bridges of Madison County* was beginning in Cinema B at four o'clock. He bought the tickets, I bought the popcorn and we lurched back in. It would end in tears. It did. I, who had read the book in a two-hour sitting and been appalled by its tacky tricksiness, was enchanted by Eastwood and Streep to the extent that my tears became a medical complaint and my body weight plummeted. I hadn't had such a good time since Bambi's mother popped her clogs.

Cambridge reminds me, subtly, of Stratford-on-Avon. It has a slight attitude problem. As in, 'What we have here is eternal. Don't like it? Don't come again. Next!' Reasonable enough if you look at it from their point of view. Why would they want 70-odd rogues and vagabonds queuing up for pasta with pesto on plastic plates from a van in the middle of Jesus Green? Take a film crew to a verdant hamlet in Connemara with a post office, a blacksmiths and a pub called The Skillet and Shillelagh and you'll be welcomed with open cash registers. This is not quite so true of historic, international centres of knowledge with one-way traffic systems. Here, mostly you just get right up their patrician noses. A violent little lady in Country Casuals asked me what was going on as we filmed by a churchyard. 'It's a TV play,' I whispered. 'What's it about?' she insisted. 'Erm...Cambridge,' I replied. 'Well,' she said huffily, 'I've never seen such a bunch of scruffs in all my life!'

One day I wandered on to the set before my own scenes were due to be shot. It was a breathtaking picture – actors Tom Wilkinson and David Ross, playing parents of interviewees, crossed the famous Mathematical Bridge into Queens' College, out-vying each other to extol the brilliance of their offspring. Two extras placed in punts on either side of the bridge were to glide past on 'Action'. The day was bright and the air heavy with expectation as the camera prepared to roll towards the bridge on specially laid steel tracks.

It was at this point that a heartfelt cry rent the air, shattering the fragile peace. 'For Christ's sake!' bellowed the director. 'Where's the fucking punt?' It was perfect. I firmly believed we might have finally found our title.

Later on in the day, leaning up against the carved niches in the entrance to Queens', there was a lull in the shooting as we waited for clouds to cover the sun. David and I decided to launch into an improvised busking session, using lips for double bass, blown cheeks for trumpets, sibilant teeth for cymbals. Obviously impressed, the crew chucked a twopence piece at our feet. Mere seconds later, the world's most malicious pigeon crapped on my head. It received a standing ovation from the crew. Do you remember the joke about the circus assistant whose job was to clean up the elephant droppings. One day he's fired. Distraught, he seeks similar employment elsewhere. 'Have you thought of working in another kind of job – in an office or a restaurant?' 'What,' says the man, 'and give up show business?'

Back to the hotel, a large Campari and soda, my one cigarette of the day and Chinese food to follow. There are many reasons why I became an actress. These have been several of them. Besides, I was never Cambridge material.

A Cat's Life

The cat was not well. Something to do with her enzymes. And her great age, of course. I bought her as a sop for my daughter when her father and I ruined her life by producing a baby brother. The ruinous boy was now nineteen and sleeping through his gap year. The cat was the same age and sleeping through the gap where her teeth used to be.

I've chronicled in the past the lengths Pushkin would go to to reduce a new three-piece suite or an old antique love-seat to a macramé trimmed with Shredded Wheat version. She had decimated seven such seating arrangements and was lively enough still to contemplate the eighth, ninth and now, the tenth, which had just arrived in plastic coverings and would stay in plastic coverings until I could find the right shade of fashionable 'throws' (or, as my mother would say, car-rugs) to protect them from her 'Streisand lookalike' nails.

Like all great British comediennes, Pushkin was 'a character' in her twilight years. She was eccentric. She always loathed competition; the sight of a neighbourly cat keen for a meaningful relationship, would elicit arching, hissing, thickening of tail and maidenly racing around the walls.

She always eschewed sex in any shape or form and since I read what a tom's spiked tackle does to the female's most intimate parts, I can't say I blame her. She obviously did it once, got herself into trouble, gave birth to the progeny of the painful union, and shut up shop.

Still, whatever turns you on, I suppose... Take my friend Lizzy's dog, Ozzie, the wire-haired fox terrier. Nothing special, character-wise; pretty as a picture with his bouclé cream and tan fur, his alert stance – as though leaning into strong gusts from the

18

coast of Dover – and, not to put too fine a point on it, his slightly suspect IQ. In one respect, though, he was utterly unique, in that although his idea of foreplay may have involved rump sniffing on Hampstead Heath, his true sexual gratification came entirely from close personal contact with a computer printer.

I swear, you had to see it to believe it. A perfectly normal canine went barking mad with lust when Lizzy pressed the printer. Yes, at the first chattering and juddering vibration, he pricked up his ears, fastened himself to the table leg, jerked convulsively, and uttered the strangest set of high-pitched moans, howls and whimpers you've ever heard.

I could live with Ozzie because, like Pushkin, he made me laugh. Although I remained stony-faced, mostly, when Pushkin slept on my head or tapped me on the forehead monotonously until I woke up dreaming I was drowning in a bale of hay. Nor did I smile when she hooked one small claw into my lip. I was known to yell 'Gerroff, you perfidious wart!' from the depths of Nod.

Also, Pushkin's eating habits suddenly went awry. She refused to eat the same food twice. In other words, halfway through a mouth-watering tin of Whiskas Turkey & Giblet, she was desperate for Tuna & Pilchard. This happened a mere seven or eight times a day and Jack was a slave to her whims. When the trash-can was filled with enriched jelly, Jack raced up the road to Toffs, Muswell Hill's prize-winning fish shop, and had a haddock cutlet specially grilled for her. This tabby was no cheap date.

In spite of this, she became painfully thin. I used to be able to brush her with a special bendy brush I bought at the Ideal Home Exhibition. For myself. Later, the feeling of the bristles on her protruding bones became too hard to bear. Actually she had been more sprightly since Mr Paradise, the vet, operated on her thyroid. So sprightly, in fact, that Lizzy swore that we were given back a new cat. But no-one could convince us that Pushkin's nature could be reproduced. The baleful looks when she was removed from the hairy mess which used to be your best coat; the unforgiving back she presented when you returned from a trip she wasn't invited to. Pure venom. Pure Pushkin.

Still, demanding cat demanding food, wouldn't eat, looked thin...so, out comes the cage and in went the cat, fighting me one remaining tooth and claw, pitiful croak emanating. 'S'all right, darling,' I cooed as we sped along the Barnet road towards the vet's surgery. 'You'll soon be better, I promise.'

She was very quiet in the waiting room, cowed by the smell of a four-month-old wolfhound awaiting its injections. Next to me a lady with a perforated cardboard box. I was fearing snake so I had to know. 'Oh, it's my son's rabbit,' she said abstractedly. 'She's got awful diarrhoea...' I clucked sympathetically, recalling something I'd heard on the radio about rabbits having only 24 hours to live once they'd contracted diarrhoea. I decided to keep quiet. Suddenly, a head and a white-coated arm popped round the door clutching a sheaf of notes.

'Pushkin Rosenthal?' said the vet, and I was overcome with remorse at giving her a name which seemed like a good idea nineteen years before but which now made her sound like a refusenik with literary pretensions. It seemed that all Jack had to do was crumble a pill into the food she refused, chase her round the house with a syringe and a can of liquid food or, inevitably and finally, force open her mouth, throw the pill in and tap her on the nose to make her swallow.

Notice I said *Jack* had to crumble, syringe and tap? I was more stroking and brushing. He was more basic. More life-prolonging. We had almost got used to the idea of letting go of our two-legged dependents, but would a time ever come when we'd ever get used to letting go of the four-legged one?

Four Across, Two Down

Finding ourselves with a yawning April gap, we decided, like Webster's Dictionary, to get Morocco bound. We stayed in the luxury of one of those hideaway hotels which you only hear about from the mouths of sybaritic friends or glimpse on labels on the kind of luggage which has been hand stitched from the skins of infant vicuna by sight-impaired Sisters of Mercy in a Tajikistan souk.

Once there, you sleep in individual stone cottages, each with its own scented sandalwood fire for the evening chill, and take breakfast on the individual frangipani-fringed balcony in the morning sun. We booked for a fraughtnight and friends, as usual, on hearing of our plans, rang to enquire of our dates and destinations then immediately booked different dates elsewhere. Our reputation as holiday 'mavens'* goes before us.

It goes without saying that on the whole they were not wrong. It had not rained in this part of Morocco for years. Suffice to say, it has now. At some stage, therefore, we moved onward to Marbella where the drought has been severe for two years. It isn't any more. We thought about hiring ourselves out as sort of bespectacled human twigs for water-divining purposes.

Actually we had tremendous fun in Morocco, although perhaps not as much as the famed English theatrical luminary who, describing his holiday in the guest book, wrote, 'The perfect is always reassuring.' Most of the fun came via the world's most fabulous couple who travelled to the hotel with us in a van from Agadir Airport. Now, you know there is a God when there are only

---

* Yiddish for 'specialists, and then some!' It's worth knowing.

ten people in a hotel and two of them turn out to be soulmates. The four of us gorged ourselves with laughter as we sat in our sun loungers, occasionally attempting heart failure in the inexplicably unheated swimming pool. The chaps raced each other through faxed copies (no newspapers – hotel too posh) of the *Telegraph* crossword and the ladies shared Jane Austen's unputdownable *Persuasion* – a real holiday vest ripper – and traded indiscretions.

Crossword-wise we had not a one in the whole holiday, which is triumphant when you consider the gag I played on 'Himself' on the plane out. He fell asleep, having filled in seven clues in the *Telegraph* crossword. Scanning my *Guardian*, I observed that the patterns for both crosswords were almost identical, although the clues and solutions were, naturally, different. Painstakingly, I removed his paper from his comatose hand and transferred every written answer from one paper into the same spot in the other. Absurdly, they all fitted. All that remained was to slide the half-filled-in *Guardian* back in his hand and wait for the Mile High Club's first clinical breakdown.

It was priceless. The world's slowest burn. He awoke, glanced at the crossword, focused, blinked, refocused, then just stared. For ever. Then he put his glasses on his head and brought the paper very close. Then he put the paper on his lap and gazed sightlessly at the roof of the aircraft. Then he closed his eyes and opened them again very wide. Then, with a look which mingled perplexity and panic, he turned to me and said hollowly, 'I think I'm going mad...' I'm afraid I cracked up completely. His relief was tangible. 'You swine!' he said, not unpleasantly. 'You out and-out villain.' Little did he know how glad he'd be of my Machiavellian bent when grounded in subterranean silence broken only by murmuring Moroccans in white djellabas and linen coronets for the next 186 hours.

We decided to leave one chilly day after watching a fourth generation video of *The Discreet Charm of the Bourgeoisie*, which looked as though a turkey was being plucked above it, and with the help of the admirable hotel manager managed to unflex our inflexible return tickets and pack in twenty minutes. We flew to Gibraltar and pushed our giant suitcases painfully into Spain inch by inch at the tail of a three-deep, 100-yard queue of migrant workers crossing the border.

Want to know why the cases were so heavy? I thought you would. You thrive on my misfortunes, don't you? Well, I'll tell you anyway. The cases were heavy because the day before we left London, Jack went to pick up all his summer clothes from the dry cleaners on their half-day closing day. He managed to locate the cleaner's mobile and extract a promise of home delivery from him, waited over-optimistically until 12.30am, then, defeated, packed two winter suits and a hacking jacket; in other words, all that was left in his wardrobe. It goes without saying that he was perfectly dressed for a Moroccan winter whereas I froze in layers of cotton and was forced to wear a stylish but limited yellow parka with everything. He was *Brideshead Revisited* and I was Big Bird.

So, after Morocco we drove to the meteorological disaster that was Marbella and phoned my mother, who happened to be in Benalmedina. '*Hello*, love,' she said. 'What's the weather like in Morocco?'

'Very nice,' I said. 'Cool in the evenings. What are you doing today?'

'We-ell,' she mused, 'we might get the bus into Malaga, or we might try Marbella. I don't know.'

'If I were you,' I said casually, 'I'd go to Marbella.'

'Why do you say that?'

'We-ell... when you've done shopping, at least you could have lunch with someone you know.'

'Who?'

'Well, for example, me, and, better still, your son-in-law.'

At the risk of sounding like a Miami T-shirt, sometimes making someone else happy is better than two weeks' holiday.

Doing It Religiously

It struck me that I'd been doing more than my fair share of clerical duties. In fact, I'd done the full canon in just one week. If there really is no such thing as a coincidence then someone was trying to tell me something.

Being that I'm troubled by the odd chronic complaint, I took the train down to Westbury with my newly graduated daughter to see a divine, in the sense of delightful, canon who specalises in healing.

It was a sunny day and Amy and I love a flapjack-and-magazine strewn train journey and the chance to catch up on our angsts. The difficult bit lay in the fact that the canon's back had been put up, or out, rather. Literally. He was in that terrible state of lumber pain where mobility involves a slow ambulatory squat. I tried laying my hands on him to help him to do likewise to me and we ended up in painful but mutual giggles.

Later he rang me, worried that he hadn't been able to give me of his best, but I could only assure him that his presence alone had done me infinite good, and so it proved.

A couple of days later I was due to cut a ribbon at my GP's newly refurbished surgery. Rebecca, my doctor, is of Greek origin and the occasion would be honoured by His Eminence the Archbishop of the Greek Orthodox Church who would bless the new surgery. So round about 5.30pm I donned my ribbon-cutting regalia and walked the 200 yards to the surgery (if I live any further from blood pressure gauges and bottles of muscle relaxants I panic and move house). There, outside, was a table laid with incense, Holy Water and fresh herbs. The Archbishop stood in his traditional black robes, high hat and full bearded splendour. Alongside was the Mayor of Haringey, in glorious chains of office and a long grey ponytail and I took my place beside them in my unstructured linen and my 'Gosh, this is interesting. I wonder where *I* come in?' expression.

The Archbishop began the Greek Orthodox chants and the actress watched with fascination as His Eminence proceeded through the swinging of incense and the blessings with Holy Water. He was now holding long stalks of fresh herbs which he dipped into the Holy Water. I wonder what he's going to do with those? I mused, interestedly. One nano-second later he had swung them in front of me, above me and finally, quite gently and somewhat inevitably, hit me on the head with them.

Well, apparently my face said it all and the onlookers made no such secret of their amusement. My hand went to my head where the Paul Mitchell spray, with which I'd soldered up my hair for the occasion, gave way under the influence of wet rosemary and capsized, leaving me looking less like the local celeb than the local yokel. Still, two days into the week and I was twice blessed.

A couple of weeks later in a small, ancient Catholic church where my godson, Emanuel José Smith-Castrelos, was about to be baptised by a stout and stout-hearted Roman Catholic Father. The parental briefing had not been entirely conventional:

'Are you married?' he had earlier enquired of the mother of the child.

'Er, no, we're not... I'm afraid,' responded the mother.

'Are you intending to get married?' he ventured.

'Er, maybe later...' she replied.

'Are you Catholic?'

'Erm, I'm not but my boyfriend is.'

'And,' he continued, taking much in his stride, 'the godparents – are they Catholic?'

'Well, one is. But he can't come...' She took a deep breath. 'The other's Jewish!'

It says a lot for the resident priest that he not only performed the ceremony but he won many hearts that day as well as one small and perfect soul. And I was to be a sort of 'long stop', he assured me in cricketing terms, by which I understood I was to be there to support the wicket keeper and be reliable, not just for the one-day match but for the whole season. It's a responsibility – but I really don't feel stumped.

And now, I take as my text for the day, a sporting parable. A man is playing golf and hits the ball into the lake. Scrabbling around for it in the reeds, he pulls out a tiny elf in a pointed green hat. 'Why, thank ye, sir, for rescuing me,' says the leprechaun – for such is what he is. 'I'm grateful, sure I am, and I'll be granting ye three things in the future. Ye'll have plenty of money, ye'll play excellent golf and ye'll have a fantastic sex life.' So saying, he tips his hat and disappears.

Three years later, the story goes, and our man is playing on the same course and, just as he's about to tee off, a little voice says, 'Well, how are ye, now?' He looks down and sees the leprechaun, the very same one, and he greets him warmly. The leprechaun looks enquiring.

'So how's the money situation?'

'Fantastic!' says the man. 'I can't seem to fail at business – a millionaire now.'

'Grand,' says the little creature. 'And the golf?'

'I'm almost scratch,' say the man proudly. 'My handicap's gone down to nothing and I win nine times out of ten.'

'Splendid,' says the leprechaun, leaning forwards confidentially. 'And tell me...how's the sex life?'

'Oh, can't complain, can't complain,' said the man, beaming. 'You know, once or twice a month, sort of thing...'

'Once or twice a month!' hollers the little leprechaun. 'Sure that's nothing to brag about! Once or twice a month...'

'Weeell...I dunno...' mumbles the man, modestly. 'You know... for a priest, with a small parish...and no car...'

Working Party

In January 1996 I went up to Manchester to play Mrs Malaprop in Braham Murray's production of *The Rivals*. It was the last show in the Manchester Royal Exchange Theatre before the IRA bomb decimated so much of the building that housed it. Amy was in her last year at Manchester University. She had been shopping at Top Shop for her summer holiday. Two days later there was no Top Shop. The theatre was damaged and closed for almost two years.

The rehabilitation work has been done beautifully. Light streams through the delicate stained glass ceiling panels and yellows and pinks and turquoises of the modern theatre-in-the-round gleam like shells in the historic old Corn Exchange. It's a bit of a triumph.

Theatre-in-the-round audiences are trained to expect a little cheek – scenery often gets moved by stagehands dressed as butlers or even cows, depending on the play, because total blackouts are difficult to achieve. Exits are long, through vomitoriums, so they tend to be declamatory or in some way taken at a run with a dastardly flourish and a rising inflection. It can encourage the show-off in us.

I'm not saying it has to be like this, or that it necessarily always is. It's just a tendency I've noticed towards it. A need to nod and wink to the audience; to fill in the gaps often elsewhere concealed by a proscenium arch.

Braham and I had a mild dispute over the soliloquising overhearing scenes which all rely on being hidden behind doors or flattened against walls. On our set we had neither.

I couldn't believe his suggestion that I should go into the audience to soliloquise. I mean, *I'm* cheap but that seemed positively penurious. He insisted it would work. I tried everything else – hiding behind the sofa, listening through a glass up against an imaginary wall. Again and again, I failed. Finally, on the second preview, I sat in the audience as he'd suggested. Amazing reaction. Huge laughter. By the time we opened I was practically doing stand-up out there. They needed a hook to get me off. Braham told me he'd never seen anyone quite use the theatre in the way I did. He never explained whether he said that in a despairing or an admiring way, and because his delivery for both would be similar, I never asked him. It was fun and stretching, the costumes were exquisite and, curiously, I have no idea whether I was any good or not.

We opened *The Rivals* to a smattering of third-string critics and those intrepid members of the Manchester audience with snow-shoes. The Royal Exchange Theatre was a cross between a three-tiered cake plate and a circus ring. The gusts of wind down your corsets as you scurried from dressing room to the hollow area surrounding the stage gave you the kind of nipples that the cast of *Baywatch* use surgery and ice to achieve.

Manchester folk were as warm as their feet were cold. 'Ello, Maureen. Y'ahright, Maureen? 'Ave a seat, Maureen,' hollered the receptionist at the BBC radio station where I'd gone to publicise the show. 'Rotten weather for you, Maureen, eh?' Now, anyone who's entered the hallowed portals of BBC Radio in London will know that the receptionist's chief job is to give you an inferiority complex as big as the building! Here, though, the word 'love' is uttered more times than in the complete works of Barbara Cartland – 'Mornin', love,' "Owar yu, love?" "Owzitgoin', love?" I reckon all that 'love'ing must seep into the atmosphere. Even the *Big Issue* sellers call you 'love', which explains why my briefcase is crammed with their wares.

My hotel was wonderfully eccentric – and I'd say that even if they hadn't given me a phenomenally good rate. The Victoria and Albert Hotel, Granada's own 'themed' hotel, is themed in the sense that every room is named after a Granada TV show. I actually began in *Affairs of the Heart* and ended up in *Hard Times*. The staff were divine and the menu must have been written by Ken Dodd's scriptwriters – 'Hot parkin with ridiculously lumpy custard' and 'Sausage and mash with no faffing'.

Back at the theatre, the first night was rife with tension and the audience cold, both literally and metaphorically. Still, I felt relaxed and fully fused with my Mrs Malaprop, to the extent that at one point I calmly observed a silence going on too long, thinking, Oh, God, he's dried stone dead, when in fact it was my line next and I was merely standing there, placidly, not saying it.

All my good luck cards and floral messages had glorious malapropisms in them but my favourite came from fellow actor Cliff Howells. 'Good luck, Maureen,' it read, 'and I think your Mrs Malaprop is truly excrement.'

Director Braham Murray gave us an accurate preview of the curmudgeonly local critic's review but the audiences were full to bursting and uproariously appreciative. Still, after the second show on Saturday night, I trudged bleakly back to the Victoria and Albert through the hurtling monsoon thinking, If there's a Scotty, for God's sake, beam me up!

On the Sunday I flew home. My son was leaving for six and a half months in India, China and other places without postcodes and Hovis. My contribution to his departure was the purchase of a medical kit of enormous complexity and an irritating stream of enquiries, all fielded at source, about T-shirts, socks, backpacks and malaria pills.

The other reason, and here I pause because I'm on shaky ground – and because my face bronzer will streak the minute I mention her name – was that Pushkin, the 107-year-old (in cat years) cat, had cancer and had to be put to sleep on the Monday. Amy was coming home so the five of us could have a last Sunday together. Wait – I'll think of something funny in a minute – honest I will. OK. Got it. Two dyslexic skiers on a ski slope. One says 'OK. Here's where we zig-zag down the mountain.' 'No, we zag-zig,' says the other. 'No. Zig-zag,' says the first. After a while a man appears near the brow of the mountain. 'Can you help us?' calls the first skier. 'Do we zig-zag down the mountain or do we zag-zig?' 'I'm afraid I don't know,' replies the man. 'I'm a tobogganist.' 'In that case,' says the skier, 'Could I have a copy of the *Daily Telegraph* and a packet of Benson & Hedges?'

Monday morning I packed my bags, passed the normally noxious but somehow precious smell of Pushkin's last litter tray, kissed her farewell, hugged my enormous boy, who finally allowed himself to be hugged, and stumbled blindly to the car. At the door he finished me off by doing an absurdly droll dance. Upstairs, his sister had been inconsolable for about nine hours.

That night a London producer came to see *The Rivals* and I did my best to pull out all the stops and be mountainously funny for Manchester, Europe and all the Cinque Ports.

Pushkin, the other one, wrote:

It's time, my dear, it's time! The heart demands its quittance –
As day flies after day and each demands its pittance –
Withdrawn from living's store and meanwhile you and I
Draw up our plans to live... and then, why then we'll die.

Upwardly Mobile

Since I was going to be away in Manchester for at least six weeks, give or take the odd day-return for a slow haircut and a quick row, it was suggested to me that perhaps I might take along the mobile phone for company. The Manchester Royal Exchange is a theatre with a staff of hundreds, and I'd be living in a hotel populated by the touring production of *Pickwick* and half of Granada Television. The risk of severe loneliness seemed remote.

Still, I took the phone. And the charger, which weighed as much as an Ogen melon, and the instructions, and just about everything connected with it save the telephone number, and off I set, jaunty jolly, for merry Manchester, the place where I first gave my heart to the man forlornly waving me off from Platform 4.

Once in my seat, with my tabloid, my *Private Eye*, my take-away cappuccino and my oatmeal flapjack, I settled down snugly to await the glorious 'white noise' that constitutes the passenger announcements. 'Britishraywelcmsyoua boade tedoclo'tray to Badchesta, callin' at Bilto' Keys, Bacclesfee, Stockporan-BanchestPiccadilly.' God only knows how foreigners ever get off at their chosen destination, let alone how they ever got on, since the relevant platform number tends to be a closely guarded secret between Passenger Information and the man who blows his whistle impatiently as a horde of frothing passengers hurtle down the said platform yelling, 'Wait, you swine! I've been sitting on the train to Folkestone for twenty sodding minutes!'

(I apologise profusely if the aforementioned abused company is no longer British Rail but is instead 'Railtrack', 'Euro-Trek', 'T. Tank Engine Productions Ltd' or 'Sansui/Time/Life/in conjunction with Lloyd-Webber Frost/Murdoch Shanghai Puffa-Trains Inc.')

But I digress. Here I was, not five kilometres north of the Watford Gap, when the girl across the aisle – long hair, heavy boots, serious briefcase, navy nails – started in with the phoning:

'Hi! It's Rose! I'm on the train. Yeah, look, erm, did you, like, get any more on the new location?' Her voice was two decibels short of that of an aurally impaired towncrier. 'OK. So as of now we, like, don't have permission to film, right? Right. Well, look. OK. Shall I call Frank? Oh, you have. Well, let me know if I can... right. Well, bye for now. Call me if... oh.'

She put down the phone for the briefest nano-second, then rapidly redialled: 'Hi! Frank! Rose! I'm on the train – yah. Grim, eh? No luck with the exteriors? Oh, sorry, I just thought you might want me to... Oh, she has? Right. Great. Well, I'm on my mobile if... Sure, OK. Cheers, then.'

This time the phone stayed down for less time than it takes to contemplate murder by insertion of small digital appliance as she repeated the whole mind-crushing routine on more unreceptive ears.

At this point, a large man in a brown three-piece suit ahead of me looked up from a sheaf of notes. I rolled my eyes upward to indicate distaste at this telephonic excess. He smiled grimly and two minutes later his briefcase started ringing. After 30 seconds' pretence, old brown suit answered and, *sotto voce*, gave mono-syllabic answers (twice, in most cases) to a string of questions regarding some heavy-duty meeting at the Co-op which necessitated three further calls. (We now had the a cappella version of Symphony for Two Mobiles, an Inter-City Special and a curmudgeonly commuter.)

Then the third mobile put in an appearance. The mobile buffet. This is a sort of hostess trolley from which two chatty stewardesses flog tea bags, coffee sachets, hottish water and elk-flavoured crisps.

I couldn't help noticing that the sandwiches on offer included Roast Beef and Cream Cheese and Cheese, Cucumber and Marmite. I came close to pulling the communication cord.

The carriage now sounded like something composed by the late Lionel Bart for an early-morning street scene: 'Coffee, tea, sandwiches, cake!' – 'Well, we'll need at least five extras for the night shoot' – 'Soft drinks and flapjacks!' – 'I've talked to the Holiday Inn about computer facilities' – 'That's two coffees and a beansprout and tofu baguette!' – 'I'll bring the flip charts. OK. I'm on my mobile if you...'

'Would you all please SHUT UP! I AM TRYING TO TRAVEL!' cried a strident new voice. SILENCE. 'Because if you don't I'm going to start my Ethel Merman impersonation!' It was, of course, *my* voice, and I must say it was pretty damned effective, albeit winning me few new friends on the 10.00am to Manchester Piccadilly.

There is a story, possibly apocryphal, of a brash yuppie in the early eighties on a crowded train performing loudly into his cellular phone to the fury of the rest of the passengers. Mile after mile they are forced to sit through, 'Well, where is the idle bastard? It's 8.20 in the effing morning! I've sewn up three deals in Tokyo by now! Tell him he gets those options or he's out on his arse! Get me Tate and MOVE IT!... Tate? Benson, B.L.P.G. Assoc. Buy! Four K simulated copper – Sell NOW!'

Suddenly, nearby, a man lurches forward, clutching his heart, and falls to the ground. It's clear he's having a heart attack. 'Is there a doctor in the carriage?' shouts a commuter. Panic reigns until someone suggests phoning ahead to the next station. The cry goes up for a phone and everyone looks across to the Gordon Gecko clone, huddled low in his seat. 'Can we use your phone?' someone yells. 'No,' growls the yuppie. 'A man's dying!' screams the spokesman. 'Will you please give us your phone!' 'No,' repeats the yuppie.

Finally, the phone is prised from his hand by the affronted passengers. It doesn't take long to understand his reluctance. The phone is a dummy. From a joke shop.

Similarly, there was a story reported in the papers about a famously pretentious boxer spotted in the bar of the Groucho Club giving someone verbal hell on his mobile in loud lisping tones. 'I don't care what the time is, you clown, you get him outa the meeting AND tell him who wants him or your job's not worth the paper it's – I said NOW, you dimwit. Do you KNOW who you're talking to...' Quite suddenly, blissfully for the other customers, the phone he was yelling into began to RING...

Must dash – train to catch. Who was it who said it was good to talk?

Ban the Bonnet

Let me shamelessly state that if any existing TV company, let's say one called 'I can't believe it's not LWT' or UK Make-Over TV, were to offer me the small but meaningful cameo of Mme de Flibertigibbit in a six-week series of Jane Brontë's *Ratings and Rateability* for Equity minimum and an Eccles cake, all shot on location in Snape on a Box Brownie, and directed by Geri from the Spice Girls, I would probably take it and offer to provide my own mob-cap and liberty bodice.

However, since I've been offered only a few roles in floor-length clothes in 32 years in the business they say there's no business like, it is an unlikely scenario. So when my non-curmudgeonly husband expressed doubts that I should write about this for fear of causing offence to those who might employ me, a snort of sorts escaped my sinuses and a chunter was heard, 'If I'm treading sour grapes, at least it'll make a good whine.'

A famous film casting agent rang my home recently. I've known her socially for 25 years. She's broken beamingly into my dressing room after more first nights than I've had gym memberships. I know her. I like her. The feeling is, I think, mutual. Lord, she once typed up and mailed us a copy of her mother's recipe for Peas and Barley Kasha – can you get closer than that? 'Oh, hi,' I said. 'Don't tell me – you've got a movie job for me after all these years?'

She sounded forlorn. She just wanted a mutual friend's number. I realised, of course, this must happen to her all the time. I wasn't remotely serious – I knew long ago that networking only works for strangers – in fact, that's a helluva good title and I said it first! But it's true. Not for friends. Or sleeping with people, of course – that'll do it. Yeah, acquaintanances and lovers. Not friends.

The truth is I turned on my television some time last year after six months in the theatre to find that in my abstinence England had been televisually cobblestoned. I'm not suggesting that classics should be rare, only that perhaps they should not be overdone.

There has undoubtedly been a surfeit of 'bonnet' drama since Ken and Emma reintroduced the word 'farthingale' into our homes with that spirited Tuscan romp *Much Ado About Nothing*. I admired the film, and its right-on heir *Sense and Sensibility* even more, although I remember idly wondering quite why it entranced the international film world when it was pretty much what the BBC have been churning out quietly with verisimilitude for some decades. *Pride and Prejudice*, the marvellous *Middlemarch*, *The Mill on the Floss*, *The Tenant of Wildfell Hall*, *Moll Flanders*, *The Moonstone*, *Emma*, *Ivanhoe* and *Nostromo* have sprung rapidly out from our TV screens with descending degrees of success and the purveyors of horse stock, frock coats and tapestry frames must be booking their second holidays in Mauritius with nary a thought to the extra supplements.

It's understandable. Bonnets sell! Even dowdy faded bonnets with last year's trimmings sell. Many, like *The Tenant of Wildfell Hall*, are pre-sold co-productions with Canadian or Australian TV, involving further sales of tea cannisters, pot-pourri holders, boxed video sets and Mr Darcy 'wet-look' shirts. Simple stories are padded out with impossibly beautiful firelit interiors, enough low-angle galloping hooves to merit a commentary by Peter O'Sullevan, the obligatory open-mouthed kiss and pedantic post-coital lines like, 'What are you thinking, dearest?'

So what with the perks and the A-level syllabus, as Mel Brooks used to say of a nectarine, 'Even a rotten one is good.' *Rhodes*, *Nostromo* and *Emma* have been vilified as much as *Pride and Prejudice* was venerated but they are probably going to break even in the end and cause the accountants, who now run commissioning departments, no real grief.

Is it justifiable? Is it hell. You show me an independent whose job involves selling contemporary new ideas to TV companies and I'll show you a person with their pockets full of Gaviscon. Calls unreturned, promises reneged on, budgets mercilessly cut, projects dropped, heads of departments switched after months of meetings – it's like the NHS. Everybody has their own horror story. *Our Friends in the North* was twelve years from conception to fruition. *Agony Again* was dropped after one series without explanation after skirting round the seven to eight million rating. *Nostromo*, I understand, pulled 'em in at the two million mark. If there's no bonnet, then they'll happily settle for serial murder or hospital drama or a combo of the two, the autopsy room, or *Only Fools and Birds of a Porridge Behaving Badly in the Grave*. Again!

There is a dichotomy. We reel back in shock from the grimy controversial assault of Peter Kosminsky's *No Child of Mind* or we hook in religiously to *Our Friends in the North, House of Cards* or *The Crow Road* because we recognise that, like it or not, they are a reflection of society today. Bonnet drama, conversely, removes us tidily from any such responsibility to a world of rules and rituals, where everyone knows their place and virtue is invariably rewarded. It's how we like to see ourselves.

Almost every screenplay, from *Rebecca* to *The Tenant of Wildfell Hall*, sports a deep but headstrong woman, a strong, silent man and an unspoken secret revealed only at the altar or the grave.

'Tell the nosey villagers he's your blinking brother, for God's sake!' I want to (and frequently do) yell at the screen. But the inexorability of the misunderstanding is, like any good farce, part of the whole long-suffering package. (The second part of *Captain Corelli's Mandolin* gave me the same problem. Someone would have told him she was on the island! And unmarried!) After all, who's the most popular and prolific authoress in England, still producing three or four novels a week and still getting herself up to look like a smoked salmon bagel seen through a lattice window? And what is she peddling, post feminism, post modernism, post your answers in a plain pink envelope? She's peddling what the punters most admire in this deeply conservative island – love, restraint and a plain gold band. This is exactly how the world likes to see us too. As some quaint, dimity-repressed little islanders from whose dusty loins sprang forth Shakespeare, *Upstairs Downstairs* and an Empire. Merchant-Ivory movies and *Shakespeare in Love* sustain the myth and thank God Mike Leigh and Ken Loach keep knocking it down through the big screen. But it was our television which led the world and that was largely built on great writing on contemporary themes.

On the other hand, bonnet dramas effortlessly do something which is arguably the most important task of all. They sell books. Classic books. In their millions as the series ends.

In the beginning was the word – in the millennium, is TV just the word processor?

The Party's Over

Dahlings –

I've been to a mahvelous party! It was so good that I was the last
one to leave. I actually left bearing two crates of Chilean red, half
a birthday cake, 21 blow-ups with captions, a large helium
balloon labelled 'It's a Girl', three black plastic bags full of gifts
and 48 unclaimed 'Going Home Bags'. That night I slept like a
hippo.

I feel an explanation coming on. Of course it was my party I'd
been to. My half-century party (no, of course you can't believe
it) held, appropriately enough, at Lord's Cricket Ground. Not
actually on the pitch, you understand, but in their banqueting
rooms, dazzling in fuchsia and dark blue, with sparkling balloons
aloft. There were Friday night candles on each table, for the
party was a traditional Friday night dinner – chopped liver,
chicken soup, the lot for 150 friends of all faiths and sizes
presided over by my beloved and much missed friend, Rabbi
Hugo Gryn.

When I'd proposed the idea weeks earlier, it was received like
an air-raid warning. Jacquie, my secretary, slumped over her WP
and began bringing home brochures for holidays to the Cape of
Good Hope. Jack said, 'If that's what you want, love...' in the tone
of a crated veal calf on its way to Europe. Mother was OK until
mention was made of the 'm' word. 'You must be joking! A
marquee? Are you mad?' Foolishly, I hadn't realised why the
hiring of tents was a sign of insanity, but mother was about to tell
me. The explanation involved blasts of freezing air every time a
waitress entered, toilet facilities spewing effluent over guests and
a lunar landscape, where the lawn used to be, for the next

seventeen years. Unfazed, I invited two marqueemen to measure up and estimate, then I booked Lord's banqueting suite. It's my party and I'll cry off if I want to!

For the next three weeks my career was in the past tense. I never imagined the day would come when I would sit in my living room of an evening, combing through boxes of balloons and seriously discussing the merits of silver foil over pearlised latex. Do you need to know where to get a banner made which reads 'Happy Birthday, Your Majesty, William Shakespeare, Sir Cliff, er, Maureen Lipton'? Well, I'm the girl who can tell you. Or 150 yo-yos? This was the moment when my secretary and I almost came to blows. I was all for giving one yo-yo per couple. Jacquie insisted on individual yo-yos. Neither of us would give way. 'But if I was giving them a silver salver, I'd give one per couple!' I cried. 'But if you were giving a bag of sweets, you'd give one per *person*,' countered Jacquie. 'We're two intelligent women. I can't believe we're standing here yelling about yo-yos!' I decided she was right on the grounds that she always is and I'm sure, at some future function, the 40 left-over yo-yos will be a real asset.

Even now, I can't discuss the seating plan without hyper-ventilating. It was in perpetual motion up to and including the moment they all sat in each other's seats.

The caterers, Mr and Mrs Sharpstone, were the sort of people you could lay on an open wound. What's more, they could take a joke. One example from our menu: Apple Strudel (From our own Strudel Orchard. Guaranteed to lie on the chest at 3am). Plus every Going Home Bag contained an Alka Seltzer. Frankly, if I could afford it, I'd have booked them to cater for the rest of my life. The cake was made by my friend, Judy Bastyra, from an idea which woke me at 4.00am – laughing. It was the front cover of OK! magazine, only on the cake it read 'O'ecK'. The headlines included 'Zelma Lipman comes out!' and 'Happy Birthday Mum' in authentic Chinese, purporting to be from my son.(What's more, it tasted great. Judy had brought two samples to choose from and, unanimously, we all chose the Sainsbury's fruit-cake mix.)

Three days before the party a parcel arrived from the missing link, son Adam, in China. It was a green silk dressing gown and the rice-paper letter said, 'I've been into seventeen different shops to buy this with no knowledge of how big you are or what colours you like. However, I have managed to master the art of bartering the Chinese from a very low price up to a very high one before buying.'

My dress was bought one mad afternoon from designer Neil Cunningham. I'd faxed him a sketch of the old Marilyn Monroe 'draught up the drawers' dress with halter neck and flare, saying, 'I suppose a frock is out of the question?' and he'd suggested I pop in the shop where the very dress was waiting for me in bronze chiffon and satin. (In my heart I lusted after the coral but I couldn't face the thought of coral against fuchsia tablecloths – yes, it had come to that!)

On Sunday in Hampstead I found a pair of bronze shoes for a knockdown price of £15. The shop was packed and everyone in it seemed to know my entire geneology so I grabbed the shoes and left, thinking, I need never shop again until one of my children gets married.

On the party day at 5.45pm, face steamed and packed, hair freeze-framed and bust aligned, I opened the shoebox to find one shoe size 38 and one shoe size 39. Naturally, both were right-footed.

'Oh, my God!' screamed my mother. 'What are you going to do?'

'Oh, my God! What are you going to do?' I screamed down the phone to the shop.

'Who's going to look at your feet?' breezed Amy. 'You're 50.'

She was right. Nobody did.

It was the party of a lifetime – or certainly of half of one. The speeches were brilliant. My brother, who flew in from Japan that day, gave his 'Reflections on being the brother of an only child' speech, which raised the roof.

Jacko did a hilarious rundown of the year 1946, including the invention of the biro which could write over 200,000 words without running out – and still not get a reply from Alan Yentob at the BBC! Amy, looking as tender as a spring violet, said she hadn't prepared anything then delivered the funniest, most touching speech imaginable, and Linda Agran – same birthday, different year – told the assembled gathering to shrieks of delight exactly why she hates me so much. I rewarded her with a T-shirt reading 'I will always be a year younger than Maureen Lipman'.

The band, Alodi, played everything from Klezmer to 'Can't Get Started With You', and people shook legs that hadn't been shaken since rationing went out and bananas came in. As for me, I floated above the evening like a benign and beaming hovercraft, thinking, It's only two years to our Silver Wedding. Now, about the seating plan...

How to Give the
Perfect Dinner Party

I was once asked to give my suggestions for how to give the perfect dinner party. In all seriousness. Me! The following poured out in one four-minute rant.

First allow guest guilt to build up to the point where you spend most of your time at social functions behind the drapes, your husband or, preferably, someone else's husband.

Then make a list of people to whom you owe invitations. When you've filled two exercise books, throw them away and invite, instead, people you've just met and wish to suck up to.

Next pick an evening which suits everyone and has an empty day before it in the diary. Over the subsequent days, fill up the said day with appointments, including some which necessitate leaving town via British Rail and some which require physical exertion, i.e. agree to abseil over Coventry Cathedral in aid of Distressed Single Lady Accountants.

As the day approaches, select a menu at 3.30 in the morning under the influence of drugs and remember you are appearing on Breakfast TV in three hours on a discussion panel about 'How to prevent under-eye bags'. Leave instructions with the inmates of the house to buy last-minute ingredients such as several chickens stuffed with chestnuts between skin and flesh marinaded in herbed wine for 24 hours and home-made mango and coconut ice cream. Leave note for daily lady to turn off the water running on the frozen smoked trout before it's pummelled into a trout purée and set table with what's left of best china.

Return in good time to bail out the kitchen and read note reminding you of half-day closing in Muswell Hill. Pause to drink half-bottle of dry sherry, run to last-remaining open supermarket, to purchase frozen fish fillets, oven chips, sliced bread, various tins and trifle with dodgy sell-by date stuck over even dodgier sell-by date and warm Sauvignon. Place wine in microwave and frozen fish in freezer, take all your clothes off and apply face pack whilst running bath. Whilst in bath remember what you've done and race down naked to reverse the contents of freezer and microwave. Body should now be mottled red from bath and nipples akimbo from freezer as your Friday gardener (own key) pops in for his £50. Only when he leaves and you try to put your purse in your pocket do you realise how you looked when you were discussing the lupins with him.

Wearing face pack and dressing gown, flour and season defrosted fish and place on table and put chips in oven-proof dish. Heat oil and oven. Tip M & S tomato and herb soup from tins to saucepan and add own herbs to point of lunacy. Likewise mushy peas. Spread copies of this week's papers on serving counter and butter thickly on slices of bread. Open jars of pickled onions, beetroot, gherkins and bottle of HP sauce. Add vinegar, salt and pepper, linen napkins and best glasses. Throw on little black dress and as door bell rings, oil bursts into flame, bottle in freezer explodes and cat eats trifle, smile brightly, cracking face pack into 4,000 wrinkles, and open door to first guest.

Hot Flush Blues

I just passed fifty/'n' I'm givin' in to gravity,
Got my tongue in a real deep cavity,
Still looking round for signs of depravity –
I'm long in the tooth/short on love.

Wanna make love when I'm not tired,
Wanna wear a bra that ain't underwired,
Wanna watch Tina Turner and get inspired,
Long in the tooth/short on love.

I could paint my own pottery – bake my own bread.
I say 'The day I do that's the day I'm dead.'
Don't want cameo brooches/organised coaches,
Wanna smoke roaches and get outa my head.

Won't see a shrink/got no neuroses,
Won't watch the soaps/'n' get my kicks by osmosis,
Won't read pamphlets on osteoporosis,
Cos I'm long in the tooth (don't have to be) short on love.

Don't give me lavender and lace/unless the lace is black,
Wanna face-lift not a stair-lift/and I ain't comin' back.
Wanna punk that's a hunk/to overdose on aphrodisiac,
Cos I'm long in the tooth, short on love.

Time to Make Up

My daughter forswears make-up. At 21, and with a naturally fresh skin, it couldn't matter less really, which is not to say I wouldn't give a flagon of aloe vera and a groat of rolled oats to get my hands, brushes and Buf-Pufs on the unchartered territory of her face. Just to delineate, you understand – to give more balance to eye and lip...and perhaps to pluck... but no, she'd never let me near her, although she purports to admire the reconstruction work I do on my own unaligned visage.

'I hate my jaw! It's repellent,' she moans. 'Why can't I have your jaw? I love your jaw!'

'What's to love?' I splutter. 'It's a jaw. It opens, it closes. It chomps, it grinds. It's a working jaw, for God's sake!'

'Yeah, but you know what I mean – yours squares off! Mine just meanders around then slopes off. I HATE IT!'

I'd like to laugh but I daren't. Besides, I know only too well the pain of comparison, being the daughter of an alarmingly pretty woman who, in her seventies, is still (blast it!) taken for my sister. For years I tried to rub away my nose to make it the same shape as my mother's. To suggest to my daughter a touch of underjaw shading would be to agree with her self-assessment – and would it be my fault if it resembled designer stubble?

'You look so much *older* on stage,' marvelled Jo Public, as I entered the bar each night after performing in *The Rivals*. 'How long does it take you to put on all those lines?'

It pained me to tell them that I didn't apply ANY lines – the ones they saw were my own, breaking through the make-up. Long ago, on the BT ads, we discovered that painting wrinkles on my skinny face made me look not older but merely extra-terrestrial. A pair of glasses, a grey wig and a permanently pressed expression was all that was needed, depressingly enough, and in those days I was a mere stripling of 40, not the woman recently asked by the *Mail on Sunday* to contribute to an article called 'Fab at Fifty'. (On reflection, it may well have been 'Flab at Fifty', in which case I would have had much to contribute.)

Each month, magazines aimed at the 'fairer sex' (a 'darkist' label if ever there was one) extol the virtues of this season's 'new, improved maquillage'. 'Forget last season's insipid beiges and tepid taupes,' they scream, 'and step into spring with lacerating lime, pizzazzing pistachio and orange with oomph!' Orange and lime. Two colours so acidic and draining that only Timmy Mallett can survive them, and still look like a vat of coleslaw. So out go the insipid beiges and in come the sizzling hot pinks, peachy whites and fluorescent fuchsias. Theoretically, that is. In reality, most of us approach the 'shock of the new' with scepticism.

My mother's generation, with their Ponds Cold Cream, spit-on mascara and Max Factor pancake, seem to have emerged with skin like a baby's, which is more than can be said for most of my fellow exfoliators racing off for their electrodes and fruit acid peels. They emerge taut as a yacht sail for two hours and then subside like the skin of a kiwi after the fruit's been removed.

Aged ten, I remember applying pancake to our live-in help's arms and back before she put on her evening dress. It seemed to me an entirely exotic exercise to buff her body parts into a smooth matt surface sans freckles, spots, scratches or vaccination marks. Above it perched her face, Max Factor panstick, powder, silvery blue eye-shadow and 'Tangee' lipstick.

Of course, no-one thought, least of all me, that under the heat of a mirror ball and the influence of Ronnie Hilton and too many crème de menthes, the inside of her black crêpe frock would turn a dark orange as would her boyfriend's shirt, tie, lapels and, with a bit of luck and opportunity, his trouser turn-ups.

My son, when aged thirteen, once informed me that the word 'gullible' had been removed from the English dictionary, then sat back to watch my blue touch paper explode. As my 'How dare they do thats!' rose to a crescendo, I realised, from his face how neatly I'd fallen into his trap. Nowadays, I often feel as though I have a PhD. in gullibility in the face of the cosmetic industry's extensive, expensive snares.

How did we face life before we had liposomes and antioxidents and exfoliators and light-reflecting pigments and sebum regulators and cell reconstructors and mini-lifts in a jar? I'll tell you how. By being young and not needing 'em, that's how!

Eyeliner goes out of fashion. Kohl pencil comes in at roughly three times the price it was in its previous incarnation as an eyeliner. Our hair requires vegetable-laden shampoos and massive doses of avocado and jojoba conditioner – with panthenol! Invest in them and voila! – on to the market comes Wash & Go, because which nineties juggling woman would admit to having time for two separate washing regimes? Meanwhile, rouge is replaced by blusher (same thing – squarer box) which is in turn ousted by sun bronzer which bites the dust when pastel blush pebbles come along.

Powder, always intended to matt down the sheen of foundation cream, comes 'luminescent' with reflective sheen, basically to make foundation... er, shiny. Lipsticks come with moisturisers which make them disappear roughly one cappuccino after application, and gel, guaranteed to reduce under-eye puffiness, will cost roughly £19.90 more than the most effective cure, a slice of cucumber.

Not too long ago, I found myself walking late at night down the Champs Elysées. There, at 11.45pm, was a state-of-the art make-up shop, open in all its minimalistic glory. We strolled around as though we were in an art gallery. Everything was black, save the make-up, which was displayed in individual items. Rows of lip colours faced front by the hundred in every shade of the palette. Counters of barely graduating blushers – it was dazzling. Long black leather chairs invited you to lay back, headphones on, and just jig about to music of your choice. Internet computers lovingly awaited your E-mail. The smell of good coffee abounded. It was so seductive that I lost all judgement, flailed about like a good-time girl and came out clutching a pewter-coloured lipstick which makes me look like I've got mercury poisoning.

When Lancôme rejected Isabella Rossellini, arguably the most beautiful woman I've ever seen, from their advertising and Max Factor took on Madonna and Estée took on Liz Hurley, one had to face facts. It's style over content out there. Kiss reality goodbye and say hello to hype. I doubt whether Audrey Hepburn would have got past the advertisers' scrutiny. What's hip is a canvas, a blank one preferably, and a very young one with not a trace of life's experience on it – why bother, when it can be painted on and 'Eraced' at will? There are botulism injections available now to paralyse the frowning lines and the smiling ones too. Collagen will give you African lips (without the possible inconvenience of African colouring) and your teeth can be whitened over in your lunchbreak. Listen, if you don't want the *Baywatch* contract, just keep drinking loads of water and eat fruit. It works for bats.

The Hanging Basket Issue

The day was balmy. I was writing in a desultory sort of fashion in the downstairs study, and every so often I stopped to chat on the phone to a friend. Feeling anxious about a few things, I unburdened myself, then returned to work. The study clock said 4.30pm. I've a deadline to meet and a date at the theatre at 7.00pm.

Then the doorbell rang. I opened it to find a florist, a basket of trailing fuchsias and a cheer up message from the shoulder I'd just unburdened upon. I rang her answerphone: 'This is Gypsy Rose Lipman with a prediction: You'll never have two halfpennies to rub together but you'll have many friends who love you.' I went outside, wedging the front door open by slipping the bolt down at the bottom to hang the fuchsias up where the existing tired basket was.

I stood on the low wall and tried to unhook the basket. It was heavy and I had to get my shoulder under it. With my head down I manoeuvred the metal ring over the iron hook which was attached to the wall bracket. Twice I nearly got it off but it slipped back and, in grabbing at it, I removed large contented clumps of allysum. I turned it on its side for easier removal and soil fell, in clumps, down the inside of my shirt. I finally removed the basket. It didn't look so tired when seen from eye level. There was a healthy pink petunia, a shy violet pansy and the promise of a fuchsia. I went down to the cellar to look for some means of hanging it on the trellis and returned with a thin metal bracket. Leaving the basket on the low wall, I slotted the metal bracket over the wooden trellis which supported the passion-fruit vine and hung the old basket over it at eye level.

It looked good but needed me to move a potted daisy tree over left to reveal some purple petunias in a wall basket. I pulled over the daisy tree and the bottom of my back sent an angry message to my calf. Ignoring said message, I climbed on to the wall and put the trailing fuchsia basket up on high. I stood back and admired my handiwork, then I turned to leave.

There was a slow creaking sound and the trellis, basket and passion-flower vine did a slow-motion dive to the ground, taking the daisy tree pot with them. I was now angry, soiled and in pain.

I lifted up the pot, hurting the other side of my calf, placed the fallen basket on the wall, relocated the soil from the step into my finger nails, returned to the house and closed the door behind me. Or rather, attempted to close the door behind me, for the bolt down to the floor had wedged solidly and the door would neither open nor close. Words were exchanged between myself and my deity.

I went down to the cellar to find a pair of pliers. Just to look at them made my teeth hurt. I got back to the front door and pulled the top of the bolt. It didn't move but my back started S.O.S.ing all over the rest of me. I braced my thighs, tried again and this time the bolt lifted enough for me to close the front door.

I returned to the study, picked up my pen and glanced at the clock. It still appeared to be 4.30pm. I raced to the kitchen where, contrarily, it was 6.45pm. I was in grubby shorts, soiled shirt, there was peat in my Gossard Maidenform and the show started at 7.00pm. I phoned a cab. There wasn't one. I phoned the theatre, which was a small one, thank goodness, and told them to tell my girlfriend I'd be late. I hobbled upstairs and lay on the floor to get my shorts off. I eschewed thoughts of a shower and removed earth with a baby wipe. What was left I rubbed into my face to look like sun bronzer. I was dressed and out of the house in ten long minutes with gas-fuelled hair tongs in my hand. I had forgotten my first-night greetings card and present for friend, Niall Buggy, whose show I was not sitting watching, and I drove like Mr Toad in a car which I'd only driven once before and whose width I had no idea of.

By the time I reached Hampstead, the mirrors of every car in North London were turned inside out.

After a peg-legged walk from the parking spot, I arrived to an empty foyer. The front-of-house assistant said I could sneak in during the next blackout – but when it came to it I lost my nerve.

I mean, there was Niall, on his own on stage, giving out with the gorgeous Sean O'Casey. I found I was incapable of clomping down four levels of stairs in a 100-seater theatre and having his beady eyes register, 'What's that dozy cow doin' comin' in at this hour?' So I sat in the foyer of Hampstead Theatre Club and read through pamphlets on Feng Shui, T'ai Chi and How to Find Your Voice, then I went to the bar to order a drink in the hope that when the audience tipped out for the interval I'd look as if I was the first one out and was dying of thirst from bravo-ing so much.

'Can I have a Campari and soda, please?' I asked the young lady behind the bar.

'Ice and lemon? 'she asked, then, 'And how did you like your hanging basket?'

Well, you could have knocked me down with a bag of John Innes multi-compost – well, actually, you could have knocked me down with much less than that – a slug pellet would have done the trick.

'How did you know I...'

'Well,' she said cheerily, 'I work in a florist in East Finchley during the day and I packed the basket up for you.'

'Well, it's your bloody fault I'm standing in the bar instead of watching the play!' I hissed, much to her amazement. 'Oh, don't ask, just pour me another – you can read about it some day in *Lip Reading*!'

Scales

I have been known to cook herrings whilst listening to Schubert's *The Trout*. It is a tasty combo.

The thing about herrings is that they are acknowledged, rather like myself, to be quite versatile. My daughter had asked a couple of friends from university to stay. They came down on the coach from Manchester and were delayed for an hour by a missing wing mirror. So supper was a bit of a mess, really. The fish had been under sentence of grilling for so long it resembled Sean Penn in *Dead Man Walking*. The hors-d'oeuvres had a uniform greyness about them and afterwards, when Amy was replacing things in the fridge, both girls were heard to remark with astonishment, 'Why do your parents have so many *herrings* in the fridge?'

And I suppose it's true. There was a jar of rollmops and one of herrings in mustard and a carton of chopped sweet and sour herring and, now I come to think of it, a pair of kippers for breakfast the next morning. Mind you, I wonder if, at their age, they realise that kippers *are* smoked herrings. I was about 38 when that piece of news filtered through to me, along with the other interesting titbits, like how near Egypt is to Africa and how the word misled, which I'd been reading for years as misled, was actually pronounced miss-led. It's a fold in my brain in which is trapped alarmingly obvious details. It's familial too. Observe the conversation I had with my mother last week.

She: Ooh, I do feel full up after I've eaten. I get so blown up.
Me: Well, don't eat bread. It's the wheat that does it.
She: I never eat bread. I don't. At home I don't ever buy it. (Pause) Is toast bread?

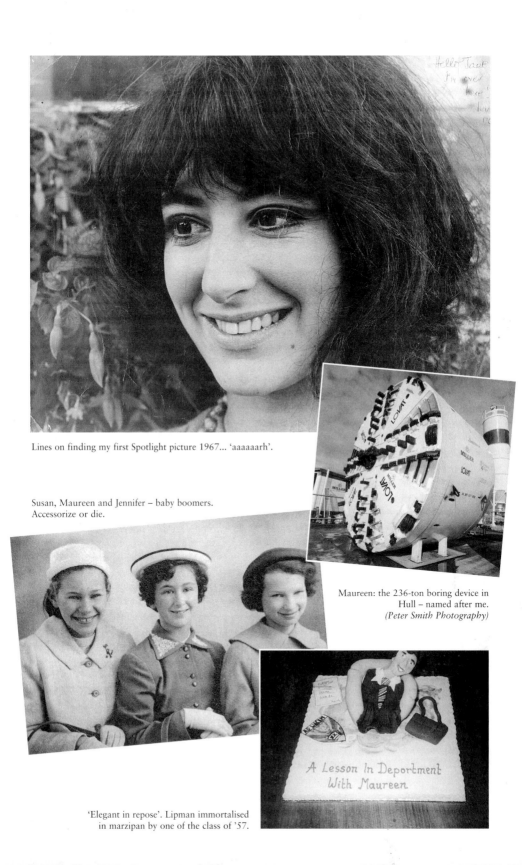

Lines on finding my first Spotlight picture 1967... 'aaaaaarh'.

Susan, Maureen and Jennifer – baby boomers.
Accessorize or die.

Maureen: the 236-ton boring device in
Hull – named after me.
(Peter Smith Photography)

'Elegant in repose'. Lipman immortalised
in marzipan by one of the class of '57.

Mo'swell Hill.

Wheelbarrow of laughs – posing for SOS, a charity for
children with cerebral palsy.

My nice Carmela, my nice Anastasia, my necessity Jacquie – at The Ivy to celebrate my Commanderment.

Bishop and actress,
Doctor and mayor,
Waving wet shrubbery
Over my hair.

Friend Lizzy and I with
original models.
(Brian Moody/Scope Features)

Queue 'ere to board QE2 – taking our gap-year lad home.

Woman in trunks – Thai paradise.

Holiday infatuation – and since
then, does he phone, does he fax,
does he email?

Travels with my ant.

Relaxing on vacation in
Cornwall. Horizon behind
– deadline ahead.

'The corn is as high as Aunt Eller's right eye.'

Prince Charles gets hoofing tips from choreographer Susan Stroman.

Many happy returns, Ma'am (and happily none at the box office).

David Ross and me in *Eskimo Day*, with 'baby boomer' author Jack Rosenthal.

Working with Hugh Jackman and Ioan Gruffyd in one year – no wonder the woman is smiling.

Absolutely Fatuous: Tony Britton and me as Sir Anthony Absolute and Mrs Malaprop in *The Rivals* by Sheridan.

Victori-us. How I press-granged Ms Wood
into speaking at the Women of the Year lunch.

The Full Conti – Tom and I hosting the 50th Year
Celebrations of the State of Israel at Wembley.

Just Williams. Is it fair the way
one of us gets handsomer
every year?

Ewen me at the Evening Standard
Film Awards.

Beryl Bainbridge, Ben Elton and
me being bookish at the
Whitbread Awards.

I suppost it's the mittel European in us which veers herringward. Or it could be the Scandinavian. If we had any Scandinavian in us. My friend Astrid's Norwegian American and she can sniff out a herring tidbit at a distance of 45 yards in a freezer bag inside an Electrolux. The Scots, too, are partial to a wee herring. Rolled in oats and fried. Delicious – you can pick 'em up and eat 'em like a biscuit. Perhaps it was just food to feed too many kids on too little income. Certainly in Russia, Poland and Germany there would have been in the streets barrels of shmaltz herring (almost like eating a huge anchovy – makes your teeth hop just to think of it), salt herrings, soused herrings in vinegar and herrings in wine and herrings in sour cream. (I'm practically dribbling.)

My husband must never read this: he's in withdrawal from that little-known but growing problem, herring addiction. His vice is to take twelve herring fillets, roll them up with a toothpick, place them in a casserole with equal parts vinegar and water, onions, sugar, peppercorns and a bayleaf and bake them brown in the oven. It doesn't seem to occur to him that what looks like grey coiled springs with brown edges floating in spotted brown onion water may taste divine (it does) but poses a hell of a presentation problem. Cornish people solve this problem with a 'Star-Gazey Pie' in which young herrings are cooked with their heads poking out from holes in the pastry topping. 'Here's looking at you, kid.'

Which brings me to the music side of things. I've often been moved to tears by precocious talent served up in the simplest of presentations. The first was during my Manchester stint when I popped in to the Chetham Music School for a lunchtime concert of Chopin and Prokofiev.

Apart from me, the audience in the fifteenth-century plaster-and-beamed hall consisted of one other spectator – and my feeling was that he was a staff member. The fourteen-year-old players were at once self-possessed and tremulous and reinvented the music for me. Every year I watch the Young Musician of the Year and marvel that, no matter what their appearance, the young players are made beautiful by their concentration, involvement, their spirit and their freshness. This year a mere sprat of a northern lass won my heart playing hers out on a mighty and sonorous trombone. She didn't win, except in my living room, but she kept coming back to me, rather like a kipper, and I mean that as a compliment. Smokey, warm and strong with a tendency to linger.

Again, we were lucky enough to see the late, great Michel Petrucciani play jazz piano at the Festival Hall. For anyone who doesn't know the work of this prodigiously talented jazz pianist, he made one piano sound like three. He wove delicate strands of improvised magic around new and classic themes, returning playfully to tease you with remembered melodies before darting off again into flights of fantasy which left you dazzled. The man made beauty tangible. Yet he arrived in the auditorium in a wheelchair, swung himself on to the stage on two tiny crutches and, standing by his grand piano, was, honestly only inches bigger than his piano stool. He suffered from something colloquially known as as 'glass bones' disease, similar, I guess, to that suffered by Toulouse-Lautrec. When he played, though, he was mighty. Michel Petrucciani died last year, far too young, but thank God he left us his work, which is eternal.

Let's face it, if there is a connection between a simple but delicious fish and great and glorious music, then it's tenuous, to say the least. I trawled a few opinions at dinner with friends the other night and nothing much was forthcoming. My friend Harriet sang a timorous version of 'They shall have a fishy on a little dishy', prompting the idea of a new CD called *Harriet Sings Herring*, or better still, as her son Simeon pointed out, *Harriet Fishman Sings Herring* – yes, it's her real name. Actually, the CD took care of the rest of the evening's entertainment as we composed titles for the disc. In terms of around the table contributions they read as follows:

FAMILIAR TUNAS FROM OPARROTO ROCK

'There's a Plaice for Us'	'Sprat'll Be The Day'
'Oh, You Are A Mucky Squid'	'Twist And Trout'
'Anchovy The Way To Go Home'	'Whale Meat Again'
'All I Have To Do Is Bream'	'Kiss Me Skate'
'There Was I, Whiting At The Perch'	'Prawn Free'
'Don't Fry For Me, Argentahina'	'Roe, Roe, Roe'
'Mackerel The Knife'	'Abba Dab Adabba'
'The Girl From Kippernima'	'Goldfish Finger'
'Here Comes The Scalloping Major'	'Teen Angel'

'Salmon Chanted Evening'   'O Sole Mio'
'Shark, Rattle And Rollmop'   'If You Knew Sushi'
'We're A Cuttle Of Swells'   Prawn Free'
'Turbot For Fortune Go You And I' 'In My Oyster Bonnet'
'Sitting On Haddock Of The Bay'   'Passardina'
'It's Only A Scampi In Old Scampi-Town'
'I Can't Do My Halibut-om Button Up'

We could have a Foreword by A. A. Gill – and that's just Side
One. There's another side. Perhaps you'd like to Mullet over? It
could just be a complete performance of the opera written by
Benjamin Britten, clearly with the punch line of this chapter in
mind: the tale of the Nineteenth Century fisherman, 'Albert
Herring'.

Since I mentioned this ludicrous example of time-wasting to
Julia MacKenzie, she has phoned roughly twice a day. The 1st call
went like this...

'Hello, Mo. "Bloater Wind Southerly", Oh, and Jerry says "Eel
Be Seeing You." 'Bye'.

And then another...

'Hello, Jack, won't keep you. Just tell Mo, "Bass You Is My
Woman Now". 'Bye.'

And one day, unforgettably...

'Hi, Mo. George Shearing says have you got "Mahi's He's
Making Eyes at Me"? It's a Hawaiian fish – '

'George Shearing? You mean as in Ella Fitzgerald and George
Sh___'

'Yeah, he lives near us, he's lovely. He also suggested "Pike Up
All Your Cares and Woes" – '

'I can't believe George Shearing is supplying me with fish
songs! Shouldn't he be brilliantly arranging something?'

'Hang on, he's on the other line. He says "Caviarno
Rusticana".'

The whole thing's building up to a slim volume – or a concert,
maybe. Who knows? It's up for crabs. Included will be works by
Coley Porter, Oscar Hammerhead and Pilchard Rogers, engaging
the services of John Dory Previn, Billy J. Crayfish, Theolonius
Monkfish and the great Jaws Shearing himself – at the piranha.

It's a Sing-A-Ling if you like, with some well-known backing Groupers like the 'Mamas & the Snappers'. Maybe Jackson Pollack would design the poster. A special attraction would be Old Dolph' Harris singing 'Tie My Kedgeree Down'. The highlight of the evening will be selections from those famous shows – 'Finan's Rainbow' and 'The Flounder Music' with – soy – Ginger Rogers and Finisterre.

EDITOR: Maureen?

MAUREEN: Yes?

EDITOR: Stoppit! For Cod's Hake, stoppit!

Part II

Mother of Two Tours England

Live and Kidding

The idea for *Live and Kidding* came from producer Duncan Weldon having a spare Sunday night at the Chichester Festival Theatre and me having an excess of public speaking at lunches, brunches, benefits and Bar Mitzvahs around the silly season, which these days takes in Christmas, spring and the summer solstice. It suddenly became clear that making people laugh to raise money for homeless palaeontologists and to provide support groups for single parents of children with risotto allergies might similarly amuse an audience of theatregoers in a small intimate space. What's more, I wouldn't have to draw the raffle, auction my underwear and eat dodgy pâté de fois long-ago-put-out-to-gras with the chairman and his lovely wife who addresses me throughout as Miriam.

The 'small intimate space' turned into a 1,400-seater theatre and the one-night stand turned into a fully fledged affair. Then, at the Leeds City of Varieties, the affair became a proper engagement with guests and a video. Zelma, should you be passing through Hull, shows the video to invited (pressganged) groups twice weekly. Otherwise you may find *Live and Kidding* slightly harder to locate than the Bermuda Triangle.

This new respectability did not involve cleaning up my act, for I intended it to remain as tawdry and indiscreet as befitted the thoughts of a girl from a nice middle-class home. I have always known that just as the natural habitat for a truffle is under a knobbly root in marshy terrain with a pig nearby, then the natural habitat for a comedian is in a back-street tenement, grimy with poverty and unemployment, with an abusive, alcoholic-dependent parent or two, eight to ten aggressive siblings and a social life centred around the saloon bar of the Cock and Pullet where aged three, snivelling and snotty, you first performed 'Does Your

Chewing Gum Lose Its Flavour On The Bedpost Overnight?' wearing a Fair Isle pullover, a pith helmet and your dad's old sparking clogs. For this you received a bag of pork scratchings and a clout round the ear.

Add to the mixture a weak, sickly frame, buck teeth, chronic asthma, myopia and membership of an ethnic minority and you are but a nano-second away from 'House Full' signs at the London Palladium.

Now, other than the myopia, the overbite, the ethnicity and a mild tendency to croup between the ages of seven and eleven, I don't have many of these qualifications. My middle-class upbringing gave me nothing to complain about, unless you count an obsession on my mother's part with matching accessories. And – oh, all right, let's get heavy – she made me squeeze a fabric tightly in my fist for many minutes to test it for crushing before purchase. And she *never* let me cast a clout (!) till May was *well* out nor let me return to the house for a forgotten item without first counting to ten and never let anyone sew anything I was, at the time, wearing, without the sewer first biting the fabric of the item to be sewn.

I've had some theatre dressers withdraw very smartly from my room after that request. But compared to Billy Connolly, Lenny Bruce and Jacky Mason, I come from the Darling family in *Peter Pan* and simply don't have the background for an opening *gag*, let alone a darkly humorous philosophy of life.

Mind you, when you look around at today's funny men and women, they are all pretty middle class. Paul Merton, Victoria Wood, Steve Coogan, Ben Elton. I suppose the buck teeth stops here, after Ken Dodd and Tarby and Dave Allen and all those 'We were so poor we had one shoe between the eight of us' – 'You were lucky! We only had one *foot* between the eight of us!' Or perhaps it's just that the new boys on the block all honed their knives at university, not at the lathe or the factory bench. Cynical observations such as 'Why is it better to be black than gay?' – 'If you're black you don't have to tell your mother' or 'What's the difference between Manchester United and Oasis?' – 'Manchester United are playing Giggs next year' wouldn't work in the working men's clubs and likewise mothers-in-law who've 'had everything taken out and a new fireplace put in' would get short shrift in the union bar. Still the message remains the same whoever

the messenger – the jesters are the boil lancers. We let out the pus of
anger and fear and prejudice, we release the steam from the pressure
cooker, and from Lear's Fool onwards it's always been a precarious
sort of a job. Yet the high I get from doing stand-up – or perhaps in
my case, 'lean-to' – comedy is higher by at least an elephant's eye
than the one I may or may not get after a well-cast, well-performed
play. Perhaps that's why I feel like such a hybrid in the world of show
biz – one court shoe in the theatre, one plimsoll in light
entertainment, one inner sole in the bookshop and not a leg to stand
on anywhere.

For a start I'm a woman who loves jokes. Loves to tell jokes.
'Tell them the joke about *Moon River*,' urged my mother in front
of a roomful of guests to my thirteen-year-old self. This in itself
was a challenge, not least because of my age and sex but because
Moon River was the *punchline* of a complicated joke concerning a
talent scout visiting the papal sanctum in Rome. Any reception
subsequently had to be regarded as an improvement.

Here's one of my brother's off-the-wall stories, phoned from a
stopover in Bangkok and swiftly inserted into Act II.

Man and woman marry, each for the second time. They resolve
never to discuss their pasts. They go to Mauritius for a
honeymoon of bliss and on the first day on the beach she kisses
him and says she's going to take a dip. He watches her walk into
the water, where in less than five minutes she swims a mile
straight forward, a mile to the right, a mile to the left and a mile
back into the shore. She walks back casually, as though she's
merely been paddling, and flops down beside him.

'Unbelievable!' he says. 'Where did you learn to swim like that?'

She looks at him angrily. 'We agreed never to talk about our
pasts, OK?'

The following day she walks into the sea again and astonishes
him by swimming five miles in five minutes, zig-zagging all over
the sea and returning scarcely out of breath.

Once more he asks her, 'Where did you learn to swim like that?'

She brushes his question aside brusquely. '*We agreed*, OK? Just
don't ask.'

After a week of watching her incredible pyrotechnics, he can
stand it no more and demands to know where she learned to swim
like that.

'You won't like it,' she tells him.

'I don't care – I need you to tell me. I need to know.'

'You'll be sorry.'

'I'll be sorrier still if you don't tell me.'

Finally, she breaks. 'OK – you wanted to know. I was a street walker in Venice.'

It always mystifies me how quickly topical jokes appear and circulate. From whence? From whom? For how much? And who rotates the legendary quips made around round tables and round Irishmen called Wilde? Did Lady X really say, 'If you've nothing good to say about anyone – then come sit by me'? Did Dorothy Parker quip, 'Here comes the good time that was had by all'? Or did they think of it later when telling a friend and omit to add, 'Gee, I wish I'd thought of that at the time!' Certainly, on the odd occasion I've been told a witticism attributed to me, I've had no recollection of having said it – which didn't stop me graciously accepting the attribution and repeating it rather more than was necessary.

Meeting Michael Jayston in a Brighton street, he reminded me of the time we were filming together in the *About Face* series. Waiting around for the right light to film in a Nottinghamshire garden, he had stopped to admire some banks of resplendent peonies and bemoaned his own meagre display at home. Apparently I had instantaneously accused him of showing evidence of *peonies envy*, a pun which he'd remembered fondly and I'd obliterated. Till now, of course. And the next book, article, theatre programme and, one day, I guess, memorial celebration.

Most jokes seem to seek me out. Life has a way of giving a comic a funny face which ultimately starts to pay for itself. Once the face is a familiar one, the sight of it provokes other faces to feed it material.

''Ere, Maureen, you'll like *this* one...' they'll say, or, 'You wanna come down our headquarters, Maureen. Laugh? You'll snap a tendon!' Or they'll simply stare at you long and pityingly and say, 'You've been on the telly!', as though accusing you of gang rape. Then as you decide whether to agree or mince self-deprecatingly, they'll add, 'I've got that kind of a memory!' 'Aren't you Richard Todd in later life?' someone once deliriously said to the actor. Family, friends, members of the public, doctors and au pairs all figure in the routine, and even the odd late-night panic call Barry Cryer... 'Here, Barry, I'm doing an accountants gig tomorrow night – any gags?' 'Yeah, how about, "An accountant is someone who's good at numbers but doesn't have the personality to be an auditor?"' 'Thanks, Bazza!' To all of these naturally funny people I owe a debt of gratitude for supplying the software for the obsolescent computer in my head.

Worryingly, there are so many one-man shows doing the rounds now that it won't be long before some enterprising entrepreneur thinks, Hey, I know what. Why not put all these 'one men' together and have the actors then talk to each other! We can call it a PLAY! Perhaps actors prefer to talk to imaginary characters rather than real ones. After all, that's how we started out, addressing our dolls and our toy soldiers. And they never answered back, came late every day, gave you the wrong line, or reeked of BO and tequila, or made you laugh as you were busy dying at Agincourt.

'Words are all we have,' wrote Samuel Beckett. Darcey Bussell and Marcel Marceau might disagree but they're all in the business of communicating.

Communication is a continuing circle of thought connections. It's as old as it's new. E-mail is just fast ER mail. Karaoke is a computerised sing-song round the piano. Fax is a papyrus phone call. CD Rom is... what is CD Rom? However, swapping and sharing mishaps and comparing cock-ups make talk not just cheap but downright cheerful. In the beginning was the word, in the millennium is the chat show – a roomful of people watching two people do what they are no longer doing themselves.

For one of the great things about stand-up comedy is the direct communication you feel with an audience. Human beings need to communicate and though we can do so through dance and through music and love-making and even silence, if it's an easy silence, I believe that when you come through the door from the gridlocked street, the automated tube, the soft hiss of the closing bank machine in your ear and the uneven camber of the newly replaced pavement beneath your soles and you call out 'Hello', then the most beautiful sound on earth is the returning call of, 'Hello, love. How was your day?' And if you're in the wrong house, what the hell? It could be even better to talk!

On the Road: Live and Kidding – A Diary

It was the last week of rehearsals for my solo show *Live and Kidding* and I crawled home, in a tailback which started in Ladbroke Grove and more or less stretched to Muswell Hill, to find Mr Roddy Llewellyn stepping out of a cab in my drive at about the same time.

He was doing a piece on floral delivery services and I was to judge arrangements for the *Mail on Sunday*. They were being delivered to Marianne Plume (it's an anagram) so as to discourage special treatment. The plus side was that it worked and all the arrangements save one were tatty. The down side is that I forgot to tell my secretary the flowers would be arriving, so she sent the first batch away – 'not known at this address'. Mr Llewellyn was delightful, the session painless and the house was filled with fauna all week.

On the Saturday of the same week, I was watching Manchester United when the doorbell rang and a bunch of white tulips and freesias came through the door. 'Oh God – not more flaming flowers!' I groaned. 'I'll have to put 'em in a saucepan!' 'Good luck on Monday,' said the card. 'You'll be brilliant.' It was from my son at university and I was suitably chagrined, touched, overwhelmed and moved to buy a vase.

Monday, we opened at Richmond. The theatre was full, the performance smooth and technically easy, the laughs constant, the ambience warm. The husband, the daughter, the agent and the producer were all visibly relieved and the actor, the pianist and the director hit the Sauvignon with élan. It was our first audience and they had shown us we had a show.

Tuesday night. Forget everything you just read. The actress was nervous, the sound crackled and every time the audience laughed I panicked. 'For God's sake,' I willed them, 'keep laughing while I THINK what comes next!' Mercifully, the audience laughed without recourse to pity. Overheard in the audience, after a man waxed enthusiastically about the show, his lady companion said sourly 'Well I don't *like* her but she's brilliant.' I love it that anyone would venture out to see an actor they didn't like – in a one person show!

The following week was Guildford and I decided to stay at Grayshott Hall, the health farm. I weighed in on Monday, got blood pressured, then drove through blinding rain into the Guildford one-way system. And out again. And in again. Finally I found the Yvonne Arnaud Theatre, more or less where I last saw it two years or so ago for *Re-Joyce!*

First night went well. Something about the proximity of audience and performer at Guildford turned the whole thing into a party. Producer Duncan Weldon, Guildford director James Barber and I had a contented, bordering on the smug, meal and I got in my car smiling and waving and set off for Grayshott in the rainy dark. In minutes I was deeply lost. It was gone midnight, I couldn't find the A3 for Portsmouth and I kept setting off for London. I drove to the A31 to Farnham and soon I was the only car for miles on a pitch-black road riding to nowhere.

My husband phoned. 'How did it go, love?' I started whimpering, 'I'm lost. It's dark. I'm driving in the wrong direction. I'm so tired. I can't see properly.' And other sentences to cheer a spouse at 12.10am on a wet Monday morning. 'Go back to Guildford and get a cab to lead you,' he barked. 'Go on – turn round now.' I did and the minicab driver said, 'Drive in front of you all the way to Grayshott? Never! It'll cost you twenty quid.' 'I don't care if it costs 120 quid.' I said. 'I want a bath.' He drove me to the A3 and waved me off, waiving the fare at the same time, bless his heart. The following night I had a motorcycle cortege as far as Godalming, courtesy of stage management, and somehow I managed to destress and detox during the day and pump adrenalin at night for a week. I also managed to put on one pound four ounces, although the nurse at Grayshott would probably hate me for telling you that.

At the end of the second show on Saturday night I was physically unable to get up from my curtsey and stayed down momentarily – both hands on the floor. The applause built up wildly. Eureka! I'd always thought the whole idea was to make it look easy! I realised Donald Wolfit may have got it right and in future I intended to cling to the curtains.

Home for sweet Sunday and a dress fitting. My second-act dress by Neil Cunningham was a marvellous stretch satin but somehow it had managed to climb up my body and become a micro skirt. When I sat down you could see last night's kedgeree. We went back to the drawing board and opted for the flexibility of organza.

Sunday night was the Olivier Awards. I worked on my face with a wire broom and some mortician's wax and dug out an original thirties black chiffon which my friend Rita had given me twenty years before. It was a hit. Jack hates these 'do's' and climbed into his penguin suit with something akin to despair. Outside the Grosvenor House, he tried, at my suggestion, to put his woolly scarf back in the car and the doorman trapped his hand in the car door. We spent the next 45 minutes in the Gents with TCP and the one strip of Elastoplast in a five-star hotel.

Monday I headed for Bath in blinding hail. The theatre welcomed me back with full houses. I was still chopping and changing lyrics and order of jokes. In a show like this, variety is the arribiata of life. At two o'clock I collapsed into my hotel bed. Some time later I woke up and looked at my watch. It was a quarter to three. A gale was blasting the window frames. I wove my way to the bathroom muttering, 'I've got to get some sleep. If I'm this tired out I'll forget all the ad-libs!' I took a Baclofen muscle relaxant and flopped back into bed just as there was a knock at the door. I wheeled round. 'Who is it?'

'Room service.'

'Room service??!!' I yanked open the door. A waiter stood there with a trolley, silver tureen, bread baskets. 'What time do you call this?'

'Erm...it's – er – twenty-five to ten, madam. Isn't that when you, er, ordered breakfast?'

I had, of course, looked at my watch upside-down – it had been quarter past nine – and I now faced a morning in a Bristol recording studio with very relaxed muscles.

Friday night I lit my shabbos candles in the Bath dressing room as ever, hoping that God would understand. Best show ever – me light as a feather and them standing two deep on two levels!

A card arrived from Mrs Browning of Bath telling me I was talented with a lovely figure. 'However,' it went on, 'I believe that all arms over a certain age need sleeves to flatter them. We were sitting in *Row F*!'

The day before, Alan Strachan had overheard a woman furiously complaining in The Hole in the Wall restaurant.

'So, madam doesn't do mid-week matinées – who does she think she is? Too much effort for her?'

'It must be quite exhausting for her,' murmured her companion.

'So what?' snapped back the theatregoer. 'It's only a couple of hours a day, for heaven's sake. It can't kill her!'

Heading for the Duchess Theatre for a five-week run with small red eyes and a luminescent cold sore, I could only hope she was right.

On my final night I tottered back after two shows barely able to put one knee in front of the other. My plastic key wouldn't open my hotel room. I went for help but the porter's master key also failed. After eight minutes' wait I ran snarling to reception and emitted wild animal noises. The night staff finally congregated outside my room trying endless combinations of key card whilst I ranted and raved. Finally the manager came running from his desk: 'But Miss Lipman, you are Room 219!'

'I know *that*!' I yelled, 'and I want to get into it and go to sodding sleep!'

'Then why are you trying to open Room 215?' he enquired.

On the road I'd drafted my own lyrics into my favourite song, 'Can't Get Started With You', and put in an announcement before the curtain went up, as a bit of a lark. It went:

Throughout the performance please ensure that your personal pagers, digital watches and musical pill reminders are fully operational and set to go. When accepting calls on mobile phones, we ask that you make sure the whole audience, not just those in your immediate vicinity, can hear your conversation.

When consuming confectionery, remember to remove both outer and inner wrappings as slowly as possible and to crinkle the cellophane in your hands for the duration of the performance.

Remember – coughing attacks are infectious, so please cough generously, particularly on or around the punchlines. If you miss a punchline because of a serious hacker, then please make sure you ask the couple behind you, loudly and clearly, to repeat it. If you see the punchline coming a mile off, then Chinese whisper it along the aisle, pointing out how much funnier it was when Bob Monkhouse told it.

Thank you for your indulgence and please enjoy the show.

And now, Hull's own answer to the closure of the docks – MAUREEN LIPMAN!

It was good to wait offstage and hear the chuckles build before Michael Haslam, at the piano, began to play in 'Can't Get Started With You...' I rather smarmily changed the lyrics depending on the location – Bath, Richmond, Chichester and finally, the Duchess. Alan Strachan, my *Re-Joyce!* director, kept a firm grip on my creativity and brought the guillotine down on any inherent sentimentality. It was vaguely autobiographical in form (Hull figuring largely enough to ensure it would never travel overseas) and marriage, kids, advising Barbra Streisand on how to sing and throwing potatoes during a royal lunch were setpieces around which to hang the odd song and sketch.

As the curtain rang down on Live and Kidding and the audience filed out, they heard the following comments over the air – most of them courtesy of Jack:

Woman's voice: What I liked – there was no nudity. *Amadeus* was the same.

Man's voice: I like her better when she's with other people.

W V: Put it away till we're outside. You can smoke outside.

M V: I haven't *lit* it! I'm just holding it in my mouth, ready.

W V: Are you hungry?

M V: I could eat a flock bed.

W V: Which restaurant did you book?

M V: I thought *you* booked the restaurant!

W V: That bit was quite amusing – with the joke.

M V: Which joke?
W V: Oh, you know me, I can't remember jokes.

W V: Oh, look, there's Gerald! Don't look!
M V: Why not?
W V: He's with another man. He looks like Trevor
                McDonald only more Spanish.

W V: You know what was really funny? That
                programme on meerkats.

W V: What did you think of it?
M V: Marvellous. I slept like a baby.

M V: She's not a patch on *Riverdance*.

We ran successfully for a limited season of eight weeks.
Sometimes it ran like clockwork, sometimes – as I wrote at the
time – it ran like the movie *Clockwise*.

Ah, the theatre! The sheer magic of a night out at the theatre.
The expectant hum of the stylish audience, the barely audible
sigh as velvet evening cloak meets uncut moquette chair, the
insistence of the third bar bell, the last-minute flurry of a long-
awaited latecomer, the settling down, the darkening
auditorium, the swish of the heavy curtain, the heavy tread of
the leading actress as she gingerly crosses the roof of the theatre
in high heels, cocktail dress, newspaper folded over her head to
protect her from the rain.

    Sorry. Shall I run that last one past you again? Yes, it was
me. I *was* that thespian, though nobody in the packed auditorium on a Saturday matinée in March would have known it as I
entered centre stage, splattered but smiling.
    The problem with the Duchess Theatre was that it was
deprived of tender love and care. A string of farces – *No Sex
Please We're British*, *Run For Your Wife* and *Don't Dress for Dinner*
– had left it with its trousers firmly nailed to its ankles. The No.
1 dressing room, at the top of 48 steps, painted in parchment

gloss, resembled a sleeper in an old Pullman Express and was all right if you like receiving guests who seem to be impersonating Dustin Hoffman, mid-gasp, in *The Marathon Man*. There *was* a lift but it was purely ornamental and not very at that. The stage, incidentally, was two more flights down from the main entrance, so nipping back to the dressing room for a forgotten inner sole required the assistance of a hyperbaric oxygen chamber and a Sherpa.

One Saturday I arrived one and a half hours before curtain up (it takes that long these days for the concrete to set on my make-up) to find my assistant Sally at the door saying, 'There's a problem...' Always my favourite opening gambit. The problem was that a shower had leaked into the electrics and all the dressing rooms and backstage were in darkness. I would have to dress and make up in a small front office. They'd rig me up a mirror, there was a point for the Carmen rollers, and Sally would feel her way up 48 steps, distinguish between Leichner No. 5 and No. 9 pansticks by touch and a household candle, and carry armloads of dresses and shoes down on a return trip.

Somehow I got my make-up and my microphone on and crept along the corridor to the loo (an interesting experience when wired up for sound!). When I got back I could hear the buzz of the audience as they filed in. It counterpointed nicely with the banging I was now doing on the office door which had obligingly locked behind me. The first master key failed to open the door and with five minutes to curtain up, in my kimono and rollers, my solo show, *Live and Kidding*, looked like it would have to be retitled *An Evening With Nora Batty*. Finally the door caved in, the frock went on and Sally led me in my coral satin slingbacks and matching frock across the flat roof of the theatre, in the rain, and down the darkened passageways to the stage. That was Saturday.

On Monday night I was sitting at the table, stage left, telling the audience the polar bear joke. (The one where the baby polar bear asks his mom if he has any grizzly in him. 'No, darling,' his mother says. 'You are a proper polar bear.' 'Well, have I got a bit of koala in me?' he asks. 'No, darling, you are pure polar,' she assures him. 'Have I got a *weeny* bit of panda then?' he persists. '*Noooo*, darling,' replies his mother. 'You are polar bear through and through. Why do you keep asking these silly questions?' 'Why?' says the baby bear. ''Cos I'm bloody freezing!') Yeah – well, it was a family show.

Halfway through the joke I realised that it was raining. Not a steady pitter-patter on the roof I'd come to love and circumnavigate so well, but on the stage on which I was damply sitting. It persisted down steadily until I was forced to ask the audience that old theatrical standby – 'Is it raining or is it me?' They confirmed that they were seeing the same weather from where they were sitting and it went on all through the first act, forcing my pianist and I to move all the furniture to one side and wringing from me a spirited version of Gene Kelly's 'Singing In The Rain'. The 'problem' that night was a four-gallon leak from the washing machine four floors up. There was a *Sunday Times* critic in that night but, bless him, he didn't mention it – or maybe his notes were too wet to decipher.

Another unfortunate critic was seated next door to my mother. 'He was writing everything down in a little red book,' she sneaked, 'but he never came back for the second half.' I phoned the press office to find out who the indolent skiver was and found out that in fact he didn't leave in the interval – he merely moved to another seat because the 'woman sitting next to me kept staring at my notes!'

So next time you settle down in your aisle seat, with your programme and your bittersweet mints, and the curtain rises in a suburban house in Maidenhead with French windows and a maid with a feather duster, spare a thought, will you, for the fact that five minutes before curtain up the French windows were hanging from the flies, the leading lady was in hospital having a disposable lens removed from the back of her eye, the Inspector was being forcibly dragged out of The Frog and Parrot in Frith Street singing 'Keep Your Hand on Your Ha'Penny' and the maid is desperately ad libbing until the door opens. All in a day's work for the profession so aptly described by the actor Patrick Troughton as 'shouting in the evenings'.

Still, I'd written, with the help of Andrew Marvel, Geoff Morrow, Jack and Joyce and a couple of composers like Gershwin and Bernstein, a variety show. The critics were kind, even fond; occasionally patronising.

'Her taste in jokes, thankfully, is refreshingly rude.'

'Marvellous observations on marriage which transform her into a Jewish Victoria Wood.'

And even, mysteriously, 'Like a brushed-cotton nightie.'

'Lipman pulls it off. Just.'

No wonder the actor's fear of someone tapping them on the shoulder and saying, 'Have they found you out yet, old boy?', grows through the years.

I remember watching a documentary showing Lily Tomlin putting her act together for weeks on the road. She changed it, sharpened it, honed it, every night a new angle, a fresh thought. Finally she hit New York and, boy, was she a hit. Why? Because she made it look effortless, improvised – newly minted. I admired the discipline; the rules followed to make it look *easy*. I dislike the acts who hang on to the curtains, dripping sweat and beg you to applaud their efforts. I enjoyed the writing and the rewriting. It was structured danger – and (no kidding) I've seldom felt more alive.

Underwired

The Queen's corsetière and I once appeared on the same afternoon TV show ('Hi and welcome to *Burbling in the Afternoon* and I'm Fifi, your ditsy blonde lightweight, and today we'll be hearing from Ainsley – how to do 101 unheard-of things to a venison escalope – and from Maureen Lipman about her one-man show, *Live and Ticking*, but first the tragic story of a woman whose face was bitten off by a rabid au pair girl with multiple personality disorder'). The corsetière was a sound, smart-looking lady called June who runs Rigby & Peller, Corsetière by Appointment. It's an uplifting tradition.

Before the camera lit up she whispered to me, 'Now, you are *not* to send me up!' I opened my eyes to their full width – about two millimetres these days – and mouthed back, 'Would I?' I didn't and was duly impressed by the array of basques separating the breasts of the surprisingly well endowed models who paraded through the tiny studio.

Afterwards, June told me I ought to pop into their salon. She'd already correctly guessed my bra size and, it seemed to me, also deduced that what was nestling under my sweater was threadbare and mangy – not to mention the state of my bra! 'Yes...well...I will,' I mumbled. 'I ought to pop in...' I paused, hoping to curtail the inevitable, but failed...'Before I pop out, as t'were.' Her smile was the epitome of patience.

'Mind you,' I careered on, 'I don't want anyone handling the goods. You know, shlepping them up and under and all around the cubicle. I had enough of that when I was a fledgling.'

'No, of course,' she said soothingly, 'but if you want a bra that fits then you must be properly measured.'

'Yeah, with my clothes on. Then shove the bras through a hole in the curtain and leave me to my own devices, OK?'

She concurred with mild amusement, so I resolved to go in the shop. But childhood trauma was stronger than the resolve. Lingering memories of Hull lingerie departments, me beige faced and sullen behind the candlewick, my mother boldly going where no man dares and, to my ears, hollering in parade-ground fashion, 'She's very small backed but VERY FULL IN THE CUP.' Then, as every eye swivelled towards me, 'She needs a lot of SUPPORT.' I did and I wasn't getting it. The purchase of firm crossover fronts, adjustable triple-strength straps, long-line all-in-ones with comfigrip suspenders and other such Humberside contraceptive devices rendered me as impregnable as a concrete fortress presided over by Roseanne Barr.

Remission only came during the sixties when, braless and corsetless, we grew accustomed to occasionally bopping ourselves in the eye with our own or someone else's renegade boob. Any shape was acceptable. High slung, low slung, wobbly, pointy, pert, pigeon or pachyderm. We let it all hang out. I was a 36C cup and proud of it. I was famed in the Manchester theatre in which I worked for being able to lace myself for period plays into corsets which made me resemble a golf bag with a bum sticking out the top. Two children and two decades later, with the whole thing resembling a well-used candle in a Portuguese bistro, I was poised to re-examine the reinforcements.

The old Warner underwired front-fastening 34C see-through saw me through the grown-up years of smooth lines under fake Jean Muir silks. Then one day in Frank's of Golders Green – one of the last blessed outposts of what used to be called a drapers, where you can buy a pair of gloves, knickers or slippers without having to negotiate an escalator or a food department – one of their wonderfully peremptory assistants told me that my bra size was, in fact, not 36B or 34C but 32DD. My face fell in line with everything else.

'Thirty-two double D!' I hollered. 'Impossible! I must be a freak. How can any woman who's five foot seven inches be a double D?'

'No, dear. You're a perfectly normal shape.' (For an emu!) 'You just have a narrow frame and large bosoms, that's all.' She moved towards the till, which still looked like it was suffering from withdrawal symptoms from the loss of those aerial tubes which used to whizz overhead, ferrying bills from nighties to naughties, and relieved me of the price of three double-D hammocks in black, white and beige. I've been wearing them ever since and washing them together for long enough for them to become a uniform shade of pewter.

Imagine my discombobulation, empathetic reader – nay, bosom friend – when I finally made it to Rigby & Peller in search of strapless support for under my off-the-shoulder *Live and Kidding* stretch satin, only to be told, quite pleasantly that they were low in stock in my size – which was a 30E cup. 'Thirty-E!' I gasped. 'For God's sake, I must look like a bloody bus stop!'

So there you have it. Going down, as they say in the talking lift. The world is divided into two sorts of women. Those, often boarding-school educated or elderly, who swim outdoors all year round and shed their clothes in the changing rooms with the abandon of a two-year-old, and those, like your correspondent, who wear a bathing costume in the sauna and put their underwear on tortuously under a towel with their head in the locker.

'What are the measurements of a mermaid?' goes the old fishwives' tale. And the answer? 'Thirty-eight, twenty-four – and eighty pence a pound.'

Oh, how I wish I could tell you the joke about the woman with the overdeveloped right breast. I would but it requires me to lurch around the room miming a large object being thrown in the air and caught behind my back, then twisted round my body and hoola-hooped back the other way... Look, it's a visual joke, but one thing I promise. If I ever get to promote this book on a late-night show, I will do it. The whole joke. Honestly. And never work again.

Perhaps one shouldn't joke about breasts. The important point is that they work. If they are remodelled into perfect scimitars it means relocating the nipples, and that's curtains for foreplay, which in itself is a marvellous title for a slim but racy detective novel.

When Demi and Melanie G, with their super attenuated boobs, are 'on top', it's probably devastating – but lying on their stomachs having a snooze must be like levitating. Weird.

The Ruby Isle

It was my friend Ruby's incredibly significant birthday. The significance of this was such that my ribs were sore from the mental nudges I'd given them and one eyebrow was permanently arched.

A brief chat with her friend, Aida, told me that Ruby didn't want a party, had never had a birthday party and didn't intend to start now at the awe-inspiring age of thingywhatsit.

So I racked my brains for a suitable gift to send to Jersey where she lives in mellow style and comfort. Champagne? Well, it's very Ruby but it's not very me (then again, you can't send poached eggs on toast through the Royal Mail – although much of what one receives through the Royal Mail arrives looking like poached eggs on toast, but that's another issue which I'm now poaching from myself). Flowers? To Jersey? I might as well send a couple of pounds of new potatoes, a cow and a postcard of John Nettles, and my guess was that the number of silk scarves and silver photo frames currently winging their way there was enough to justify laying on a special charter from Stansted.

So, with the arrogance of long-standing affection, I decided to give her the thing that was easiest to send over and guaranteed a warm welcome. Me.

The plan was that on the Monday in question, my mother and I would board the early flight to St Helier Airport where Ruby's son, Julian, would meet and secrete us somewhere about his small, beachside hotel, then, whilst his wife Martha took Ruby to The Potteries Restaurant for lunch, he would follow on, with two heavily bearded Lipmans slumped low in his back seat. Once at the restaurant, I would enter the dining room via the kitchen, where the staff would provide me with a waitress's uniform and a portion of Dover sole.

So far, so well timed. But much of my timing is only in my head and to deadhead a long story, we missed the plane. Well, no, we got to the airport in time but the gate was closed and whereas I might have legged it, Linford Christie style, through Terminal 2, scattering domestic flyers left and right like Schwarzenegger in Chinacraft, it was unfair to ask my mother to do the same. Matricide seems a high price to pay for a prank.

Anyway, miss it we did. Which was OK with me because I put us on standby for the next plane at 12.35, which could still deliver us in time for me to deliver the tarte citron. I say OK with me because my mother has never missed anything in her entire life. Not an appointment. Not a bus. Not an opportunity, not a trick, not nothing. She was mystified by my apparent sang-froid. Her jaw, which had dropped a handsbreadth at the news, remained so for minutes on end. Her eyes took on a black and haunted expression only seen in early Ingmar Bergman movies and her brow furrowed into readable excerpts from the Torah. Zelma was in shock.

'What's going to happen?' she breathed hoarsely. 'What can...? What will...? I mean...Will we get...? I mean... What if we don't...?' Her knees sagged and she visibly aged as I led her, mumbling and stumbling, towards the VIP lounge, where she continued to ponder the unponderable for the next three hours. Out loud, and on a loop. (I read *Hello!* magazine with a casual abandon that I didn't entirely feel.)

'Do you think if we hadn't stopped when you saw Emma Thompson....?' (We had actually chatted to her for all of six seconds.) 'I mean, why *did* you tell the car to come at 7.15 instead of seven o'clock? Did you think the plane went at 9.00 not 8.25? Do you think if we'd run for it they'd have let us on? Shall you bother with the 12.35 plane? Do you think we'd even get on it? What if it's completely full to bursting? Do you think if we hadn't stopped for Emma T...?'

We got on the plane. Our docket said 'Attending 80th birthday party' – ooops, sorry, Ruby – cats and open bags all over the place. We arrived in 35 minutes, sped across the quaint winding and largely unsignposted roads to the back entrance of the beautiful Potteries Restaurant and hissed meaningfully through the kitchen windows at the staff to let us in. A brown pinny went over my white shirt and some kind helper emerged from the vapour of a frantic lunchtime kitchen (I mean, they needed me and my mother like Nicholas Soames needs a treacle pudding) and clipped on a tie.

'Can I have a hat?' I gurgled. I'm never happier than when I'm in extravagant disguise or an animal suit. *Voila*! A small pastry hat manifested itself low on my brow, giving the missing barmy look to my regalia. Glasses went on awry and as I stood waiting for my props, I could feel the spirit of Su Pollard entering my bones. The Jersey accent is, amazingly, gutteral like a South African one, but at that point I hadn't found that out, so the character remained firmly rooted in East Lancs.

By this time, in the excitement, Ruby's Dover sole had been cooked to the consistency of something requiring Blue Watch and a three-man pump – but, *cela ne fait rien*, I carried it on high into the clattering chatter of the restaurant.

Ruby had her back to me and was in conversation with Martha and Julian as I executed a painstaking bob, banged down the plate, tapped her on the shoulder and over-enunciated, 'I'm ever so sorry, Mrs Bernstein, but the gefilte fish is off, so will you settle for the sole?'

She gazed at me with absolute blank bewilderment, not an expression I've ever seen on her wonderful, humorous face, as if to say, 'If this is what they call Care in the Community, then I'm changing communities.'

'You see, we can't get the carp, luv,' I continued, as Ruby held my gaze with faltering politeness. 'But' – and I nudged her knowingly in the ribs '– Chef does a marvellous pork lung fricassee if you've a mind...'

She slowly withdrew in her chair to verify what she already knew, then, in the gesture which made it all worthwhile and which is forever freeze-framed in my mind, she took my hands in hers and in her best Lady Bracknell voice, boomed, 'Dahling! You came,' managing to give both the first and the last word about twelve syllables.

Zelma emerged from the shadows and more kisses and syllables were exchanged, glasses clinked and Emma Thompson's responsibility in our airline horror story discussed. I winked conspiratorially and gratefully at Ruby's son and daughter-in-law and breathed, 'The bagel has landed!'

Old Boiler

It was during a particularly cold spell that our central heating chose to pack in, sling its hook, give up the ghost, whatever, leaving man, woman and graduand huddling pathetically around the gas coal log effect fire in the dining room.

If this sounds cosy and familiar then I must point out that, of the five descriptive and emotive words gas, coal, log, effect and fire, it is the word effect which mostly describes the item in question. I was wearing a vest my mother once forced on me when I was four months pregnant and night filming in Ormskirk. My daughter, whose teeth would chatter in Rangoon, was wearing leg warmers over most of her body, and even Jack, the human furnace, had dug out a maroon sweater that may once have been cashmere some Christmases ago. We all hugged glasses of lemon tea and gazed at the steam of our own breath and if Anton Chekhov had happened to stroll past, there may well have been a sequel to *Uncle Vanya*, called *Uncle Vanya and His Old, Frozen Dependents*.

Of course I'd phoned the Gas Board as soon as it happened, pointing out to them our status as holders of their new Three-Star Service 'Keeps you in the safest possible hands' Cover, where for a mere £109 you become a top priority call for their engineers to be there, desperate to get their hands on your boiler, within 24 hours.

Thirty-six hours later I picked up the phone in gloved hands and began a series of complaints to a phalanx of disinterested voices. I'm 'on the computer', I'm 'off the computer', I'm 'on yesterday's computer', I'm 'on tomorrow's computer', I should have been, would have been, could have been... I 'held the line' more times than a trainee tightrope walker and still I was living in Lapland. After day two I did the unthinkable. Jack had gone out of the house to get an emergency haircut – or perhaps to get warm – and I phoned up Customer Service yet again, only this time not as irate Mrs Rosenthal but as Ms Lipman. I explained that I was writing an article on their exclusive priority service which had let me down badly in the freezing weather and did they have anything to say before I condemned them?

'The recent weather has made our task...'

'Recent weather!' I hollered. 'It's cold... It's just cold! I mean, what do you expect in an English winter? Pineapples?'

'I have no comment to make at this time,' the young man at the end of the line countered skilfully before transferring me to the PR department.

My dears, it was like mentioning Fat Cats to the Yorkshire Water Board. Not ten minutes had elapsed when the first van arrived and not eleven when the second screeched to a halt. For some reason this made me madder than ever.

'I mean, it's all very fine you turning up 'cos someone who's on the telly makes a fuss – but what if some little old lady is freezing her dentures off in Pinner when she's forked out her life savings to your...'

'Madam,' he said patiently, 'you seem to be a bit upset. HOWEVER, it's no use shouting at me or my colleague. Five minutes ago I was yanked off a job in Potters Bar – '

'Oh, yes? And how long had *they* been waiting for Three-Star Service? I mean, why can't your office get a rota which works, for God.'

'I'm sure you're right, madam, and if you could just take me to your boiler, I'll make sure that there's no more need...'

'Certainly I'll take you to my boiler!' I thundered, turning on my heels. 'Follow me!' A thought was striking me but my dudgeon was too high to acknowledge it, so I continued striding to the utility room followed by the two engineers. 'I mean,' I chuntered, 'we haven't even had any hot water! It's simply not good enough. Here you are. The Boiler!' At this point I flung open the door of the airing cupboard exposing three rows of clean towels.

'Erm... that's your airing cupboard, madam,' said the engineer pleasantly.

I looked at the piles of towels – and continued emphatically, 'I know, I know. I *know* my own *airing* cupboard. I'm just saying...

the... the... HEAT... from, er, the boiler would... normally, er, come up from here.' I flung open the lower cupboard door for his inspection and we both surveyed the enclosed tank in silence.

'Erm... and that would be your hot water tank, madam.'

I looked. To my mind it was a tank. A lagged tank. What did he want from me – boiler expertise?

'Well, yes. Obviously, it's... the hot water tank. I was just showing you... how... how... dry these towels are but, yes, *the boiler...*' I flailed. 'Follow me.' I doubled back into the kitchen.

'Yes, the boiler, madam, with the fuses and...'

'Fuses!' I seized the word and turned sharply back into the utility room, causing him to jump on his colleague. 'Up there on the wall! That's what I'm saying.'

He scratched his head and studied some forms with rapt interest. 'Not the electric fuse box, madam, more the actual gas boiler... If you could just...'

'The boiler with the fuses, you mean?' I barked. I hoped that I had implied that it was his tone of voice which had confused me. 'You should have *said*,' I added, and led him to the cellar where I vaguely but pleasantly showed him my ironing, my children's pottery, a floor-to-ceiling pile of clothes for the hospice and, finally and most dramatically, a cupboard containing LPs. It was a tour de farce of staggering ineptitude and there was nothing to do but admit defeat and trudge to the telephone to call Jack. Which I set off to do, with the engineers following at a respectful, or maybe wary, distance. Halfway up the cellar steps, having neatly closed the Boiler Room door en route, I thought, I wonder if we call that the Boiler Room because there's a... *boiler* in it?

Well, the engineers did the trick and we had a merry house-warming that night. The Gas Board sent an apologetic letter and we stayed on the scheme until the next time because every poor gas person deserves a second chance at doing what they are supposed to do, quietly, in an expert fashion. Like knowing for certain that a five-bedroom house is probably not heated by a pile of towels and some LPs.

Meanwhile my conscience continued to throb at the thought of the frozen unknown in Potters Bar. Should I have sent an apology? Flowers? A storage heater? Just thinking about gas queue-jumping makes me hot all over.

Out of Towners

Born within the sound of cow bells? Not me. The nearest thing to country matters in my formative years was a short market street incongruously named 'The Land of Green Ginger' and an aborted trip to Burton Constable when Dad tried to steer us into a golf club for our picnic. It was Passover at the time and I remember my mother wailing after his departing back: 'Maurice! You can't take matzos on a golf course!' We ended up eating our hard-boiled eggs on the hard shoulder and I can hear to this day my dad's doleful murmur as we drove home: 'All me life I've wanted to see Burton Constable Hall.' Sad, but not insoluble, since the said hall was a mere sixteen miles from his home and his days were pretty free. I know for a fact that he never went.

Over the years, many of our towny colleagues have bought second homes in the country and some have gone so far as to make these second homes their first homes and stay there for the duration. I must say I've never been tempted. Living in one home is a full-time occupation for a woman who has to consult the manual each tir e she uses the washing machine.

Anyway, they've all settled in nicely and they talk about how trips to London are such a *treat* now that they don't have to drive into it every day, and how, now, they see more of genuine friends because they come down for whole weekends and you can really talk, how much more relaxed they feel and how much improved their skin is and how miraculous the Aga is – heart of the house and all – and it's at this point, after eating three wholesome meals, sharing a labrador walk/pub stopover and picking up my egg from under a moving chicken, that my man and I drift towards the local estate agent and put ourselves on a list for brochures we both know we will never look at.

Certainly Muswell Hill has lost some of its charms for us. There's now a fight to the death between the building societies and the pizza palaces as to which can open the most outlets in the shortest time. Pizzas are winning seven to six at the time of writing but I suspect their rivals may have a card in hand and are about to open a Deep Pan Building Society with extra topping. The streets are gridlocked to and from M&S food, adding fifteen minutes to every journey. London is often a mean city. Perhaps my spectacles are rose-tinted when I go to New York. I can see four shows, one movie, two museums and 27 friends in five days and still have energy to shop. In London I have dinner with friends once a week, stomp out of the local Odeon because the sound system has tinnitus, watch crap TV till I can taste its acridity in my sleep and draw no real succour from the city which inspired Wordsworth to write 'Earth has not anything to show more fair'. To my son, however, newly returned from six months in the Far East, Muswell Hill is Jerusalem and Shangri-la rolled into one. He rhapsodises about John's fruit shop and sings the sweet charms of the Earl Grey tea in the Highgate Wood cafe.

Perhaps the countryside has much to offer that is not just wellies, point-to-points and mulch.

For a start there are sheep. Sheep are hilarious. Sheep are not a flock, they are a ladies committee. Old maidish, truculent, spiky, territorial and cliquey. It's so perfect that they should effortlessly spawn the very stuff which facilitates the clicking of needles and clucking of tongues. My friend Dorothy and I, whilst perambulating around the fields of Sherborne sucking on a grassroot and regurgitating our pasts, saw a lost sheep bleating outside the field's parameters. Between us we headed it off at the pass, waved twigs and bracken behind it whilst performing Native American dances and somehow frightened the big daft thing back into its enclosure. We then watched it buttonhole every munching matriarch in the flock, crying, 'Did you see? Did you see? I was completely stranded! Miles from civilisation! It was bleak! It was... I say... it was bleak... it was...' 'Bog-oo-o-off, dimwit,' snorted the other sheep, disdainfully. But does the little bleater give up? Not he. Instead he accosts the next group, tail flailing: 'No, listen, you won't believe what's just happened to – You see, these two demented townies started brandishing weapons and –

no, honest – it was field rage!...' 'Yeah, yeah, yeah, we've heard it all before – sod off, will you, macramé brain!' And as he forlornly tottered away: 'God, the younger generation, eh? Chemicals in the sheep dip, if you ask me...'

'What's the difference between PMT and BSE?' said my brother on the phone from Brussels. Sensing chauvinism, I professed ignorance. 'One's mad cow disease and the other's a serious agricultural problem.'

I have witnessed in the last few months the splendour of French sunset in a beauty spot in the heart of the Lot et Garonne and the madness of a parochial goat lady who has turned a row of houses into something resembling the end of a five-day rock festival with 10,000 fans and one toilet. I have watched a wedding blessing in a shady dell in the Victoria Pleasure Gardens deep in Dorset and been caught in the crawling hell of cars vainly trying to skirt Stonehenge and get home. I have avoided balsamic vinegar in stone jars in Bourton-on-the-Water and been stranded on Bures Station when the train to Sudbury decided to go no further that day on account of a lorry colliding with a bridge. It is possible that my Russian forebears may have tilled the land but sometimes I can understand why they chose instead to man the till.

Inventory

The fact that my son learned to read with the *Professor Branestawm* books by Norman Hunter is something of a miracle because I adored reading them so much that he could never get them away from me. The Professor was an inventor of marvellous Heath Robinson-like 'necessities' and though I say it and shouldn't, my rendition of his housekeeper, Mrs Flittersnoop – all chin tuck and pigeon flurry – was one of the finer moments of my long, and largely unseen, reading career.

Also, I've always harboured a sneaking desire to invent something myself, and an even sneakier suspicion that I could if I just knew how to turn daydreaming into patents. For instance, I was chuntering on for years about housing for TVs and videos before they started swamping the repro shops with their hefty ugliness, and CD stacking jobs were in my head from the day I bought my first CD – Dvorjak, since you ask. Recipe holders, pressurised toothpaste containers – old-fashioned radios to combat the bleak blackness of the ghetto-blaster – all Lipman losses in the 'Oooh! I thought of that first!' stakes.

In Hull there is an industrial estate where small businessmen, and indeed those of average height, are given grants and even offices to encourage their inventiveness. I understand that someone has triumphed with a folding golf club which can take on the world, not to mention Japan, where there is so little room for golf courses that golf has to be played virtually in the mind. I heard only recently about a scratch handicap Japanese amateur playing at Gleneagles who couldn't tee off because he was crying so convulsively. It turned out that this was the first time he'd played golf on an actual course.

In Berwick Street market once I was recognised by a family of

Hullovians. We chatted and I asked if they were enjoying their
weekend in London and had they taken in a show? Somewhat
bashfully, the father informed me that he was in town to collect
an award for inventing a security system of great simplicity which
was set to knock spots off every other system in the world. I was
so flabbersmacked that I found I had bought a £60 outfit from a
stall for my daughter which not only fitted her like a glove – i.e.
like it was made for someone with five limbs – but which she later,
fatally, pronounced, 'The sort of thing that *you'd* look good in.'

Has anyone ever invented something to prevent mothers from
doing and saying the wrong thing every time they speak which
doesn't involve a large black plastic bag and some double-sided
tape?

Here's a few things I think need to be invented, not least
because they'd look so great in the pages of those publications you
wish to hell wouldn't drop all over your feet every time you pick
up a Sunday paper, i.e. those advertising His 'n' Hers Matching
Monogrammed Tennis Elbow Supports, Pewter and Onyx Key
Ring and Lottery Number Selector and Disposable Stair Lifts
which double as Plant Waterers.

For a start, I'd like every car to be fitted with a device which
signals, 'I'm sorry, that was my mistake.' It could be a red light or
a bassoon sound or even a little pop-up sign saying, 'Oops! I'm a
nudnik.' It wouldn't cost much and if it diverted *one* road rager
from pouring nail polish remover over someone's shiny bonnet, it
would be worth its weight in anti-freeze. While we're on the
subject, how about another sign signalling, 'Thank you for your
courtesy'? Admittedly it would be used as often as a Rastafarian
uses a Carmen roller, but it could only take the heat out of
driving, and if that's not a mixed metaphor then my name's Tarara
and I'm an 'IT' girl.

Right. Now I'm warming to my theory. Next, I want a device to
help the house-person to change his or her duvet covers. I know
there's an easy way to do it involving turning the thing inside out
and gripping the far corners of the duvet as one does with pillow
cases, but I've yet to do it without personal ligament abuse. I've
no suggestion but if I had I've a suspicion that strong magnets
might come into it.

Necklace clasps. I've said it before and I'll say it until my editor gives me a final warning – they are the worst designed item since birth canals. Invariably it's the last thing you tackle before gliding gorgeously out of the door and it's the one thing which makes your lenses fall out. They need to be bigger and simpler and not rely on one hand holding down a millimetre of hinged metal while the other hand gropes myopically for the space created by said manoeuvre. Oh, and chuck in butterfly backs, would you? They are rarer in our house than a Red Admiral in Moscow and they never fit the post! Every earring should come equipped with attached post clip. Let the bloody butterflies migrate back to Lapidoporus. For ever.

I can feel my temperature rising – which brings me to thermometers and why can't I read them? Why is my mercury downwardly unshakeable? Without a tennis elbow support, that is. And why can't I see any mercury when I remove the tube from my mouth? I realise he was the god of flight but where the hell does he go when I'm trying to read him? I had a forehead patch for the children but it was so definitively black or red that I never knew whether to send them to school with a clipped ear or throw them in a bath of ice.

Oh, here's a whimsical one. Politically incorrect as this may sound, has anyone yet invented a warm, attractive, stylish but appropriate outer garment for ladies who wear saris? Just asking. I mean, the garment is gorgeous but it's meant for Bombay weather and the addition of an M&S cardigan and/or a navy-blue anorak just doesn't do it. The garment needs to be curvy and fluid as well as functional, warm and ethnically in keeping. Royal College of Fashion – go for it! I shall award a slap-up dinner at Jamash, our local Balti restaurant, to the winner.

And where's that sliding plastic device for the end of the clingfilm box you promised me? So I'll never lose the wretched end again. And the self-cleaning tomato ketchup top? Finally, a daughterly conversation between my mother and me – which left me no option but to invent a new kind of body brace:

Me: I've renewed your subscription to *Good Housekeeping*.
Her: Oooh, I'm not sure...It's a bit heavy for me.
Me: *Good Housekeeping*? Heavy? It's all articles on how to keep young and furnish your house and take control of your –

Her: Noooo. I mean when I'm in bed reading, it's too heavy for
      me to hold up.

I rest my inchoate inventory.

Backs to the Cornwall

Call it corny, but Cornwall never lets me down. As a traveller I am a seasoned whinger. Hurricanes, earthquakes, dung beetles in the porridge – you name a hazard and I'll ignore it warning-wise. People ring us up solicitously on our return and say, 'Was ANYTHING all right?'

Recently, however, my husband and I swanned back from God's own county refreshed, revitalised and with at least one of us as brown as a mahogany chiffonier. Needless to say the mahogony chiffonier had kept his face down over the *Guardian* crossword for ten days, whilst his partner, your whey-faced, pink-nosed correspondent, had kept her head at a jaunty angle and consequently walked constantly into capstans on the corners of Cornish quays – and just try saying that quickly after a pint of scrumpy.

Of course the weather helped. It was insanely sunny. Warmer, said Sian, the Welsh meteorologist with the shrunken fringe, than Athens on the same April day. With the top of the car down and Mendelssohn up, I felt like a late sixties movie star in some jaunty British film about Eng-a-land swinging like a pendulum as we tootled blithely down the B roads to places whose names evoked memories of *Five Go Pigging Out in Penmorthan*.

Our hostelry, Nansidwell, where we lodged for the duration, was an elegant country house with sofas at right angles to each other, assorted porcelain wall plates and copies of *Country Life* on low tables in front of a roaring inglenook. I wasn't sure for the first couple of nights whether our host Jamie's greeting gear of Black Watch trews, embroidered 'wesket' and Pooh Bear bow-tie would throw Mr Rosenthal's dusty sneakers and cords into low relief, but soon realised the place was so blithely carefree that, frankly, it wouldn't have mattered if he'd worn fishnet tights and a Teflon cardigan.

The house sported a non-resident black and white cat of ample proportions called Thomas, whose splodges were so eccentrically placed that he looked like he had one eye, no mouth and several noses. All the cats in Cornwall, I came to realise, have a similarly batty, off-kilter look as though they've just sampled a Tia Maria in somebody's bicycle basket before sloping off for a Morris dance behind the rune stones.

The neighbouring gardens, open to the public, sported copious species of bamboo as well as several displays of what looked like giant rhubarb but turned out to be Gunnera – at least that's what they called it. We had the first of many excellent cream teas in the company of local residents and house guests, who seemed to have at least three dogs per person. Conversation took place around, through and in spite of canine intervention: 'So have you been across the river to – MARBLE, THAT CAKE IS NOT FOR YOU – Constantine yet? I think you'd find it fraffly interest – OH, LOOK, HE'S TRYING TO PLAY – HATTIE – NO! NOOOO! – It's charming and the little village shop sells hundreds of malt whi – DOWN, BINGO, I SAID! – Yes, and do you still do your Joyce Grenfell show or have you moved on? I remember seeing her when I was a – SAUSAGE? SAUSAAAAGE! MUMMY WON'T TELL YOU AGAIN – child. She was so...marvellous. NOT ON THE GRASS, HECTOR. NO! Of course, we've had no rain, the place is bone dry – HE'S WAGGING HIS – YES, I DID SAY BONE, YOU CLEVER BOY – He's sooo intelligent. Oh, are you awf?' Most people said 'awf' instead of off, including the dogs, who said it instead of 'woof'.

When we did, finally, head for the tiny village shop in Constantine, we were thrilled to find that the rumours of booty on board had not been exaggerated and there were, indeed, around 300 different species of malt whiskies on the back shelves and a bottle of Napoleon Brandy modestly marked at £875. We bought some more than reasonable Islay and set awf for Gweek.

In this neck of the woods, you keep finding yourself on the road, past the road or approaching the road to the charming fishing village of Gweek, patently named by a rhotacism sufferer. In fact, at dinner one night, we suggested to Jamie that he held a Gweek evening during which we could dance around a Wetsina bottle and fling all his wall plates on the gwound.

After a week of fine food – panfried rosettes, medallions and duxelles 'nestling in beds of warm wildebeest' – we did begin to hallucinate slightly on the thought of *'Les flagellots dans le sauce de tomate sur le pain grillé'*. But this is comment not carp. In fact, we had no carp with the whole week.

It was pre-election April and my one commitment was to turn out in Camborne and Falmouth for the local Labour Party. Candidate Candy Atherton warned me that the local paper would never use the photos because they loved the Conservative candidate, Sebastian this-one-will-run-and-run Coe. Indeed, their reportage of the afternoon's canvass was hilarious. 'Miss Lipman, in cream trouser suit and pendant earrings, was followed at a respectable distance by her husband, Jack Rosenthal, wearing dusty sneakers.' (They should have been witnesses to the scene Jack and I had played previously outside a branch of Bally, when I'd suggested he might buy a rather dashing pair of shoes in the window. He stared at me uncomprehendingly and said, 'But I've *got* some shoes.')

We ended up in Camborne Labour Club to receive a cheque on behalf of the Labour Party. It was a traditional Labour Club in the Keir Hardie and pool table sense and if Tony Blair had walked in he'd have felt even more of an alien than the woman in the pendant earrings with the dustyfooted husband. Heigh ho! Still, like Candy and the other members, we had a magnificent break.

Elsewhere, we sailed down Frenchman's Creek and heli-coptered to the Scilly Isles of St Mary's and Tresco for a perfect lunch at the Island Hotel. There were only twenty people on the helicopter – and one turned out to be the son of Roy Callow, our decorator, and another had lived for ten years with my best friend from school. Isn't it a small heliport? We visited the architecturally stunning Tate Gallery in St Ives to be dazzled by the light within and without and sat meditating on the strength and purpose of the sculpture in Barbara Hepworth's beautiful garden. The costumes which had fitted me ten days before for the BBC play I was about to embark on suffered grimly from the clotted cream teas I came to fixate on daily – otherwise, the holidaymakers from hell had had, for once, the perfect break.

A Shiver Down Your Spine

You know how it is – well, I hope you don't know how it is, but if you've had a serious medical condition then for the next few years you are monitored to make sure the 'thing' hasn't recurred. Well, that's how it was with me. Every year I'd slide into a steel spaceship called a scanner on the fifth floor of a hospital with the slowest elevator I've ever encountered. (I mean, you could conceive before ringing for that lift and deliver a healthy bawling full-term infant by the time you reached the fifth floor.)

I've often raised money for MR scanners in the past and I thank God that I did because they have one job in life and that is to save seven or eight lives a day. A couple of weeks before my half-century birthday, the scanner revealed that my neurofibroma, niftily removed by a surgeon two years before, was back. And he was ugly. It wasn't that the tumour was growing but that it was filling up with fluid and pressing up against things inside my spine which might well start reporting it for harassment.

So I did what any mature woman with a devoted husband, caring kids, a hyperventilating mother and a simmering career on the front burner would do. I ignored it. By that I mean I ignored it in a Jewish kind of way and sought a second, third and ultimately fifth opinion whilst auditioning surgeons on all sides of the Atlantic. (Did I dream I saw a card on a surgeon's door which read 'Please get your second opinion before consulting me'?) One was against the op as I had no actual symptoms. Some were optimistic but gloomy about the prospect of having to sever the nerve to my right hand (the writing, lacquer spraying and pansy-potting one). Others, like the glorious Fred Epstein in New York, six foot three and stunning in snakeskin boots and bleached blond hair, chuckled, 'Come ON, Marine – get without! So you lose a little feeling in your pinkie – I mean, what the heck?' (He made the operation sound as dangerous as having your eyebrows plucked.)

The heck was that, instead, I saw gifted faith healers from the great Matthew Manning who laid on hands to Charlie the veterinary healer in Potters Bar who normally does horses but took stock of my long face and my whinnying and felt at home. And for fifteen months things stayed stable.

Until the last few days of filming the sequel to Jack's *Eskimo Day* before beginning rehearsals for Noël Coward's *Blithe Spirit* in Chichester, when I casually rang the neurologist's office for my latest scan results and got them. Right between the shoulder blades.

Fellow actors Tom Wilkinson and David Ross caught me weeping in my winnebago and it all came out. Tom immediately recommended a neurosurgeon friend who lived in nearby Muswell Hill. I told him I'd got five surgeons on the go already and needed another like Bill Gates needs a benefit – but I ended up dropping my X-rays in to Mr Bradford on my way home. His words were Balm of Gilead. 'If it were my wife, you'd have had it done yesterday.' (On reflection, of course, any actual doctor's wife must snort with scorn at that particular expression as 'For God's sake, woman, take an aspirin' seems to be the general prescription for members of doctors' families.) He went on to assure me that Alan Crockard, my second, second opinion had taught him all he knew and if it made me feel better he would assist him. I relaxed. My neck and hand were in safe hands – four of them. I had the dream ticket.

Meanwhile, rehearsals for *Blithe Spirit* were proceeding to their second week with me sitting on this bombshell. Madame Arcati was springing on to tables, falling backwards off stools and dancing eccentric tangos. The usual laughing, lunching and luvvying sessions were all happening between Twiggy, Belinda Lang, Stephen Pacey and the rest of the small cast. In short, we were bonding. Part of me, though, was drifting above it all, and on the morning of my withdrawal I'm afraid I withdrew to the toilet and just hid there whilst the cast were told.

I read somewhere that Harry Enfield doesn't believe that actors are brave. I can only assume that Mr Enfield has never been in a stage play. With two weeks to go before opening night and no replacement for Madame Arcati, the cast was only concerned that I got better. Septuagenarian star Dora Bryan had ten days to learn a huge part and complicated illusions. The management wouldn't delay the opening by a day. One night she rushed off stage, leant panting in the wings and said, 'Well, I think they got the gist of it.'

Harry – you're right. Actors aren't brave. They're flaming heroic.

The operation was booked for Monday week. Meanwhile, things were coming to a head and not just figuratively. I had a throbbing abscess under a large section of bridgework and root canal work was the next day's projected treat. Walking away from the endodontist with a lip like a buttock, I bumped into the first surgeon who didn't think I should have the operation. Confused? Who, me? Where was my passport and those South African rands Lord Lucan sent me?

The decision made itself. A date was fixed. The weeks went fast. 'When shall I come?' said my mother on the Hull extension. 'I'll cancel that appointment I've got on the Monday. I'm only going to Bernard's for a blow-job.' There was no answer to that.

'Come Tuesday,' I said. 'It's not going to be much fun here.'

'Don't be silly,' she said. 'I'm not expecting FUN!'

'For me, Mum, for me...' All the medics talked about trying to save the nerve to my right hand, until one night my doctor read out a letter which more or less admitted that the nerve to my hand would have to be severed during the op. For the first time I freaked. I threw the phone across the room and started shaking. Once I started I couldn't stop. My teeth began playing ragtime, my knees a sort of counterpoint.

Now here's the spooky bit. Two days earlier I'd cancelled an appointment with a psychic healer, thinking perhaps I should leave well enough alone. At the start of *Blithe Spirit* I'd visited Belgrave Square Centre for Psychic Studies as research for the part of Madame Arcati, the medium. Rather alarmingly, a message came across, for me, from the psychic in charge of the demonstration. 'You have had some bad health problems and it's not over yet. But it will be OK.' Right now my surgeons were saying the same thing. I felt secure with them. A second psychic opinion I didn't need. I thought.

My teeth were still chattering when the phone rang. It was my friend, Layla. It was she who had recommended the psychic healer. She didn't like the sound of me and phoned again the next day to say she'd reinstated my appointment and if we could get to Twickenham – twelve miles away – in 50 minutes, he would see me. I was dressed, out of the house and picking her up in six minutes.

People will always be sceptical about faith healing. How could they not be? There is no scientific proof, it works for some people and not others, the methodology is often suspect, the practitioner often bizzare. All I know is that for two hours I was manipulated physically and cajoled mentally. There was a strong sense of my late father in the room. I became quite disturbed and at the end Graham told me casually that he'd drained the tumour and moved it slightly so it could be removed more easily from the nerve. Layla and I went to a tea room afterwards and just sat there stunned for an hour until I could face the drive back. She had prayed for two hours. She was more bushed than I was.

Something must have worked. The first thing I did on waking up, post op, was to wave my right hand at the family. Truly, madly, deeply, they waved back. Mr Crockard was delightfully open-minded. 'Whatever it was,' he said smiling, 'the forces were with us.' Someone who'd been present during the surgery told me the surgeon had, actually, consulted a third surgeon when they realised the tumour was in a slightly different place. It was felt that, because of this, they could scrape it away instead of cutting the nerve. I had had so much support. Groups of nuns had prayed for me. People sent tapes and cards and even a slip of paper which had been blessed and which 'you must wear in your bra during the operation'. I felt twice, thrice, a hundred times blessed.

Lying in Intensive Care, my throat like a felt duster, I watched the cup of tea I'd begged for grow cold in the corner while I made feeble mewing sounds to attract the attention of the nurse in charge. Later, she astounded me by confiding, 'I'm not often in Intensive Care – I'm usually in Admin, but I like to keep my hand in.' Gulp.

My first meal was days later because, as ever, the migraine kicked in after the anaesthetic. In my mind's pink and bleary eye, I could see crisp lettuce, fresh, barely ripe tomatoes, translucent cucumber and fresh, salty cottage cheese. The reality when it came was limp and over-ripe, and the cheese was rancid.

I called the general manager, who came bustling and beaming round the door.

'Hello, Mrs Rosenmumble... Are you enjoying your lunch?' 'Mr Hassid, this is my first food in a week. The cottage cheese is rancid. This is a hospital – I'm a patient. What are you thinking about...?'

To my amazement, his grin only widened. 'Oh, yes – you are she, all right. Ha! Ha! You are just the same as you are on TV. You are Beattie, right? Very similar – very funny – I will tell my wife.'

I looked at my right hand. Was it strong enough to squeeze a throat with? I wondered

Whilst I was recuperating, every live, dead, hovering-in-the-spirit-world, fanciful, exotic, quixotic form of flora to ever grace the borders of Kew or the display brochures of Interflora came my way. Like Patsy Kensit, I was up to my neck in oasis.

Don't misunderstand me. I was wildly, pathetically grateful to the myriad friends, relatives and relative strangers who were generous enough to cough up everything from Phalaenopsis orchids to whole magnolia plants for little old wobbly-necked me. My hospital room looked like a float in the Jersey Festival. I could hear people getting out of the third floor lift and going, 'My God! It smells like a tart's boudoir up here!'

Inevitably, there was one hugely gorgeous all-white arrangement which arrived without its card – so whenever the phone went I said, 'Thank you so much for the gorgeous flowers,' just on the off-chance. This of course embarrassed anyone who didn't send flowers into frantic florist phoning and the whole thing started over again.

Somehow, my friends the Morrows managed to smuggle a traffic cone complete with floral centrepiece and a 'No Loitering' sign into my hospital room.

On Sunday, a couple of days later, I took myself out of the place and started for home. There my mum watched me, marvelling, as I chopped up veg for a casserole.

Another friend, Tom Conti, phoned me at home just as I was frantically trying to find a chair – any chair – that was high enough to support my post-operative neck. For weeks I wore the deepest neck collar the hospital had had in stock – one usually reserved for Zulu tribeswomen and contortionists. 'I feel like one of those wobbly-headed beagles which hang in the back windows of Volvos,' I told him. Twenty minutes later Mr Conti was to be seen shlepping a large wing chair up my front drive. My mother almost passed out. For a moment she thought she was headed for a Greek island...

I was even sent a tape from a complete stranger who sang me, unaccompanied, Gershwin in Greek for 45 minutes. Extraordinary.

Looking around, I felt absurdly grateful. So, my surfaces were never going to be pristine nor my ambience minimalistic. I was never going to drag-finish my dado or stencil my own parquet and I'd still have to ring Carmela in Marbella when she took her summer hols to ask how to open the tumble dryer door and where the piccallilli's kept these days.

There were, however, compensations. I could still make an excellent chicken and barley pot roast. I was a brilliant doodler. I could make a surgeon laugh immediately after anaesthetic and remember a colour in my head three weeks later in a hat shop. I was married to the finest, funniest and most relieved man in the history of men being relieved. I was alive, I was kidding, and the luckiest, lousy housewife in the whole wide world and Hessle Foreshore.

The Emerald Isle

Question: Where would you send a whey-faced post-operative
            woman in a surgical collar and her devoted husband,
            who for some reason has stopped breathing naturally
            and started blowing through imaginary gills like a
            sperm whale, for a recuperative holiday, when the
            woman won't fly for more than an hour and is
            comfortable only when her arms are hung backwards
            over a billiard cue?
Answer: Anywhere but your place, right?

Actually, the answer was in my lap, in book form – *Angela's Ashes*
by Frank McCourt.

I'll come clean. I'm not big on Irish fiction. Dramas about 'the
Troubles' drive me straight into the omniplex showing *Babe*. I
never can fathom why Irish plays are always greeted with rapture
reserved for an English tennis player reaching the first round at
Wimbledon. *Angela's Ashes*, however, I devoured. You don't just
read it, you're immersed by it.

Taking this as an omen, I phoned the Irish Tourist Board and
gave my brief to Katrina of the honeyed voice. Bobbing fishing
boats were mentioned and words like 'family-run' and 'sleepy
fishing village' and, before you could say Dingle Peninsula, we
were boarding an Aer Lingus plane with our usual vacational
accoutrements – a suit bag for Jack and a gargantuan grip, which
appeared to have a white rhino in it, for me. This time we had the
welcome addition of a sheepskin backrest, an inflatable neck
support and a selection of surgical collars. I felt like a pervert.

Ballycotton. 'How that name comes up mixing memory with
desire,' as J. D. Salinger once memorably wrote. Ballycotton.

Three pubs, one shop, a few B&Bs, some pretty terraced houses in sugar-almond shades and one hotel, white and gleaming, looking out to sea over a tiny natural harbour. 'Now that's the sort of place I'd love to stay in,' I sighed, as we whizzed past, without realising that's where we'd booked.

We had five bliss-filled days at the Bayview Hotel. The manager, Stephen, possessed the kind of eyes that are wasted on a bloke, and the guests were the wondrous eclectic generational mix that characterises Irish social life.

Our imbibing habits became the stuff of legends. If I wasn't at the Guinness by midday then there wasn't a 'd' in the day of the week. The first taste of a pint of Irish Guinness in Ireland is like your first kiss – tender, smooth, exploratory – and you know it's going to get even better.

One day, after visiting our friend, James Roose-Evans, in his clifftop farmhouse, Jack developed that good old holiday standby – raging toothache. 'There's a marvellous dentist in Middleton,' said James. We looked at each other in alarm – Middleton was one street of shops and the usual pubs. Visions of string, doorposts and feet on chins crossed our minds. 'I'll hang on,' said Jack.

And hang on he did until Saturday, when the pain took hold and propelled him towards the nearest Phil McAvity he could find. Mr O'Sullivan filled an enormous cavity completely painlessly, while a video screen showed a blow-up of the tooth being worked on. The next day, Sunday, he reopened the surgery to extract an enormous wisdom tooth, after which the patient returned to the hotel for an enormous plate of liver and onions. He's thinking of booking in at the Middleton dentist for a fortnight every summer.

I wish I had time and space to tell you about the night in the bare and tacky bar in County Limerick, when I started out sipping Irish coffee and ended up dancing and singing until 2.30 in the morning with twenty tanked-up golfing men. *Never Do a Tango With an Eskimo* never sounded more Gaelic.

Our last few days were spent driving through the Burren, a lunar landscape, as we drove to Ballyvaughan. (Wherever you drive in Ireland, they tell you it takes 'about an hour and a half'. This covers any distance.) Mile after mile of flat, pumice-stone plateau and curving cream beaches like the head on a Guinness.

I was soon in the Atlantic jumping the surf like a woman who'd never been near an intensive-care ward. Jack, asleep on a sand-dune, looked so rejuvenated that I didn't bother to tell him there was a dead mouse by his head.

My lasting memory must be of the White Thorn Restaurant opposite the twinkling lights of Galway. As the sun sank, vermilion, into the bay, the young harpist was strumming '...*and watch the sun go down on Galway Bay.*'

'This place really puts you in touch with your roots,' I said as we left, 'and I don't even have any.' I patted my hair...and remembered that appointment I'd made to get them done. I smiled. When the hairdresser inevitably asked, "Ave you 'ad yer 'olidays yet?' I'd finally be able to say, 'Nor 'alf.'

Crazy Raving

I think I may be losing it. The plot; the denouement; the lot. The signs of inherent lunacy have always been there. For years I've been talking not just to myself, in the car, but to other people who don't happen to be travelling with me at the time. For even more years I've been blithely addressing inanimate objects as I put them away in cupboards.

'In you pop, young gravy boat,' I'll chunter as I shove a piece of china into a tiny space between the soup bowls and fruit plates. Then a thought crosses my mind: would the gravy boat perhaps be happier – yes, happier – if I put 'him' with the other jugs so he's got more people on his wavelength? All this without a trace of irony.

In similar vein, clothes are yanked out of the wardrobe and clutched possessively to my breast on the grounds that they haven't been worn since Shrove Tuesday 1976, and must be feeling overlooked and unloved. It doesn't seem to occur to me that an organism constructed by Taiwanese seamstresses out of fibres of worsted and worm droppings is unlikely to have 'feelings'. Nor that if I wear these clothes after all these years I will look like ostrich dressed up as mutton. No, all that seems to matter at that given moment is to save the sensibilities of a blouse.

Add this to the guilt I feel every time I take dying flowers out of the vase and put them face down in the bin with all the pongy potato peel and pasta, all of which have just as much genetic right to be treated anthropomorphically as has a dead snapdragon. Plus the way, increasingly, that anything makes me cry. Anything. I don't just mean films in the afternoon with Deborah Kerr. This one you simply won't believe – Doris Day! I did. *Calamity Jane!* With horses and t'baccy and 'make mine sarsaparilla!', for Pete's sake! As true as I'm sitting here typing with three fingers and appalling posture – when Calam' rode into town and nobody would talk to her 'cos they figured she'd been meaner than a coyote to Katy Brown, I blubbed into my blackcurrant and vanilla teabag. My ducts are out of my control.

Coming back on the train from York I bought the audio cassette of the BBC's radio play *Spoonface Steinberg*, about which I'd heard so much extravagant praise. This'll pass the journey home, was my innocent thought. Pass the journey home! I almost swam the last 100 miles. It's the interior monologue of a seven-year-old autistic child, breathtakingly played by Becky Simpson, and, like all great art, both moving and inspirational. By about Retford I was in serious disarray. With no handkerchief and a much-loved suede jacket or a Lycra 'body' to choose between for absorption, I decided just to let it run. It ran down my chest, down my bra and, finally, when my trousers started to show signs of incontinence, I settled for shoving a crisp packet up my nose, which more or less got me to King's Cross convenience station and a stint with my head under the hand-drying machine. Still, it is a major life-enhancing 'listen'. Just remember to pack a roller towel, that's all.

The other scary thing is that I keep finding myself in the bedroom/pantry/fridge without the foggiest idea what I'd gone in for. There I stand. Waiting. For what? Just a clue, the merest nudge saying, 'Yes, Maureen, my little fogbrained flower, you are in the pantry because the pantry is the most likely spot to lay your hands on the stock cube without which the jug of hot water you've just poured out will remain just that – hot water.'

So I'm taking stock. Exercise clears the mind wonderfully. Last week I started again. Again. I went to the gym at 3.30pm, spent an hour on the machine and twenty minutes over a freshly squeezed carrot juice and a tabloid I wouldn't allow in the house. At 6.10 I arrived home to find it totally overrun by cables, lighting equipment, loading boxes and a film unit who'd arrived as agreed, by ME, at five o'clock. Jack had kept them in beverages and good humour for an hour and a half. There was little for me to do but apologise and blame my oestrogen level.

Fortunately, Jack is mad too. In a different way. Why, for example, did he lurch to his feet last season when Ryan Giggs scored against Juventus and jubilantly yell 'Grimshaw!'? Why does he mutter 'Couch' when he accidentally bumps himself, or say 'Beige' to disguise a gentle burp? I mean, it's no wonder I'm the way I am, really, after 25 years of such close proximity. (I can't tell you the pleasure it gave me just then to use the 'x' in 'proximity' – ooh, there, I've done it again – because, well, do you ever feel so terribly sorry for the 'x', getting such scant attention on the keyboard?) Or is it me?

Then there's Ant, the beanbag ant-eater, whom Amy pushed into our luggage before we left for Ireland. Since then he's accompanied us on every holiday in spite of our combined age being 121. Recently, when Jack went to Berlin, we posted Ant in a jiffy bag complete with passport (Age: Indeterminate. Sex: Not yet! Previous countries visited: Antarctica, etc.) and he failed to turn up at the hotel. Amy phoned every day from Manchester to see if he'd been found. It was beyond embarrassment explaining to the German receptionist that we were expecting...er...a parcel... The contents? Er, well, how is your sense of humour? Forget it. By the time Ant returned he'd crossed Europe more times than the Kinnocks and was in a sorry state. Still, we took him to Cornwall and he seemed to perk up. It's us who are the worry. Retarded growth? Nous?

Then there's my bad housekeeping. I'm getting no better at planning ahead and my juggling is deteriorating. I order meat and fish by phone and provide the wadges whereby Carmela can Tesco for me. I only stray into M&S and the local delis to buy the luxurious frivolities that remain in the pantry for six years whilst I await the perfect opportunity to serve them. 'Marrons Glacés with Coconut Frappé, serves 36.' 'Virgin cold-pressed Olive Oil from the graded groves of Tuscany with Green Peppered Anchovy and Coriandered Ugli Fruit – eat before Spring '74.'You know the sort of thing. My wine cellar has three bottles of first-night champagne (I'd sooner have a Vimto) and a variety of colourful and misshapen bottles of liqueurs which were heaven in Ibiza and hemlock in Muswell Hill.

I rarely have any ice in my ice-making compartment other than that stuck to the freezer compartment door and my saucepans would discombobulate Delia. An old acquaintance visiting from California once asked to borrow my Teflon skillet to demonstrate his culinary skills. I confessed I didn't have such a thing and he went into shock.

'YOU *DON'T* HAVE... A TEFLON SKILLET?' he intoned, whilst shaking a bewildered head. I joined in and shook mine so he repeated the question in the same tone but a couple of dozen octaves higher. 'YOU *DON'T* HAVE A TEFLON SKILLET?'

Again I confessed that I had no such thing. It was as if I'd confessed to being without The Beatles' *White Album,* or a front door or nostrils. 'But, Mo,' he gasped, 'HOW DO YOU *LIVE*?'

Only when I assured him that I'd be queuing outside John Lewis basement at 8.40 Monday morning to beat other desperate skillet buyers did he come near to closing his mouth. Since then, I've often hovered around the saucepan section in Amy's 'Ardware (why does that name IRRITATE me so much?) and considered purchasing said item but then a combination of thrift and ignorance of what you'd do in it that couldn't be done in an English frying pan or a grill overcomes me and I buy a plastic tablecloth instead.

Now there you're talking housewifery. Do I love my blue plastic tablecloth or don't I? I view with resignation the neatly folded serendipity of frayed sheets and shrunken duvet covers and deeply stained tablecloths, I ask you from the bottom of my linen cupboard – where in hell is the genius in waiting who will finally invent the wipe-down sheet? I mean, how difficult can it be? For years I resisted my mother's fervent invective in favour of plastic tablecloths. I haunted antique shops for guipure lace and broderie anglaise and fresh white linen with hand-stitched embroidery which probably deprived an entire community of welders' wives in the Gower Peninsular of their twilight vision. My kitchen table looked like the set for *Under Milk Wood* with its cracked blue and white jugs and chipped china cheese platter. It was perhaps after the nineteenth or twentieth glass of cranberry juice fell foul of my son's gesticulating and reaching hand that I succumbed to the pleasure of the 21st century and bought a round blue soft plastic mock marble-ised fluffy-backed labour-saving mommy's little helper. It's as ugly as a bollard and I bloody love it.

The other thing which marks me out as Queen Slut of the Sluttish People are my surfaces. Every inch of Casa Rosenthal is covered in stuff. The odd silver filigree dish. Chinese worry balls, a dried terrapin, a goblet inscribed 'With grateful thanks for all at W.T.A.S.Z'.(Who?)

Which brings me finally to Two Nose. Should you glimpse a

woman in a taxi or waiting at a traffic light with two crossed fingers (fore and middle) stroking the tip of her own nose, then you can more or less assume it's me. It's one of those weird neurological things. If you cross your arms in front of you and clasp the crossed hands, then bring the crossed hands through and up the middle of your arms, you'll find a similar effect. Told to raise your left forefinger, you'll invariably raise your right. With the nose, because your fingers are crossed, your brain gets mischievous and informs you that you have two noses. You are feeling, in other words, a nose with each finger. It's kind of addictive once you've got it.

Unfortunately, it puts you in a sort of trance and people look askance at you as if what you're doing is vaguely masturbatory. Funnily enough, only Amy and I ever do it. The boys don't seem to need it.

Still, one of them pats his head every time he eats bread and the other recently phoned from a Budapest hospital to say he was having a great time but he had been bitten six times whilst rescuing a Chinese dog from a swirling river. He doesn't like swimming and he doesn't particularly care for dogs. Why am I surprised? Well, they're supposed to *rebel* against familial stereotypes, aren't they?

Thighland

Is there a perfect suitcase? For your basic ten-day trip? One that expands and wheels and is liftable by women with 'wear and tear' in their lower backs. One that is instantly recognisable as it lurches towards you, beneath several PVC backpacks and a set of golf irons, and sturdy enough to withstand the utter contempt of your average well-pissed-off baggage handler.

And if I lashed out two hundred or so quid on one which appeared to have all the accoutrements required, would I care more when it ended up in Guernsey when I was in Phuket, than I would if the leatherette and canvas job from a Hackney pavement stall did the same vanishing act?

I seem to be constantly buying baggage. 'This set will cover everything,' I tell myself as I lug luggage back to Brent Cross car park. 'The suit bag for Jack, the overnighter for us both and the big roomy one for posh holidays.' Meanwhile, up in the loft – or excess baggage depository – sit a dozen malevolent malcontents with dodgy zips, buckled wheels, ruptured sides and bent innards. Why I don't chuck them all is a mystery, easily explained by the lunatic notion that a suitcase repairer may suddenly choose to open any day now in Muswell Hill. Maybe in that empty restaurant on the Broadway – the one that used to display the curious sign, 'Greek fun downstairs'.

People come and *borrow* my suitcases for their hols and I always seem to have the perfect choice for *their* requirements. But for my own – never. The children of course are no help here. Each successive term at various universities requires them to abscond with the best and most flexible of my valises, a fact which I never realise until three-quarters of the way through the term when I've scoured the loft from rafter to rafter and accused every friend who's got an unexpired passport of long-term memory loss or flagrant theft.

(Here's an interesting but irrelevant statistic. How many Americans have a passport? Answer: three per cent, and one per cent of those have only been to Mexico or Hawaii. Isn't that staggering ... when you consider that their elected President is the dominating power in World Politics?) There are still a few Clinton jokes which defy topicality. Clinton returns from abroad and comes down the plane steps clutching a piglet under each arm. 'Welcome home, sir,' says the aide. 'I see you have a piglet under each arm, sir.' 'Yes,' say Clinton. 'I got them for Hillary and Chelsea.' 'Good trade, sir,' says the aide. 'Good trade'. The other concerns a genie granting a wish to Monica Lewinsky. 'I'd like to lose my love handles,' she says. There's a flash of light and her ears drop off. Or, have you heard? They're going to impeach him. From the waist down.

'There are places I'll remember all my life though some have changed,' sang The Beatles, and though they took us on a few trips up East during the mind-slipping sixties, they were probably referring to the mouth of the Mersey, not the Gulf of Thailand.

Yet the song was running through my mind when I boarded a Thai Airlines plane at Bangkok Airport to come home after a hedonistic week at 'Chiva-Som', the Thai health resort which puts the 'ah' in Spa. I had been massaged, covered in seaweed and mud, thankfully not at the same time, had my eyes read – yes, you read that with your own eyes – and my feet kneaded, which they were sorely in knead of. How did I feel? Well, if they'd carried me off the plane for a compulsory further seven weeks in the same spot, I would not have shouted 'No! No! Please let me get back to Muswell Hill – the Christmas lights are up and my agent may call!'

It had been a bumpy year. People said, 'You've had a bad year,' but I felt I'd had a good year.

It was time to sit back and take stock, and enjoy being well again. Having recuperated in Southern Ireland for two weeks, along came the offer of a travel article – a health club in Thailand with nothing but sun, sand, spoonfeeding and Gavin, the *Hello!* photographer, as my beach accessory.

Oh – and Val. I took my childhood buddy, Val, because if I'd been on a learning curve, then she'd been on a figure-of eight, with domestic upheaval following divorce and a daughter's seriously complicated pregnancy. Our last holiday together was a trip to Israel. By cargo ship. Coming back, we stood all the way from Naples to Paris on a fully booked train. Thirty-five years later, I felt I owed her some luxury.

I started laughing as I left my front door. One moment my husband and secretary were waving me and my taxi goodbye, a second later the cab had crashed side-on into a lorry. We had not even left the drive.

'You won't believe this when I tell you my name,' said the driver ruefully, after the ritual exchange of insurance companies and abuse.

'Why? What is it?'

'Bean,' he moaned. 'Mr Bean.' The die was cast, or maybe miscast.

It's an eleven-hour flight to Bangkok and three-hour journey by car to Chiva-Som (or Haven of Life) and its promise of rest, relaxation and rejuvenation. Hua Hin itself, where the revered King and Queen of Thailand keep their summer palace, is a bustling, noisy, market town of souvenir and silk shops, teeming with people. The odd 'cardboard behind the eyes' feeling of jet-lag was upon me and I craved soft water upon my neck, something cool down my throat and something flat to wake up on.

The Thai people are the most courteous people I've ever met, and some of the handsomest. We were greeted at Chiva-Som by delicate, beautiful girls in narrow-skirted traditional outfits, hands pressed together, eyes smiling, and let through the cool teak interior to rattan armchairs and sweet, fragrant lemon tea.

All the food was calorie labelled, but I convinced myself that the higher my score the shapelier I'd become. This is known as the 'Ostrich syndrome' – nothing to do with sticking heads in sand but everything to do with having a bum like an ostrich. The Thai masseuses who stood in giggling groups waiting for their clients were extremely gifted and, thankfully, there was none of that, ''Ave you 'ad your 'olidays?' speak which passes for conversation in your average Brit-spa. I was only slightly taken aback by the one who asked me when the baby was coming.

'Er...baby?' I asked, involuntarily pulling my stomach muscles in. 'Three months?' she enquired. I gave in. 'Yeah – three, four, ten, maybe eleven,' I told her. 'Like elephant.' Helpless laughter.

There was an actual elephant in the Hua Hin high street the next night. (I fed him a bag of bananas and he showed me how he could make them come straight out of the other end. It was a fair exchange.) We had gone in to see Daniel, the Sikh tailor, for trouser-making purposes. I mean, you can't go to the Far East without coming back with English tailoring – people would talk – so we arranged for Daniel to come to the hotel after he finished work at 10.15pm for the first fittings.

The following day, the day before the *Hello!* photographs were taken, I conveniently developed a sun allergy of pinprick red spots. Gavin would have to be bribed to airbrush out my entire body. Ana Maria Tavares, the elegant hotel manager, took charge. 'I'll send three bowls of cold yoghurt to your room. Cover yourself in it, let it dry and shower it off tomorrow.'

(This is what they mean by immersing yourself in their culture?) Sitting in bra and pants, smelling like a goat, the phone rang. Val took it.

'It's the tailor – he's in reception!'

'Stall him!' I yelled, rushing to the shower. 'Or he'll think I'm a pervert!'

'Can he wait five minutes, please, then come to Room 212?' said Val.

I turned on the shower. Then turned it off and screamed, 'Val! This is Room 221!' The thought of some elderly German tourist sleeping off a blissful 'Chiva-Som Loofah Scrub' being wakened at 10.15pm by a man in a turban clutching a pair of scissors and a bag of trousers was too much for us. By the time he arrived, we were too hysterical to stand up.

Laughter is the most therapeutic of treatments, and as I left Chiva-Som, I felt I'd given everyone their full share. Still, I was choked with regret when, five minutes before leaving for Bangkok Airport in a hire car, the zip on my case exploded on me. It simply separated from itself like an egg white from a yolk and ceased to function as a means of keeping thirteen times too many clothes in the same spot. With strength, initiative and forbearance, Andrew the Australian chef bound up the offensive container with heavy-duty string and ugly but effective masking tape. The two-and-a-half-hour journey to Bangkok took four hours and we raced into check-in fifteen minutes before departure time with a dry mouth and a banging heart which entirely negated the ten days of massage and relaxation I'd experienced at Chiva-Som.

'I'll try and arrange an upgrade for you,' the PR person had said kindly. 'Just mention I've spoken to Mr Cook and see if it does any good.' We raced into line, my suitcase now looking like a piece of rolled and boned brisket and hoiked it on to the machine. The beautiful Thai ground-staff girl eyed me as though I was a Cuban entering Miami and made me sign a disclaimer form allowing anybody to rip, maim, steal from or simply laugh at my luggage, with no responsibility to them. Then, limp-haired, unwisely dressed for both London and Bangkok and suffering still from an aggressive and highly attractive strain of prickly heat (I looked like Häagen-Dazs Raspberry Ripple), I had the temerity to ask for an upgrade to first class. The Thai people are the most gracious and courteous people on earth, but even she had to place a discreet hand over her mouth to hide the huge guffaw which was about to emerge.

The name of 'Mr Cook' had slightly less effect than if I'd said, 'Actually, my mother would like me to have an upgrade because she thinks it's important for me to get the full eight hours' sleep.'

Curiously enough, the case arrived at Heathrow unscathed, totally intact – and first off the carousel. My small hand luggage with the retractable handle took a bit longer, largely because having claimed it, I found it actually belonged to a Mr Wright who'd been staying in a Hyatt hotel in Bangkok. It was identical to mine but for the obvious giveaway that it had no purple tinsel on the handle. I had put the purple tinsel on to make my case instantly recognisable. And then completely forgotten I'd done it.

Oh, how I long for a soft, malleable, attractive bag with seven or eight uncrushable silk items, mixable and matchable in co-ordinating colours, one small make-up bag, a gas cylindered hot-brush and four paperbacks as my only travelling companions. When I returned I drank more water, enrolled in a T'ai Chi class and ate more fruit – though I let my basic fruit-carving skills slip somewhat. People kept telling me how well I looked, which was nice, except they invariably do that when I'm 10st 4lb instead of 9st 8lb – and I was more convinced than ever that I needed never suffer from illness again if I had the right set of mind, or the right set of luggage – I rest my case.

Part III

Actress Celebrates Silver Wedding

Class of its Own

'Forty years on and afar and asunder, parted are those who are singing today...'

Except we weren't parted. On the contrary, we were reunited. Newland High School for Girls, Hull, class of '57 and every one a variety turn. How Lesley Duggan née Watson (fleet of foot and handy with a hockey stick) managed to locate and unite 72 51-year-old women with different surnames from those they had answered to in Forms 3A, 3B and 3W from the five corners of the globe, I cannot begin to imagine.

But unite us she did with the help of her five-women committee and one of their cake-making daughters, a year's supply of stamps, and the tenacity of Ranulf Fiennes. I wasn't sure until the week before that I would be able to make it, determined as I was to do so. I was in rehearsal until the day before the event but the director turned his back to eat a Hobnob and I escaped into a hot BMW and headed for the Ml, with my trusty husband who went along just to watch my reaction when I saw the old gang after 32 years.

I had seen a few of them over the years. There was the time I was signing copies of my first book in a Leeds bookshop and a familiar figure appeared at the desk:

'I 'eard you were 'ere, so I've come to 'ave a look at you,' said the large imposing figure before me. 'Janet!' I yelled. 'Janet Dagwell! My best ever leading man.' She harrumphed a bit at that, but it was true. Janet with her strong voice and excellent timing had played a chilling Mephistopheles to my spine-shuddering Dr Faustus in the Marlowe play of that name. Her Lady Bracknell still rings in my ears whenever I see her successors.

'Look at this,' I burbled, and opened the book to a picture of the two of us in *The Lady's Not For Burning* by Christopher Fry. 'What a small world.'

She looked at the picture and harrumphed some more. 'Fancy,' she said, and put down the book. 'Well, I've seen you now so I'll be off.'

They're women of few words in Yorkshire, all but one – me – and I use their share.

Paddy Tanton I'd seen only a few weeks before the event after an absence of years. She came to see me when I was recuperating and made my jaw descend to carpet level with the list of her achievements. Shoemaker, semaphore teacher and loft converter, she had hoovered up academic letters to the extent that her headed notepaper – had she had any – would have had to be a metre wide. 'What next?' I asked her, in some awe. 'Ship's navigator, rhinoplasty, goat keeper?' 'No,' she laughed. 'I'm off to the Philippines to research my Ph.D. on Fillipino brides.' Glad I asked. Within minutes of meeting, Paddy and I slipped painlessly, unless you count the pain of laughter, back into our traditional roles of clown and clown feed...as we roared our way through the dateless years, when we would roller her straight blonde hair and make up her make-up-less face for a night out and she would scrape it all off again for a night in.

Well, you can take the girls out of Hull but you can't take Hull out of the girl, and at 5.30 on Saturday night in the Willoughby Manor Hotel, in spite of years of elocution and expatriation, the East Yorkshire vowels were blessedly present. 'Are you stayin' at herm?' and 'Which rerd did you come on?' were clearly discernible over the shrieks of recognition and non-recognition which turned the sober lobby into the encore of a Chippendales concert.

(They say Hull is the only place where pearls are people who come from Poland – Perland, I mean.) I was almost totally hoarse after four minutes. It took a while to be sure in some cases and no time at all in others:

'Leonie! Leonie!' I yelled to the girl coerced into doing an Eartha Kitt impersonation on a wobbly sofa on stage in front of the entire school. 'There's Kay Spivey!'

Her screams rang out as she charged across the lobby shouting, 'Kay! I don't believe it!' – and hugged to death a somewhat bemused and blinking Paddy.

There was Marilyn, the artist and natural comedienne, whose stunning Cliff Richard impersonation complete with curled lip and obscene hip had set the lower school screaming to such a point of hysteria that Miss Wright, or Tiny Alice as she was known, had been forced to stop the show, Jarvis Cocker-style, and dismiss the school to the school playing field to get its collective breath back. Once there, the injured party set up a throbbing chant of '*The* Horse *The* Horse *The* Horse' until your correspondent, never backward in hurtling forward, was quickly persuaded to perform her famous party piece. The one which ended with the performing 'child' peeing all over her mother. They were not a hard house to please.

And Janet, the beautiful and brainy, made a prefect and torn between her responsibilities and her love of a jape. And Jenny the pretty one and Pauline the sensible one and Hilary the toff, who could swear in the most exotic accent, and Kay, the worldly and wise one who was never ruffled and knew the value of a good pause:

'Where is your homework, Kay Spivey? Mmm?'

Pause while Kay stared back unblinkingly but without cheek. 'It's behind the clock on the mantelpiece, Miss.'

'And why, may I ask, is it behind the clock on the mantelpiece?' Pause.

"Because I put it there, Miss.' Mass sniggering was about to ensue, but not from Kay, who remained quite grave. 'To remind me to bring it in, Miss.' Game, set, match and new balls to Kay. Every time.

Two coaches took us, in our third-form groups, back to the old school. We saw it from the front as opposed to from the bike sheds. Gosh, it was pretty. Ivy covered and as neat and quiet as a convent. Inside the front door, quietly past Alice's door, where we'd so often waited for a lecture or a detention.

'Remember when we got caught smoking on the bus to the Wembley Hockey Finals? When Margaret Clubley told Alice she had period pains and smoking was the only cure and Alice was so embarrassed by the use of the word period in any context other than free or double that she let us all go...?' 'Remember how you had to stop talking when you crossed the lobby – halfway through a bloody conversation – till you reached the other side, then gab gab gab?... A Martian would have thought we'd short-circuited.' Down to the toilets. 'There's a Tampax machine! My God! Remember Miss Herman, the eighty-year old gym and hygiene teacher? Told us if we used Tampax we wouldn't be virgins when we married?' Scream.

'Remember when you came into our German class, Lipman? You sat under Hilary Brown's desk and every time anyone said "Bitte" you said "Shitte".'

'I didn't.'

'You *did*. I was one of the *good* ones till I met you.'

I wish I had a confit of duck for every time I heard that sentiment.

'You used to crawl under the desks to the front and steal Miss Hunt's paper while she was writing on the blackboard. You had a deskful!'

Back on the coach, memory and nostalgia mixed with curiosity. 'Two children at university reading PPE and Russian... Moved to Inverness in '68, with thirteen cats. The girl is married with a three year old... She's teaching Innuit children in Seskatchuan... Still single, no kids and very 'appy, thank you.' I was awash with some strange emotional excitement...in a minute we'd be singing 'You'll Never Walk Alone' and swaying.

We were and we did – but not yet. First we found our tables – 'Marilyn, over here! Paddy, quick, we must be together.' Already we were back in the dinner queue, the only difference being it was chicken and fruit salad instead of tinned mince and fly cemetery.

Lesley Duggan, née Watson, clapped her hands for silence and as normal got it from everyone but Table 4.

'Marilyn Atkinson, will you pay attention! What did I just say?'

'I don't know, Miss. I wasn't listening.'

'I said, after the first course three people move up a table, three people move down a table and three stay where they were.'

'We can't do that. We're arts. It's not fair.'

The noise on Table 4 was prosecutable. After the first move I had Janet on my right. She asked me what I was doing next and I told her I was filming in Whitby.

'What on?' she bartered back. '*Dracula*?' There was no way, in this hallowed company, I was ever going to get beside myself, let alone above.

Whinger Takes It All

I love films. Not all films, obviously, but as an actress they are quite the best of all mediums to work in for a basically lazy lout like myself. I love the endless waiting around for sun and cloud, and the camaraderie on the lunch bus, and the evenings spent in the bar saying, 'I've really *got* to go and learn my lines.' It can be exhausting but not in the same way as doing theatre. It's not inexorable. You don't have that 'feeling' hanging over you all day, like the last period at school when you know you have a dental appointment and the dentist has halitosis.

Mostly I love watching films. Always have. It still amazes me, the way you can just walk in, spend a few quid and see the exact thing you wanted to see, with no forward planning, no booking ahead, no 'You are in a queue. Kindly listen to some heavy metal until someone is free to insult you . . .'

From the Saturday morning adventure films and Gaulloise-strewn '*Un film de* . . .'s of my youth to the 'chick's flicks' and blockbusters of my dotage, I have remained a dedicated buff. Nowadays, though, I have a major complaint. And one you may not associate immediately with me. As Joyce Grenfell once said, 'I'm not shockable but I am VERY offendable.' The language. My dears, the language in the average screenplay is nothing short of appalling.

The 'f' word is now used as a verb, a noun, and no doubt (in *The Big Lebowski*, no doubt at all) as a preposition. What in the name of Mr Chambers has happened to the English language? Every script I read and every film I see is so effing full of effing 'f' words, for eff's sake, that I'm effed if I could effing recognise what the eff a sentence means without an eff in it! (Just writing that has left me effed!) And the last thing it ever means is anything to do with the good old Anglo-Saxon word for making love.

It has got so that, to the ears of the producer, the rhythm of a sentence sounds wrong without it. Its excesses strike me as much more dangerous on screen than either sex or violence.

There are so many incredible words not being used! The late Kenneth Williams used to learn three new ones a day. *Call My Bluff* has been running for hundreds of years and they still have an endless store of words we've never heard of.

The screenwriter's excuse is, 'That's how people talk,' and my answer to that is, 'Well, mate, not round my way they don't!' They say things like 'fragile' and 'curmudgeonly' and, now and again, just for emphasis, 'bloody 'ell fire club' – and when things become utterly unbearable, they might just eff and even blind, while simultaneously saying, 'Ooops, sorry, just slipped out.' In such a case its use actually *means* something.

That's not just me and my lot either. That's the majority. The scatalogically silent ma-bloody-jority. The radio listeners, the broadsheet readers, the library card owners, the thinkers, the medium-fliers who don't attend the Versace show in perspex micro mini nor the Henry Dent-Brocklehurst wedding in a dress that shows their episiotomy scar and don't watch *Eurotrash* whilst eating gulls' eggs and arugula pesto. I mean, the people for whom there is nothing on TV. The undervalued, overexperienced, overaged, class-challenged, middle-of-the-motorway public. We may not be 'youf' and we may not be sexy but we are dangerously intelligent and we deserve better.

Still, I must come clean. Woody Allen's latest film *Deconstructing Harry*, arguably his best, his most inventive and warts 'n' all funny, is also his most expletive splattered. The man is as complex as a Chinese carpet and as deliberately flawed. He's the man who put the wimp in whimper. Also, he fails to see the risibility of the love objects in his movies getting younger and fairer as he grows more and more to resemble the late Marjorie Proops after the London Marathon and a steam bath.

But when he tells us in *Deconstructing Harry* that the most wonderful sentence in the English language is not 'I love you' but 'It's benign'; when he writes a scene where an actor (played by Robin Williams) quite literally 'goes out of focus', both on and off screen; when he remarks in *Wild Man Blues*, the film documentary of his clarinet tour, that he's scared to play at the Royal Festival Hall in London because the audience will hate him in his own language, then I could almost kiss him myself. I said 'almost'.

F-F-F-Phew! I know. I said I'd do *anything* to be in a movie but I effing qualified it. OK?

Shipped Ashore

The nearest I've come to cruising since I first owned a separate passport was a five-day sail on the *QE2* to New York to pick up our son and his backpack from the ritual trip to the Far East, which, along with a Bar Mitzvah, is every North London lad's rite of passage. He was very thin, very hungry and *very* pleased to see us.

The ship was elegant and the weather bracing, and I worked my passage by delivering a couple of lectures to and from. So it was with good memories and a happy heart that with our good friends, Marilyn and Geoff Morrow, we set out to celebrate our Silver Wedding on a Holland America cruise ship called the *Ryndam*.

The cruise line has several other liners: *Stadendam*, *Veendam*, *Rotterdam VI*...As Susan, our drily comic cruise director commented, 'You can cruise to Alaska, the Panama Canal, the Mediterranean or the Caribbean on any "dam" ship of your choice.' I have no idea why my particular foursome chose the Caribbean – it certainly wasn't for its unspoilt beaches and uncommercialised ports of call. In fact, the whole package chose itself because of dates, availability and because nobody mentioned that Miami Airport was in any way involved in the proceedings.

I say that because one of my recurring travelling nightmares was of the time we were dumped blearily in Miami, with small kids, en route to DisneyWorld:

'Any plants, fruits or seeds?' barked the customs men as I scrabbled to conceal Adam's apple (as it were) before being allowed into a transit area literally carpeted with the thrown-in-from-a-great-height baggage of four separate flights. Pick your own packing.

Things had improved: the Virgin flight was the first improvement. I like this airline. There's a wonderful informality about the staff and service both in Upper and Economy. We travelled both – one of the advantages of a user-friendly face (albeit thinner than expected) at Heathrow, and the disadvantage of an unknown beige one, with a bright red nose on it, on the way home. Either way up, the food and the service were commendable. The overbooking on the return flight is only what *all* the airlines do – and it's loopy. I could have been a rich woman if I'd agreed to be bumped off the flight home and stay another night in Miami, but I didn't since (a) Mr Rosenthal likes his own hearth and (b) they sweetly gave us the seats with the leg room on account of my shopping his dodgy hip to the authorities. (He was not well pleased with the wheelchair that subsequently greeted him at Heathrow.)

But I'm slipping my moorings. We transferred from Miami to Fort Lauderdale by prearranged limo and stayed overnight in a faceless, faultless Marriot Hotel prior to boarding the ship the following afternoon. We dined on kosher franks at the nearby Bimini Restaurant overlooking the twinkling boat-filled Keys.

It was the first stage of maritime overindulgence which collectively gained us 23lbs in ten days. If my husband, perpetually in the shade reading in glasses, panama and long trousers, was 'The Professor', Marilyn, who finds out everyone's life story in twenty seconds, was 'The Confessor', and I, with my suitcase which appeared to be holding enough clothes for twelve weeks in Monte Carlo, was 'The Dresser'. Which just left Geoff who, with little competition, won both the nomination and the award as 'The Fresser'*. His excitement over a waffle, a blintz, a bowl of oatmeal or a midnight buffet proved contagious to the point of epidemic.

Before boarding we spent the morning getting ship-shape on a mini-cruise around the fabulous houses of the rich and marginally famous around the Keys.

'If you glance over the side you will see a rare sighting of the giant manatee, one of the oldest and shyest species of sea cow in the world.' Thank you. I now have at least half a dozen murky snaps of two long, brown, cigar-shaped underwater blobs which, frankly, take quite a bit of explaining.

Now the *Ryndam* was a big girl who boasted 1,500 passengers

---

*Yiddish word for one who lives to eat.

and 500 crew. Her chefs made 5,500 meals a day – and that was just for Geoff. No, it's a staggering turnover and for the most part the food was beautifully and artistically presented and tasted good in that chargrilled/broiled/sauteed/pesto-and-torn-icebergy sort of way.

Talking of torn iceberg, I took the precaution of not seeing *Titanic* before embarkation, owing to having an overactive imagination, especially after cooked mozzarella. Still, the life-boat drill was more *Carry On Cruising*, really, as no-one at that early stage knew where their cabin was, let alone how to get to Station 4, and when we did get there in our cubist life-jackets, we all looked like cornflake boxes on legs about to burst into song.

It takes a disorientating day or two to sort out your gilded dining-rooom fore from your self-service aft and another one to find ways to avoid the casino en route to almost anywhere. Any fears about my anonymity being assaulted were soon allayed by the awareness that 1,400 of the passengers were American or Canadian and – now let me put this kindly and wisely – of a certain age. One of the first comments I heard on leaving my cabin on evening one was, 'Mervyn, did ya check ya blood sugar before ya came out?' My husband, who numbers a bus pass amongst his most treasured possessions, said he'd never felt so young and frisky in his life. Things were looking up.

The four of us had definite views on how we would not be dragged into on-board entertainment. We chose our deckchairs in a quiet section of the deck, well away from poolside jollity, walked a bracing mile daily around the lower promenade and ostenta-tiously took out our serious holiday reading.

It took three days tops before we were pushing our way into the Explorers Bar, keen as mustard for our team to win the Trivia Quiz (No, we didn't – *you* try answering who was the star pitcher for The Mets in the '95 season!) and one more day before Marilyn and I almost came to blows deciding whether to do 'sarong tying' in the Crow's Nest or line dancing in the Ocean Bar.

I must say the on-board entertainment was excellent and, as you can imagine, I'm not that easy to please. The nightly shows were professional, fresh, well lit and beautifully costumed by Bob Mackie. A Canadian juggler/comedian did things with a machete, a carrot and a bicycle that defy description and the dance bands were as good as it gets. Like any enclosed community, one becomes involved with the staff – how hard they work, how little time they get off – and the Filipino crew's late-night show rehearsed between the hours of 12 and 3am made me weep. It was excellent – funny and sincere. Holland America have an asset they should be proud of.

(Conversely, the passenger talent show made your hair grow inwards. Large-bellied crudity, pace-makered Groucho impersonations and evangelical lady pianists made one long for the pole with the hook at the end. Until all was redeemed by the child passengers' version of 'Y.M.C.A.', performed by the few, maybe ten, kids on board to a pulsating beat and a jumping gesture per line. Blessedly, a four year old in a huge stetson and regularly descending gun, reduced us to pulp by executing every move perfectly – but backwards. They faced front, he faced back. They jumped right, he jumped left. It was bliss.)

'You – rike Rucas,' said our droll Indonesian table steward to me as he served up the 'Groene Erwten Soep' on the special 'Dutch Evening' menu. (Jack was wearing a muslin Dutch cap on his head – of the Muslim variety.)

'Me, rike Rucas? Sorry?'

'Yeah,' he insisted. 'You rook rike Rucas – Channel Twelve.'

It took a while to sort out that he watched *Agony* in his cabin on the high seas and had noted the similarity between me and Jane Lucas. I pointed out as modestly as I could that I WAS Lucas, but he refused to believe it. 'No, no,' he refuted. 'She *funny*.'

I have to say that the island stops filled me with less joy than the gentle, rhythmic life on board ship. Half Moon Cay is a tiny, uninhabited isle, owned by Holland America, on to which they throw a calypso band, souvenir shops and snackbars half an hour before you arrive. It's very Ealing comedy. St Thomas and St Lucia probably have much to offer if you explore them thoroughly beyond the diamond-flogging tourist centres, but there is little chance to appreciate their culture in the six or seven hours you have to tread their soil. St Maarten, half-Dutch, half-French, was perhaps the most interesting, with the Orient Beach on the French side showing enough style to list as one of its attractions 'Clothing Optional'. It gave sight-seeing a whole new dimension.

Phoning home from the ship cost several limbs, so since Geoff and Marilyn have six kids between them and the same number of in-laws, we generally left them at the quays with a bag of dimes and met them several hours later in a prearranged cove for a glorious dip and more french fries.

We reached Barbados on 18th February, the day of our Silver Wedding, and headed straight for the beautiful 1654 stone shul in Bridgetown, built by Jews fleeing from Recife in Brazil. With its marbled Doric columns, trellised gallery and magnificent brass chandeliers, it still manages to convey a coolness and a simplicity which makes the visitor stop and reflect on the vastness of the diaspora and the achievements of unique individuals.

We taxied to the Glitter Bay Hotel where (and we hardly dared to hope this would work out) my globetrotting brother Geoff hoped to meet us for lunch. He was actually at a Caribbean conference on tourism in Barbados for two days only. When his dear, weary head appeared under a palm frond I could have leaped for joy. And I did. Later on, back in the ship's two-tiered dining room, Jack and I were presented with an anniversary cake which I carried gingerly downstairs to distribute. On the way back, I managed to distribute it even further by falling UP the stairwell and smearing it all over the balustrades. There's a joke in there somewhere about having your cake and obsoleting it but I'll spare you it. Later still, after the legendary Rosenthal shuffle around the dance floor, we peeked in at the midnight buffet to watch the nightly cholesterol overdose. It was an incredible sight. Fish carved in bas-relief out of water melons, vast leaping dolphins out of ice and plaited baskets of roses baked out of dough. Nowhere else in the world, the chef confided, could he have the freedom to create such a banquet.

Like most people, I'm fascinated by dolphins, and particularly by the idea of swimming with them. It seems absurd that proximity to these cousins to man can actually have a therapeutic effect on us, but then, hell – I'm still getting used to the idea that aspirin is derived from tree bark! Everything is out there for us – cause and effect, yin and yang, perfect balance – just waiting to be discovered.

I couldn't wait to put my name down for the Swimming With Dolphins Expedition at our next port of call. Some years ago during a tour of the play *Lost in Yonkers*, the newspaper in *Newcastle Upon Tyne* reported a sighting of dolphins in the local waters. Though the month was October and the weather nothing short of inclement, my co-star Ms Rosemary Harris, a lady of formidable constitution and iron will but not – mum's the word (Jennifer Ehle's mum as it happens) in the first flush of youth, decided to hire a wet suit and a fishing smack and go out there into the freezing Atlantic for a dip with a warm-blooded mammal or two.

My first reaction was disbelief, my second was to suggest electric tagging. Why would anybody want to do this? I mean, swim with a big wet fishy thing? I didn't know then that dolphins are hugely intelligent, friendly to humans and spiritually healing. Neither did the theatre management, obviously, because they gave the project a massive thumbs down and Rosie was, oceanically, gated.

Since then, much has been written about dolphins. I'd seen the odd performance – they used to have them on Brighton Pier. One of them, when confronted by a giant toothbrush and the question 'What do we do when we've cleaned our teeth?' barked out 'Rinse!' It's true. It may have been blowing through its gill, it may have been clearing its nasal passage, it may have been breaking dolphin wind, but that dolphin shouted 'RINSE' at every show and twice on matinée days. It made me cry.

One thing is certain, the dolphin brain is every bit as impressive as the human one and may even be more sophisticated in some ways. For example, dolphins can't actually sleep the full eight hours – they'd fill up with water and drown – so the right-hand side of their brain stays awake whilst the left one sleeps and vice versa. I told my husband that astounding fact and he just said, 'Like me...' I've no idea what he meant but on the day of the tour, he stayed by the quayside with a mango juice and the other couple of mammals we'd travelled with.

It was an organised tour leaning heavily on the selling of videos and tempting offers of keyrings, framed photos, T-shirts and mugs all emblazoned with you and your mammal. Finally, you were allowed to stand in line in three feet of tepid water and shiver until the dolphins were released into the pool. Then it was worth every cent.

'Put out your arms to him,' yelled the keeper. I couldn't even see him but I put out my arms and, suddenly, theatrically, 'Jake' appeared from under my feet and slowly nuzzled up against my cheek. I couldn't believe it. 'Oh, you're *so* beautiful' I heard myself gasp.

'Give him a hug!' yelled the keeper, oblivious to my mystical moment.

I gave him one. A hug, I mean. He let me. Then he 'stood' in front of me waiting for a kiss – and, almost certainly, smiled quizzically.

'Hold him by the fins and dance with him,' said the man with the mike. I held his fins. They were rock hard where I'd expected something limp (there's another joke in there somewhere but I'm not going to descend to your level), and for a few seconds we danced. For a brief moment I was his and he was mine.

Then, like the typical male mammal that he was, he grabbed my sardine, did a lap of honour and left me covered in salt water. And, like the soft female mammal that I am, I clapped my little fins and held my breath till he decided to return. Sigh. My hero. Smooth, firm, satiny to the touch ... so far he hasn't written, he hasn't phoned, but I feel sure the bond between us is permanent.

Professor Steven Pinker in his book *How the Mind Works* tells us we are programmed to search out the most handsome, charming, genetically suitable, rich partner with whom to breed. However, life being what it is, we have to settle for less. Easy. But to stop us continuing to search the computer scrambles the wires. Makes us chemically unbalanced. We're gaga. The hardware's gone soft and vice versa. Another way of putting it is we've fallen in love.

This sprang to mind as I watched a shipboard romance over several days. She was lithe, blonde and touchy-feely. He was balding and smug like a cartoon bear who'd won a year's supply of Golden Syrup. The long moony looks, the sudden disappearances – this had to be honeymooners, high on their own endorphins, surely?

But no. One forgets most honeymooners have lived together for long enough to have had the JUST FOR ONCE CAN'T YOU PUT THE PIGGING TOILET SEAT DOWN row at least once.

As it turned out, these two were boss and employee and SHE was the boss. His wife thought he was on a golfing trip and if he said he'd scored a hole in one he wouldn't be lying.

Let's face it, the time limit on their love-in was what was

fanning their lust. But would it last, on dry land, back in the paperclip cupboard? Will his wife find a packet of three in his five-iron pouch? Will I ever forget what she did to him in the steam room? Will the first half of this chapter bear any relation to the second part? Dolphins – endorphins? Sounds awfully fishy to me.

Look. Cruising is what you make of it. There's a touch too much queuing, too many thumping great liners in dock and you can't go swinging too many cats round in your cabin. Still, you can work out, be massaged, gamble, play bridge, shop til you drop anchor, or just sit and watch all human life waddle past. Would I go again? Certainly I would although, perhaps, to a different location. The cruise staff were enchanting. Although I must say I jumped when I heard one of them say, 'I'm dealing with the Jews.' It took a moment before I realised he meant freshly squeezed grapefruit, orange or pineapple. When hundreds of Indonesian table crew filed out carrying flaming Baked Alaskas on our last night, then stood to sing their National Anthem, my eyes filled up *again*, and I realised I'm just a sucker for, as my dad would have said, the whole *mishegass*.

Back on dry land, the laborious transfer from boat to coach to hotel with luggage was almost enough to make me eat my words – but thanks to ten days cruising I was too chunky to eat anything.

Silver Salver

It was my Silver Wedding. Twenty-five years since we tied that reef knot – well, 29 years if you count the four years I spent pretending that marriage was not on my prioritised list.

Then you blink, put a few thousand meatballs in the oven, appear on too many touchlines, parent-teacher lines and headlines, then you stop being able to learn your lines, then to conceal your lines! And the next thing you know some of your contemporaries are showing you mugshots of their little Jacks and Chloes – their grandchildren, for God's sake!

And hey presto – it's time to consider how to celebrate 25 years of conjugal bliss. And, actually, it was no time at all. It was all very clever, really, because all the wedding presents had just more or less run out. I wouldn't have a wedding list in 1973 because it was 'boring and bourgeois'. I didn't realise then that lists occur to prevent couples receiving 23 stainless-steel dishes as gifts. Which is, in essence, exactly what we received. Mind you, as I say that, they've been carted off to various universities as ashtrays, or just disappeared into a tea chest as a dish and come out as a twisted piece of modern sculpture worthy of a place in the Royal Academy's 'Sensations' exhibition.

Except I didn't want any. Presents, I mean. I didn't need anything, and if I did I would have absolutely nowhere to put it. In fact, what I needed were things to house the things I'm overrun by. I'd like to trundle every old object off every surface of every mahogany 'what-not' down to the hospice shop and start all over again. New Labour, New Millennium, New Minimalism. The only comfortable old knick-knack I'd keep would be the comfortable old knick-knack I married all those years ago. And even he could do with a quick squirt with a can of Shake 'n' Jack.

As for me . . . as for me. Well, after seeing myself on TV over the Christmas period, I wanted a new attitude, a new hobby and a new nose. Honestly, I think I've hung on to this one for a heroically long period of time. I understand that your nose is the one part of your body that keeps growing *for life* and, frankly, the prospect is not appealing. So, if I show up in the late summer suddenly looking amazingly like one of those aliens at the end of *Close Encounters*, well, you read it here first.

I thought about having a wedding list at our local chemist. Imagine the phone call after a friend receives my invitation to our Silver Wedding party:

'Hello, the pharmacy? Yes, I'd like to enquire about the present list for Mr and Mrs Rosenthal . . . '

'Certainly, madam. What price range?'

'Oh, in the £25 margin.'

'Yes, indeed, madam. The bumper economy Nurofen pack? Ah no, sorry, that's already been reserved by Lynda Bellingham. What about the fourteen-pack flu powders or the elastic freeze-and-heat elbow support – or did Miss McKenzie reserve that? No, that's still available, or the hot water bottle with vibrating cover . . . ?'

'Yes, I had wanted something a little more *personal*, actually – '

'Personal, yes, madam, quite understandably so, madam. Well, there's a year's supply of Oil of Evening Primrose capsules for those violent shouting fits she gets every month, with integral his 'n' hers monogrammed earplug . . . '

Click. Friend replaces reciever. 'Den can you drive me to John Lewis? They've got a bargain offer on stainless-steel dishes.'

My mother had promised me a knife sharpener, which I really did need, although there was something distinctly ominous about the offer. I put in for a bird table, to pass the lonely empty hours – and what Mr Rosenthal was getting was between me and my mind. But it would be musical. There was no better sight for me than that of Jack torturing his violin, with my singing teacher Jane Edwards in full flow on the piano. His face was glowing, his eyes were shining, his heart was thudding, you couldn't hear a single note he was playing, and it mattered not a jot.

One thing I wouldn't be giving him was a party seating plan, because never again in my life was I going to face such a thing. People could sit on top of each other for all I cared – they could superglue themselves to the person they'd least like to share a desert island disco with, they could make vertical columns like a tired old Halifax commercial, but never, never again would I mix and match my guests into formal choreography. Why?

'Hello, Maureen, we *are* going to be there tonight but is it all right if my Auntie Gloria from Estonia comes with her guide dog? I promise she won't eat much and we won't stay for the dancing...'

'But, of *course* – it will be a pleasure to *see* her again after thirty-five years. No trouble at all...Lovely...' Click.

'Hello! Franco, can you get a large woman and a St Bernard on to Table 14? Well, I know, but Mr and Mrs Burns won't mind going on the Biggins table. They *are* in amateur dramatics in Slough...'

Never again. This time we would crush up with elbows in our kidneys and red wine and salt all over the floor. Just the sort of party which makes my partner head for the one chair in the room and not get up again for the duration.

Funnily enough, whenever he does this all the really interesting people in the room seem to gravitate to his chair. Can he be an aparty animal, I wonder?

Evenin' All

I find I increasingly miss the community life at which I used to sneer. The sense of a group of people, meeting and re-meeting for reasons of contentment. It's not that I don't have a social life – oh, good Lord, I'm here, there and everywhere. Phew! I mean, the wear and tear on opaque brownish-black tummy-control tights is unbelievable and my evening gowns are in and out of the closet more often than Michael Barrymore!

It's just that I seem to spend a great deal of time exchanging witty badinage with people I will never see again, or eating suppers I can't taste because afterwards I'm going to have to sing for them.

Returning home from one such expedition, I couldn't help remembering how my parents entertained their circle in Hull. They had 'Evenings'. I know we all have evenings – it's the bit between *The Bill* and bed, isn't it? – but theirs weren't just evenings, they were 'Evenings'.

We kids were scared or bribed off for an early bath after a leanish tea of spaghetti on toast while the house was perfected and bridge rolls covered with greaseproof. Dad's job was to make himself smart with Brilliantine and change one pristine shirt and tie for another and to lay out small glasses for the Scotch or cherry brandy that was to be offered on arrival to the guests according to gender.

Around 8.30 the doorbell heralded the first '*Hellooo!*', always delivered in a tone of intense surprise and delight as if the participants hadn't seen each other only the previous day in town, but rather had just returned from a four-year sojourn in Botswanaland teaching native children how to make potato *latkes*.

Soon the 'How ARE you?'s began to harmonise with the '*Hellooo!*'s. One always knew that Jean and Leslie would arrive first because Leslie was obsessed with punctuality and that Freda and David would arrive last because Freda wasn't. The murmur changed consistency as the men drifted to one side of the room where politics, religion and racy dialogue held sway, and the women drifted to the other to gently trash their men, their kids and whoever hadn't arrived.

Our one appearance downstairs was the occasion for more shrieks of '*Hallooo!*' and much cheek pinching and height admiration. 'How are you getting on at school?' was asked ritually and rhetorically as we set out 'occasional' tables – this almost certainly qualifying as an 'occasion' – and passed around pots of tea and bridge rolls with chopped egg, chopped herring and cream cheese fillings on doillied plates. All the crockery matched and all the spoons shone. Finally, the home-baked biscuits went the rounds on a three-tiered plate also boasting Madeira cake from the Be-Ro recipe book.

'I don't know why, but it just didn't rise this time ...'

'Well, it tastes marvel ...'

'No, the last one I made was like this [gesture]. I mean, really ... this thick – I don't know what I did differently. I used the Be-Ro.'

'Oh, I always use the Florence Greenberg for sponge.'

'Really? Oh. Well, I think I will next time. Mind you, the last one I made was like this – ' [gesture]

'Listen. They're all knocking it back, aren't they?'

Laughter all round.

During food the sexes mixed. Sometimes the 'Evening' mysteriously involved cards – 'Hearts' for the men in one half of the inter-connecting living room, 'Kalooki' for the women in the other. The laughter linked the whole concept.

Later on, around midnight, the whole thing went into reversal as Jean and Leslie left first and Freda and David lingered last.

'It's been a *lovely* evening.'

'Have you enjoyed it?'

'Oh, it's been *really* lovely.'

'Drive carefully!' (Home was all of two streets away.)

'We've *thoroughly* enjoyed it – haven't we, Mike?'

'Marvellous. G'night.'

'Thanks for coming. God bless.'

And that was that. Fourteen plates, cups and saucers and spoons to be washed up and replaced in the cupboard for 'best'. A quick go-over with the Ewbank, an enthusiastic postmortem on the proceedings from the washer-up and mumbled replies, too late, from the one shifting the furniture back. Then Dad went to bed and Mum shifted the furniture to where it should have been.

'I don't know why that cake didn't rise – I did exactly what I did for that last Evening . . .'

'Oh, give over, will you? They ate it, didn't they?'

'Still.' Lights went off. 'I think on the whole it went well. Don't you?'

Silence.

'Yes. I think it did. Everyone seemed to think so...Anyway. I won't have to do another one for seven weeks, thank God.'

After surviving 'the dinner party years', where I flailed about hopelessly in a sea of salsify, salt cod, salt tears and 'never agains', and the 'Let's try that new Etruscan/Macedonian minimalistic brasserie on the Holborn Viaduct' years, where I paid off a dinner guest list as long as Jeffrey Archer's 'Must dos' at a squillion quid a night, I'm all for reverting to type. As they used to say in Dock Green, 'Evenin' all.'

Part of the Furniture

When I set off for Birmingham, it was to combine two jobs and a parental visit. Not that I've anything against two separate visits to the city my daughter describes as 'light and airy and incredibly upbeat' – but my own memories of touring in Birmingham were coloured by the journeys to and from the theatre which seemed to entail going underground, emerging on a central island, returning underground and coming up to find myself where I hadn't intended to be.

As I drew up outside the massive Metropole Hotel, I noticed a now familiar phenomenon. All over the enormous lobby were living mobile sculptures. Not Gilbert and George successfully cloned, singing 'Underneath The Arches', but life-sized business-men with mobiles clutched to their ears, all barking at the ground. Honestly, if an alien anthropologist landed there he might have mistook the lobby for a flamingo park. With very drab flamingos who live on grey and white food rather than salmon-pink, and feed constantly, through their ears.

What was I doing in this ruched and ragrolled hotel ducking radio waves? I was hosting the Furniture Industry Awards, to be precise: best products, best motion furniture (yes, I thought that too – the return of the commode?), best all-round improvement in knobs, you know the sort of thing. Yes, it could have been dull, but I always get something out of these events, even if it's only a story to tell you.

The next day I would pick out a likely bed for us to buy at the NEC. I would also buy some boots and lunch for my daughter in town, record two episodes of *Call My Bluff* and head for home before I was missed. Thirty-six hours in the life of the last woman to think she can 'have it all'.

In preparation, I'd been studying back issues of *The Cabinet Maker*, which was actually rather riveting. For example, I found out that 50 per cent of all waterbeds fail the inflammability test. I've never really checked out waterbeds – not since the sixties – but I reckon you'd have to be pretty skilled to set fire to 70 gallons of water.

I also learned that Tony Blair bought a Swedish bed for £3,500 and that Freddie Starr met his girlfriend, part-time sales assistant Donna, whilst furniture shopping in Redditch. 'I used to think he was a hamster-eating monster,' said Donna, 'but he's *lovely*.' I'm desperate to know what piece of furniture he was shopping for. A flammable waterbed, maybe.

I spent the afternoon rehearsing the procedures in the banqueting hall with producer Chris Cree. My job would be to present half an hour of comedy (I'd racked my brains to think of stories with a furnishing bent but, aside from my mother's observation that Princess Diana may have been bumped off by 'MFI', had come up with nothing. Years ago, there used to be a saying, 'Why is MDF furniture like Cecil Parkinson?' 'One loose screw and the whole cabinet falls apart' – but I wouldn't win any topicality prizes with that one), then I would present the fourteen awards, pose for pictures, introduce the brilliant Jeremy Hardy, then knock off for the night to my suite.

After the rehearsal the sound engineer gave me a battery pack and microphone to attach to my evening gown. It was a heavy pack and, as I was wearing a long dress with no pockets, I asked for a belt with a pouch to contain it. He didn't have one. Nor did he have tape or string. I was about to phone housekeeping when he emerged with six or seven lengths of black plastic cable-ties. 'But they're too stiff and too short!' I remonstrated, not for the first time in my life. He assured me that they would clip together and three or four would make a squarish circle around my waist. Dubious but willing, I took them upstairs where I undressed, put on the hotel dressing gown and continued working on my jokes.

At 6.30, as my bath was running, I clipped three cable-ties together and hoiked them around my waist, which used to be 26 inches and is now – well, suffice to say four cable-ties did the job with the remaining slack looped down inside the belt. Fair enough – invention had been successfully mothered again by NECessity.

Except I couldn't get it off. The reason I couldn't get it off, I later found out, is that cable-ties clipped together *never* come apart. The more you tug to remove them, the tighter they become. I was stark naked and trussed up like a Haggis in mourning. I should have phoned for help – but if I got anyone, how would I explain that I wasn't a politician caught in an auto-erotic exercise but a perfectly normal naked actress, who wanted to be cut out of four black cable-ties?

I took my bath wearing it, got made up wearing it, put the black velvet dress over it and decided the engineer could cut me out of it after the show. Unfortunately, the black velvet dress was too tight to incorporate the battery pack, and the fourth cable-tie kept slipping its loop and erecting itself of its own accord inside the dress. 'Is that a cable-tie in your pocket or are you just pleased to see me?' was a phrase that came to mind.

Finally, desperately, I located Chris Cree, whom I'd met just once before, and he kindly agreed to come to my room with a Stanley knife. I took off my dress, he sawed me out. And that's the end of my statement, M'Lud.

As it happened, my introductory shtick went well and I felt more than relieved as they began their meal and I returned to my room to order my Dover sole and chips, after which I was to rejoin them for the awards. After 45 minutes, I phoned down in my 'ring of death' voice. "The meal is being plated as we speak, madam,' I was told. 'Is it now?' Ten minutes later, the chef rang to offer me *any meal* of my choice to replace the Dover sole which was now lying on the floor of the lift accompanied by a limping waiter.

I'd taken one bite of its mozzarella and tomato replacement when the chef rang to ask if it was OK. I'd taken two bites when Chris Cree rang – was I ready to start the awards ceremony? I'd had three bites and one gagging action when my daughter rang for a serious chat about life, the meaning thereof and a proposed new haircut . . .

I was transported back to the banquet on wings of ire. The perfect recipe for good comedy. 'What have you had to eat?' I asked the audience, and told them about my food. Everyone seemed to enjoy the show incredibly and cries of 'See you next year!' rent the air. The following morning, I prowled the furniture show and lay on eighteen different beds intended for the marital bed chamber. Coil-sprung, pocket-sprung, Vi-sprung or sprung chicken, I hadn't a clue. It was 25 years since I'd bought a bed and that one was roughly £1,850 less than most of the ones on show there. Still, the lying down was nice. Always enjoyable to do something you're really good at.

After all that, *Call My Bluff* was a breeze. Years ago, we sold our first house to my team partner, Robin Lustig, so there were many creaky floorboards to discuss there, and our team, under the bright and bonny Sandi Toksvig, resoundingly trounced the other side. I got to shake the hand of Douglas Hurd, share a glass with Jancis Robinson, flirt with Norman Pace, patch up a rift I never even knew I had with Francis Wheen, and still be home in time for Jack's home-made chips. *And* find Amy some fab boots in Jones of Birmingham for £19! And they call this work!

Did I buy a bed? Not on that occasion I didn't. I was offered a fabulous electric one (three grand) free if I opened someone's shop in Ealing. Jack was consulted and declined on the grounds that I'd always have my half up in the air, with my nose in a book, and he'd roll over to be friendly and find *his* in an electrified hinge.

It was at least a year later when Jack's half of the mattress breathed its final terrible wheezing gasp and both rose and sank at the same time. Coincidentally, I had just read an article by Emma Thompson in the *Standard* about how her long-term insomnia had been alleviated by one night in a bed at the Savoy Hotel. (She didn't say whether she was accompanied.)

She had tracked down the handmade bed to the Savoir Bed Company, ordered one and slept, ever since, like a baby. The price was astronomical, although compared to a small car it was a snip and you'd spend a helluva lot more time in it. And probably have as much fun with less fuel. I resolved to have one too.

I phoned the firm who were unworldlyly polite and suggested we visit their factory in Acton to see how the beds were made. We duly trundled around the North Circular (noting as usual the sudden smell of fried onions between Brent Cross and Ikea) and disputed our way through to a large and extremely ugly industrial estate and ultimately to a small garage-type door and a bell which read 'Savoir'.

A brown-overalled manager showed us courteously through the various stages of mattress construction from hourglass springs which are 'star lashed' together with strong string, through ticking and tufting to double stitching with a lethal-looking needle and layering with cotton felt, fleece and curled horse hairs. Gosh. We did our level best to look fascinated. I tell you. At the end of the demo it seemed churlish not to order a batch of beds but we settled for one. It would be ours, in no time at all, but this being the world of ordering furniture, no time at all translates as sixteen weeks. It was January. Rest assured we'd be sleeping soundly by May. Or, as an ex-boyfriend of mine used to say, 'If you fall through the mattress I'll see you in the spring.' *Ex*-boyfriend, you'll note.

How to pass the intervening months with Jack in Sleepy Hollow and me up in the air and rolling rapidly downhill? We decided to sleep on it. Next day I ordered a mattress from John Lewis which was delivered almost immediately. It would deliver us sixteen weeks of devoted service then transfer without demur to our son's room, along with our old bed. This would help to overcome the fact that he was now six foot three and, thus, a foot and a half longer than his beloved old disappearing wall-bed. Every time he came home from college his mattress would be out on the floor, along with eight boxes of books, seven of CDs, rucksack, sleeping bag, condemned laundry, assorted wall posters, inflatable armchair, music centre, guitars, fake oriental rug, several unidentified fleeces and a very pretty girlfriend. It was clearly time for one giant step for a kind man.

In the intervening weeks our anticipation became feverish. A new duvet was mentioned. A discussion was held about where to store all the summer clothes, at present in the divan drawers, which, in our case, we would no longer have. Ottomans were mentioned for the first time since the Empire. About halfway through the gestation period we put our coats down on a friend's bed in Hampstead, marvelled at the width of it and changed our mattress order from five foot to six foot. 'It's really worth it,' said the bed's owner. 'You can really get away from each other.'

'But they're too stiff and too short!' I remonstrated not for the first time in my life.

It came, we saw, we're bonkers for it. It dwarfs the bedhead, which was originally a baroque mirror in an elaborately curly mahogany frame used above, not at the head of, its owner's bed.

Not ours, needless to say. The new bed required not only a new duvet but new sheets, duvet covers and, while you're at it, get some pillows which don't have deep yellow circles round the ticking fabric, will you?

True to form I did this the day before the bed arrived in the twelve minutes I had between the physiotherapist in Harley Street and the 6.30pm *Oklahoma!* warmup. Everyone declared my choice of John Lewis's ownbrand duvet cover incredibly dull and the wrong blue for the room. 'Just help me gerrem on and shut it!' was my measured response. Later I indulged in a second set. For best. These have cream embroidered pillows. When I wake up from my marvellous night's sleep I now have a cream embroidered face. As I'm a woman of a certain age, the pattern takes HOURS to fade from my skin and makes me look like an old Kathcali temple dancer.

So now I just need the ottoman for storage and to stop me having to crawl into the underbed drawers in Adam's bedroom whenever I need a pair of shorts. Soon after the bed's arrival, I saw Emma Thompson briefly in the street while driving through Hampstead. I was in my white birthday car with the top down and wearing a white dress, so there was much sending up to sit through and no time to mention what she'd just cost me. She looked incredibly glowing and pretty and I remembered afterwards that she was going to have a baby. Oh, Lord – all those sleepless nights . . .

Cricket Test

Driving to Berkshire one Sunday with the radio tuned to the last Test Match in the Caribbean, I became aware that my husband and I were listening to two different languages. His comprehension of the patois was total. Mine was total incomprehension.

'What does he mean, "The night-watchman bishop has just been dismissed"?'

He looked both amused and superior. 'It means he's out.'

I looked at him, not amused. 'Who's out?'

'Bishop.'

'Bishop's a person, then, is he?'

'Yes, he's the bowler, really.'

'I thought he said he was a night-watchman?'

'He did. He is. He was – Last night when the Windies . . .'

'Pardon?'

'Sorry, the West Indians were batting at close of play. They use him cos he's a tail-ender.'

There was a pause whilst I regrouped myself.

'He's a tail-ender who they used as a night-watchman?'

'Yes. It means he's an eight or nine – so they put him in, rather than risk losing a three or four in bad light.'

I considered this. It was patently lunatic. Like putting a terrible warm-up man on stage to make the comic look better.

'So why don't they take people to the West Indies who can bat *and* bowl?'

'Well, because world-class all-rounders are very hard to come by. Boycott couldn't bowl. Bradman couldn't bowl. Atherton, the captain, can't really bowl.'

'He can't bat either, by the sound of it. But do you mean in the whole of England they can't find . . .'

'Botham could do it – but mostly they specialise. Even fielders specialise.'

'Pardon?!'

'Fielders. They can be best in the slips or in the covers...'

I had the W. G. Grace not to say 'and dynamite between the sheets'.

'But,' he went on, 'well, yes, they usually have a couple of rabbits with them...'

That did it. 'Rabbits! He's here with his rabbits now! What in all that's sacred...!'

. He was now helpless, shaking at the wheel and a danger to the middle lane.

Meanwhile, the commentator commentated on. Apparently, to start with, Tufnell was giving the ball 'just a bit more air', but now it would seem 'he'd flattened out'. The umpire swayed away, which was his way of saying 'not out', and someone else was exploiting the rough: 'He'll have sore fingers tonight,' he chortled knowingly, and his colleague joined in the chortle, adding for good measure, 'Yep – he just floats it up...'

Oh. Right, then, that's OK then.

I fixed my husband with a baleful look. He beamed back. Men are from Mars and women from Venus. He was loving this. As well he might, being a member of the inner circle. Those of us with noses up against the window pane of the inner circle merely sigh, harrumph and fix the knowalls with the baleful looks.

Still, when I think of the hundreds, the thousands of drowsy afternoons I've spent with Brian Johnston or John Arlott droning pleasantly but incessantly on in the background, it's shameful that I've picked up nothing of the meaning of their jargon. I mean, I've watched and enjoyed a few one-day matches, and I've even been excited by the *Daily Telegraph*'s showbiz Fantasy Cricket Team. (I chose the team name – The Kricheters – from the Yiddish word to *krich*, which means to walk slowly and purposefully) and my neighbour, Colin Shindler, chose the team members. By astounding luck our team knocked the *kishkes* (intestines) out of 25 other teams and we won a non-existent trophy. I was completely overexcited by my imaginary victory. I mean, I really like the sound and the sight of the game, but my knowledge of its rules and rituals could be written on one bale and still leave room for a stanza or two of Kipling.

And it's not just cricket. Take the shipping forecast. Now I love the shipping forecast. When it comes on my radio I feel soothed and warmed. I said this to my fellow actor, David Horovitch, on our way to Cardiff to film a Welsh/Yiddish picture. 'I know exactly what you mean,' he said. 'Whenever I hear it, the temperature goes up just a bit in the car.'

It always seems to come on when I'm putting on make-up or slicing veg for soup, one ear on the news and one side of my brain somewhere in another hemisphere. 'And now here is the shipping forecast for today, Wednesday 1st April, issued by the Meteorological Office at 18.00 hours. There are warnings of gales in Dogger, Fisher, German Bight, Scilly Automatic, South Utsire, North Utsire. Winds fresh to moderate. Gale force ten Greenwich, Rockall and S. Utsera, Finisterre.' To me it's a mysterious mantra. To sailors everywhere it's a matter of life and death. Put a map of Europe in front of me and ask me to locate Fastnet and I would probably giggle skittishly and point to Sark. Yet I've probably heard the forecast's rhythmic prose several thousand times during my lifetime.

My continuing ignorance astounds me. Where's my ruddy curiosity? I ask me. I mean, if I'm told a joke it goes straight in the brain file that holds useless information for ever. Yet I'll never know my Fastnet from my Farve.

Nor will I know my Footsie Index from my Dow Jones or my Hang Seng from my Nike. Yet I read newspapers and books, listen to the radio constantly and watch the TV when there's nothing else to do and the fridge is empty.

I blame my place in the family. My elder brother was Science and Sport so therefore I had to be English and Art. I'm numerically dyslexic. As Victoria Wood once memorably said, 'We didn't have dyslexia when I was at school. You just sat at the back with raffia.'

(A tutor hammered basic maths into you to get you through your 11 Plus and after that you bluffed it until you could give up the sciences and concentrate on three 'arty' subjects. Two years later you've whittled it down to one subject, which basically means you know what's going round the West End but what makes the world go round the sun ... or the other way round ... or whatever ... well, frankly, you're stumped.)

I suppose there may be some poor soul on a remote isthmus who doesn't know the Brian Johnston commentary which goes into history as the funniest ever. Well, I'll retell it, just for you, dear.

Peter Willey was bowling for England against the 'Windies'. The next batsman in was Michael Holding. 'Johnners', with all the aplomb in the world, announced, 'And the batsman's Holding the bowler's Willey.'

Oklahoma!

I met Trevor Nunn one evening in The Ivy. We hadn't met for years but it must have sparked off an idea in his head because he asked me to meet him to talk about Aunt Eller in *Oklahoma!* We had a good, friendly, funny chat for half an hour at the National, then I read the book and felt the buzz of curiosity. He told me how Eller was central to his vision of the show – 'the matriarch, tough, fair-minded and a character the community looked up to.'

'If you don't have a song in a musical,' I told him wryly, quoting my friend, Julia McKenzie, 'you ain't in the musical.' He promised me a couple of extra verses and I trusted him. Rightly, as it happened.

I took some singing lessons from Janet Edwards. I can sing like I can play tennis. I know the rules and if I forget trying to be good and enjoy the game, I can get away with murder. If I watch myself you can hear the catgut snap.

The readthrough was tentative. Curly was a tall, beautifully proportioned, bright, sweet-faced Australian, Hugh Jackman. Laurey was a pale, black-haired, tentative ballerina, Josefina Gabrielle. Jud, the villain, was Shuler Hensley, a mad, massive, mop-haired baritone from Atlanta, Ado Annie was a slight, just-out-of-RADA, raven-haired orthodox Jewish biologist from New Jersey, Vicki Simon. Will Parker was a sandy, pugnacious Welshman. Jimmy Johnston and the pedlar from Persia was black-eyed Anglo-Cypriot, Peter Polycarpou. Old pro Tony Selby was a smokey-voiced cockney Pop Carnes.

In short, not one of us was typecast. Not one of us fitted the bill as posted on the front of the hustings in any production of this oft-performed classic, including the Broadway production in 1943. We all sat down in a circle, coffee cups in hand, large floppy bags constantly dived into, pencils sharpened, throats cleared.

First off, Trevor asked us to go around the circle, saying who we were and giving one fact about ourselves. When it came to my turn I said, 'My name is Maureen Lipman and I told my friend Pam that Trevor had cast me as Eller because he was calling the show "*Oy*klahoma" and it was all set in a kosher prairie. She completely believed me and immediately arranged for two coachloads of elderly Jewish people from day centres in North London to attend the opening.

When we could put it off no more we read the text. When Hugh's glorious tenor rang out the first notes of 'Oh, What A Beautiful Morning' ('And he can sing too,' was Trevor's comment), my heart started to do double time. Each new voice was revelatory but right. The chorus was rich and deep. Oy! We were on to something.

For one day Trevor talked and we listened. He covered land-rushes, pioneers and the hardship of survival. The second day we improvised. There is nothing more embarrassing for an older actor than pretending to be a wristwatch or a horse trough in front of 25 twentysomethings. Tony Selby and I put our heads down, smothered our smirks and got on with it. At one point we were kneeling on the floor facing each other, telling and listening to stories simultaneously. I can't remember a word of his, but mine concerned a red fluffy pencil case named Biscuit.

Later we became our favourite cartoon characters. I Olive Oyled myself into a knot of legs and arms, loping across the room squealing, 'Oh, oh, oh, Popeye!', double-taking and doubling back on myself as one-dimensionally as I could. We were not, fortunately, asked to watch each other but only to get involved in our own scenario. At the end of the session I got the famous Trevor hug. I was, rather pathetically, thrilled by this.

Three weeks into rehearsal I tried to resign, feeling thoroughly inadequate. Trevor, thankfully, ignored my plea. I gamely exercised, warmed up, stretched and kicked with the kids, but asked to count eight beats before executing a four-beat shuffle and my eyes would fill up and I'd convince myself that Susan Stroman, the choreographer, wanted my knees in a viola case at the bottom of the Thames. Somehow I managed to busk it by a mixture of bravado and eccentricity. Only weeks after opening could I suddenly hear the prescribed beats and know when to start. It was as though my ears had relaxed. And still, whenever Stro was out front, I'd lose it again. I'd know I was going to lose it, then I'd lose it – then I'd look sheepish, as if to say, 'I told you I'd lose it!'

Don't misunderstand me, these were all tiny moments which an audience would hardly notice, but to me they were the equivalent of saying, 'Now is the winter of our discontinence...er...made glorious... – ooops – I've dried.' Eight weeks' rehearsal was a luxury I'd never even contemplated before. I needed every minute of it.

Because of the scale of the venture, there would be much waiting around. Shuler Hensley would sit on the floor, behind some makeshift prop, like a marooned giant. We'd all forget about him until he'd suddenly appear over the top of a cupboard and slither down the front of it in vest and sweatpants and along the floor brandishing his prop knife like a malevolent six-and-a-half-foot toddler.

Peter Polycarpou would fret and worry away at his lines, doubting himself, his ability, his received place in the company. Often we would prop each other up on a bench outside on the embankment.

'Pete, you're getting it – honestly. The accent's there, it's truthful – just believe it will be funny with an audience, cos it will...'

'You really think so? I dunno...He never seems to like my suggestions.'

'Well, I know. It's the same with me – I'm so used to chipping in and suggesting stuff and...'

'Yeah, well – you should – Who knows more than you about comedy?'

'But this is musical comedy. Who knows less than me about musicals?'

Tony Selby, playing Ado Annie's father, was as enervated as me by the hours of waiting, followed by sudden intensive action. One day his car exploded on him, showering boiling water over his arm, and for weeks he painfully danced and sang sporting a large sling. A couple of weeks later the male chorus danced straight into him, elbows akimbo, and cracked his ribs.

I have that look in my eye as if the wet clay scene from *Ghost* might follow... The Writer, the Sculptor, the Actor and the Cantona Maker.

I couldn't help thinking there were three of us in this marriage.

George and Louie Baker, writer Perry Portal and I hang on to words above Ruby's.

Actress Sara Kestleman: 'I went to Maureen Lipman's party and all I got was this blousy T-shirt.'

Three tall women – give or take the short one.

The late Rabbi Hugo Gryn, a man you could lay on an open wound.

The Two Degrees. Sally and I Da Do Ron Ronning.
(Jacquie Granditer)

Mike Haslam, my accompanist on *Live and Kidding*, and me 'completely out of it'.
(Jacquie Granditer)

My brother Geoff, the conservationist, and his wife Mei-Mei.
(Mark Mawson/Scope Features)

Come as You Were (even if what you were was not yet born).
(Mark Mawson/Scope Features)

A rare table sighting of two lesser-spotted progeny.

Is that a microphone cable or are you just pleased to see me?

I'd like to look like this again
before I die.

Jewels by Butler & Wilson; dress by
Neil Cunningham; photo by Cass
Latimer; decolleté by design.

DUNCAN C WELDON
Presents

MAUREEN
LIPMAN
LIVE &
KIDDING

Directed by
ALAN STRACHAN

Musical Director
MICHAEL HASLAM

RICHMOND
THEATRE
The Green, Richmond, Surrey TW9 1QJ

MONDAY 3 - SATURDAY 8
FEBRUARY 1997
BOX OFFICE 0181 940 0088

'Dear Miss Lipman,
I enjoyed your
show but I feel I must
point out that women
of a certain age should
not bare their
upper arms.'

Anna Raeburn gracefully accepting a Sony Radio Award from former Jane Lucas.

'I should never have had that last cup of tea, Ma'am.'

Accepting After Dinner Speaker Award from
the Princess Royal – the Princess and I in mix
'n' match mode.
(Doug McKenzie)

Two Commander Family – looking for a frigate.

He made a valiant attempt to return but the pain overwhelmed him. After three weeks he'd missed so much new choreography that it was impossible. Annie was right – it's a hard-knock life. Sid Livingstone appeared one day, word perfect, and took his place, temporarily, and then permanently. Poor Tony missed an incredible year.

The technical week was desperate. The actors were in full costume, wigs and make-up for eleven hours a day, Monday to Friday. In retrospect, this must have been a godsend to the lighting mavin, David Hersey, at present sailing his boat around the entire world. (Come back, David! We didn't mean it.) At the time it seemed crazy and pedantic. Most productions have one day of technical rehearsals and the actors are in street clothes and save corsets and make-up for the dress rehearsal. On the Friday night the call went out for the cast to be back in costume ready to go at 11.00am.

As the technical rehearsals reached a climax I found myself shop-stewarding the cast against the management. 'My cast are going home,' I told deputy stage manager Barry Bryant. 'They are going home now before they fall over.' I'm not sure this was appreciated. Susan Stroman came to my dressing room:

'We have to go on,' she told me. 'This isn't for the actors, it's for the crew. It's a technical. You know what a technical is?'

I stared at her.

'Stro,' I said, 'I've been doing techs since you got your first pair of block shoes. I know what a tech is. There are no corsets in a tech. These actors have to open the show and it's best if they do that alive.'

We went home at eleven. Couldn't sleep. Wouldn't sleep. Would I be branded unprofessional? I went back the next day clapped out and panicky. No-one mentioned my rebellion. The tech went on. Trevor inexhaustible, living on Ryvita and coffee, never lost it, never raised his voice, and was always reasonable.

We opened calmly and confidently. I sat 60 foot under the stage, rooting my feet into the wooden earth, smelling the butter in the churn. Squinting into the scorching sun. The floor came up and revolved into place, and the audience applauded the whole opening sequence of sunrise, overture, dustbowl, flying clouds, birds and tiny wooden houses in perspective against the sun. We were off. Curly came on, singing, and the bantering began. Two months later, the laughs peppered every quip we made. That night, though, our sincerity was our trump card. We were not expecting any reaction, so any laugh we got was a wonderful bonus. (You know what they say, 80 per cent of acting is sincerity. And once you've learned to fake that...) I believe Trevor preferred the show when it was in this tentative stage. Once the seasoned pros had nailed their laughs, it became more of an ordeal for him to watch it.

My experienced dresser, Elise, led me like a child from one side of the stage to the other, from exit to entrance. Seldom has a cast been so cosseted. The canteen fed us, the car park coddled our cars, costume and wig department dressed and fitted us, the publicity was made painless. The voice coach, Patsy Rodenberg, warmed us up, the dialect coach checked our accents: 'Emphasise by lengthening and hitting the volume, not by inflection.' It was a working community and it worked. No-one was ill. No-one was off.

I remember, back in 1971, riding my bike ecstatically over Waterloo Bridge on my way to work at the Old Vic theatre. I was a junior member of Sir Laurence Olivier's National Theatre Company. I worked eleven hours a day, rehearsing, playing and understudying. I was very happy. We all hoped that when the new National Theatre opened on the South Bank, we would all transfer with it. I could think of no more inspirational sight for creativity than the sweet Thames flowing past my dressing-room window.

Cue sound of Gods laughing at best-laid plans. Not only did *I* not transfer, but Sir Laurence – architect behind the architect – Olivier didn't transfer. Sir Peter Hall got the job. Furthermore, the dressing rooms, uniform concrete cells, were all built around a square and empty atrium. Our inspirational view was to be of each other.

Still, gazing out of my cubicle, some 28 years later, it could be that they were right. There was a corsetted and bewigged Caroline Quentin feeding her dog whilst the rest of *The London Cuckolds* cast dropped fag ash on their white tights and jabots. To the left Samantha Spiro and Geoffrey Hutchins turned themselves miraculously into Barbara Windsor and Sid James for *Cleo Camping Emmanuelle and Dick*. Up and right rollicking Irishmen chased kids from *Tarry Flynn* and down centre Sinaed Cusack warmed up melodically for her solo *Our Lady of Sligo*. All human life was strutting its stuff, to full houses in three auditoria. The concrete external hid an internal foundry of creativity.

Aside from some carping about why the National would want to spend 'our' money on a musical like *Oklahoma!*, the reviews were marvellous: classic book, score, lyrics, choreography, original play. Why would anybody want *not* to stage it?

For four months we enjoyed being on the Hit List. There were endless rumours of transfers to the West End. Most people wanted this. They needed the money and the exposure. I wanted it because I couldn't bear to think of them doing it without me. Trevor had a plan to make a video of the show in the months of September to November. The Lyceum, which was the only theatre big enough to house us, had a six-month gap before *The Lion King* arrived. TV producer Richard Price had three months to put the project together. It would take at least six. He did it in eleven weeks.

Every Friday we would have a company meeting with Richard and Trevor. Every Friday there would be optimism but no news. It became a company giggle. 'Was that a definite maybe?' someone was heard to say on their way to slap on a false hairpiece and a prairie pinny... and that was just the menfolk. The day before the last National Theatre performance, the news came through. Richard Price had pulled off the impossible. Money was in place from Australia, from Japan, from Sky, Italy, Germany, Sweden, Norway, Denmark, Finland and probably a damp briefcase under a Sicilian bridge for all we knew. Or cared. Yeeehay! We were on.

Everyone scattered to the five corners of the earth. Jack and I had a huge, fat, glorious week at Ballymaloe in Southern Ireland, forcefeeding ourselves on inimitable food and knocking back the Guinness at all the unsociable hours under Cork skies, and two weeks later the company reassembled for the video, quivering like greyhounds and utterly 'up for it'.

Just as well we were prepared. I think we stopped once a day for lunch from a standing trolley. The rest of the hours that God made we danced inches off our frames. The video crew were knocked senseless by our stamina and we by their fortitude. Every shot had a deadline. Every deadline had a sell-by date. If it couldn't be got into the day, then the day had to have a hairline extension. Some of the dancers were rising at 4.30am to catch trains and lifts to Shepperton, then leaving for home at 11.30pm, dragging their make-up and wigs off in the car park. This job required a designated dormitory on the studio floor. We shot nine minutes a day. Most TV dramas shoot three. But still we cut no corners.

Trevor and Stro and video director Chris Hunt were not compromisers by nature. It was done and we all went home with bags under our chins and a Christmas bonus. The bonus was that the transfer from stage to screen looked honest. True to what it was. What it was, was a stage show on film. The first shot is an aerial pan down the Thames, past St Paul's, into the crowded foyers of the National Theatre. Shots then cut in from audience to stage – we did an extra Sunday matinée to achieve these shots. Unfortunately they were mostly of friends, nurses, off-duty stage-door keepers and mothers.

My mother adored it. After the screening I heard her raving over the phone to Hull: '. . . and it starts with this wonderful view of the *whole* of Oklahoma all seen from above.' Yes, siree! Oklahoma alrightee! St Paul's, Waterloo Bridge, Sweet-Thames-run-sweet ol' Oklahoma. Indian territory.

Another closing. Another show. Christmas came and went, and then, ultra-violet rayed, we reopened the whole caboodle at the newly refurbished Lyceum and ran for six heady months. I won't chronicle the joy of it because it was a once-in-a-lifetime thrill. We got used to people telling us how they first saw the show on honeymoon in bleak 1947 war-ravaged London and how it was an unimaginable oasis of colour and optimism in their lives. We got used to the letters which wrung out the hearts of seasoned troopers because they came from folk who'd felt blue or depressed or bereaved or just plain didn't wanna go out that night. 'Thanks,' they wrote. 'For three hours I forgot myself totally, ' or, 'I haven't stopped singing for days,' or 'That's the best tonic I ever had.'

Two, though, stand out in my mind. One because of the guilt I still feel. The other because the letter writer was an agoraphobic who found it well nigh impossible to sit in a theatre surrounded by strangers, a condition which had been worsening for years and had effectively put a stop to her nursing career.

Friends bought her the ticket as a birthday treat. Yeah, OK, some friends, I know, but listen. She tried to get out of it, she finally agreed, she shook all the way in on the bus, her heart pounded, she sweated. In her aisle seat, she experienced panic symptoms and almost bolted, but from the moment the curtain rose, she lost herself, lost her fears, lost her proximity to others and became part of the whole experience. 'I sang the songs all the way home,' she wrote, 'and never noticed that I was on the dreaded Tube.' She was promising herself, by the end of the letter, to look into returning to nursing. The letter was eloquent and moving and sat on the noticeboard, melting the mascara of whoever passed.

The second letter was from a man whose name, I think, was David, who'd seen the show, loved it and talked about it on his weekly visit to his father, an Alzheimer's sufferer, in a Birmingham home. His father, who showed little or no interest in any conversation or any recognition of who was talking, suddenly became animated and said, 'I'd love to see that.' By a remarkable series of permissons and complicated arrangements, he transported his father to a special aisle seat, alerting the theatre staff that he might wander off somewhere. As with our nurse, his father sat for three and a quarter hours in rapt attention, barely moving but to laugh or applaud.

All the way home he clutched his programme to his chest, saying, 'I've got to remember this. I've got to remember this.' David wrote to the cast: 'I just want to thank you for giving me my father back for one evening.'

So why the guilt? I put the letter on the board. It disappeared. I was never able to write back. I tried writing to *Home Truths* and a Birmingham paper to no avail. It's on my conscience, so David whoever you are, if you ever read this please believe that the letter meant a helluva lot to us too.

The Lyceum run differed from the National one in one other way. It was five weeks before we played one night with the full cast. My notepad reads: Monday: Jimmy off – groin strain/Peter off throat/Amanda migraine/Mark back but hoarse/ David off/Ben off. Tuesday: Hugh off/Phil off/Vicki bad throat – and on it went...Every time Jools Gardener, the company manager, arrived in my dressing room it was to tell me of new missing persons. And, of course, when the guy playing Slim was off (six line scattered throughout the show) then Chris moved into his part and Ben moved into Chris's part and suddenly you were playing an auction scene with no idea who the hell Slim was and from under which stetson the next voice was coming.

Maybe we were tired, maybe we were less well cared for than at the National. Certainly my migraines were on the march. I missed two shows in the six-month run. I sat at home one Friday night, rigid with nerves, as 7.30 came and went without me at my churn. The pain of the loss was almost worse than the pain of the migraine. I knew my cover, Marilyn Cutts, was a brilliant singer and played the part marvellously. Still, I had several letters: 'I had brought my mother, who is, or *used* to be, a fan of yours, all the way from Cheshire – I had checked with the theatre, who assured me you would be appearing. I hope you realise the disappointment and misery you caused to people who were unable to get their money back' etc.

Sometimes on a Wednesday afternoon I'd be carrying my carrot juice into the stage door when groups of Welsh people would howl at me from a coach, 'Oh, you *are* going to be on – there you are, Hew, I told you she wouldn't take the matinee off!' Chance'd be a fine thing!

The last few weeks became corpse-ridden – giggly – as last weeks do when actors are 'all tuckered out', as Aunt Eller might say. One night I laughed so long and loud in the crucial trial scene that I couldn't do anything but squeak and wave my arms around like a beached bream. It was tragic. Most of the cast joined me. Afterwards, on my way home, I was congratulated by a group of theatregoers. I apologised profusely. They had neither seen nor noticed anything unusual.

Curly's horse tended to change names. 'Don't sell Dun, Curly,' became considerably funnier when the horse's name was 'Hurly Burly' and a complex and highspeed auction became a bowel churner when the starting price was eleven dollars instead of ten. A scene where Eller and four or five farm workers ran into the smokehouse after a gunshot was fired was even more dramatic when the gun failed to go off ... 'Pant, pant – who fired off that ... er ... who made that loud thudding noise?' And the presence in the smokehouse of one cowboy onlooker in full drag – with cherries on his hat – worked WONDERS for the progress of the plot.

The wings were crammed with wit during the romantic duo 'People Will Say We're In Love'. Fergus Logan and Nicola Keene were masterly in their attempts to corpse Curly on his line delivered into the wings, 'Anybody out there? I want you all to know that Laurey Williams is my girl!' After the Kama Sutra repertoire had been trudged through, they stood Nicola on Fergus's shoulders with her skirt down to his boots. The next night she was two foot one with shoes on her knees and another night found her topless with vast plastic breasts. Hugh Jackman had a way of incorporating open-mouthed laughter into Curly's sheer pleasure in the actual moment envisioned by Rodgers & Hammerstein.

I, of course, took no part in this revelry. Except to drag a huge cardboard cow into the wings and spend every interval planning worse and worse tricks. On the last matinée I dressed Hugh's real-life wife, Deb, in my first-act costume and as he sang 'Don't Throw Bouquets At Me', she stood in the wings brandishing a rolling pin. Hugh was captivated. Just clapped his hands and laughed out loud. As we all piled on stage to congratulate him and Laurey, there was one tall, statuesque blonde in a lace 'fascinator' who got more than the average hug and kiss.

It always seemed to land on Hugh. We knew he could handle it. How he kept straight-faced and sung 'And a little brown maverick is winkin' its eye' when faced with twelve mooning cowboys in the wings with dropped 'chaps' and G-strings I don't know. Pop Carnes, actor Sid Livingstone, was stony-faced throughout. We couldn't get him. God knows we tried. In the trial scene he stonewalled a fluffy glove puppet, a left breast, a hairy claw hand, a false eye and, painfully, a long grey retracting tongue. The only thing which finally wiped him was when they shortened his stool, so that his head barely came above the courtroom table. Fortunately, he quickly regained control, whereas the rest of us lost it permanently.

The last week was perfectly wonderful and the last Friday, Howard Keel, the original London Curly, (in those days, Harold Keel) now almost eighty, was brought round after the show to see us. Stately, urbane and silvery handsome, he twisted his programme around in his hand and spoke with care: 'I don't know if I'm gonna I be able to say this – 'cos I'm an emotional old fart – and 'course I didn't see the production I was in . . . but that was the finest *Oklahoma!* I've ever seen or will ever see in my life.' He was enchanting. And enchanted by Josefina doing for the first time ever both the singing and ballet.

The only sadness between the opening and the last performance was the attitude of American Equity to our show. They refused us permission to take the show over. Broadway was swamped with English actors, Kevin Spacey had begged and bargained for five from the cast of *The Iceman Cometh*, Dame Judi and Samantha Bond were being *Amy's View*'ed Zoë Wanamaker was *Electa*-fying Times Square. There were more. Alan Cummings, Corin Redgrave – it was time to start Brit-picking and send 'em Brit-packing.

Oklahoma! An American show – a pedigree! Composer through to librettist. Hammerstein, Rodgers, De Mille (middle European immigrants but let's not carp). How bloody dare we? The arrogance of it. I could understand their proprietorial feelings, but in giving way to them, they lost American actors two years' work. Trevor's schedule had no hole other than immediately after we ended. Our company could have gone for three months then left it to them to play on for however long it lasted.

It seemed to me that they refused us, as much as anything, because of the 'Tony' Awards. The 'Tonys' run what runs. 'We don't want trophies,' I wanted to tell someone. 'Just let us show you the show we've created then you can give us tea in Boston and we'll go home.' When the man who ran us out of town, Equity boss Alan Aisenberg, came to see the show, he visited our dressing rooms. Too late to admit us, he stood, chastened, and confessed he'd been knocked out. By a real community of players in a landmark production.

I waxed empirically my theory about the melting pot casting being just what the actual Indian territories would have been. I didn't have to tell him the detailed work which had gone into that easy grouping. He could see that. A subdued man said bye and thanks to a wry cast. What the hell? When David Hockney or Lucien Freud exhibit their work in the States, nobody suggests it should be repainted or remodelled by Edward Hopper or Andrew Wyatt. The same applies to musicians from Menuhin to Vanessa Mae. Nobody suggests replacing Charlotte Church with a twelve-year-old soprano from Poughkeepsie. There are enough indigenous borders in our own country, religious or class or kind. To have them in art, especially in international art, to have a 'special relationship' which includes weapons but fails to include art, is a shame and a waste.

The last week began with a normal Monday. We tried hard not

to think, Well, that's the seventh but last time I'm ever going to hear that song, because frankly it gets you no place but down.

Tuesday was a special lunch given by the Variety Club for American actor Richard Dreyfuss. I had met Richard and his co-star in *Prisoner of 2nd Avenue*, Marsha Mason, over dinner and bemoaned the fact that neither of us could see the other's show, as we played the same matinées. This Tuesday I was to make a toast to him at the lunch.

I thanked the Variety Club for giving me the opportunity to welcome Richard to this small, sceptred, newly devolved island, ruled, quaintly, by Scotland, Bill Clinton and Rupert Murdoch. 'With our customary native charm we offer you tube strikes, anarchist riots, a soaring pound, inner-city riots, a Balkan War, Man. Utd supporters in Trafalgar Square fountains and, soon to come, after the torrential spring rains, the summer drought and the hosepipe ban.'

After watching clips from his film performances over the years from boy actor in *The Apprenticeship of Duddy Kravitz* to white-haired character actor in *Mr Holland's Opus*, it was not difficult to praise his talent.

'You seem to have absorbed what no teacher can teach, the ability to enjoy. And to dare to keep the channels open whatever the danger.' (There's a quote from the choreographer Agnes de Mille's autobiography which I gave to the *Oklahoma!* cast, because it hit me between the eyes when I read it:

'There's a vitality, a life-force, an energy, a quickening that is translated through you into action and because there is only one of you in all of time, this expression is unique. And if you block it, it will never exist through any other medium and the world will have lost it. Keep the channel open.'

These were the words of dancer Martha Graham as she cajoled Agnes de Mille to use more of her talent. Agnes replies:

'But when I see my work I take for granted what other people value in it. I see only its ineptitude, unorganic flaws and crudities. I am not pleased or satisfied.

'No artist is pleased.'

'But then there is no satisfaction.'

'No satisfaction whatever at any time,' cried Martha passionately. 'There is only a queer divine dissatisfaction that keeps us marching and makes us more alive than the others.')

The last joke of the day concerned the agent who went round to congratulate the director after a show and said, 'The show's great, the music's great, the sets are fabulous but where did you get that awful leading lady? She can't sing, she can't act, she looks like a dog...' The director says, 'I'll have you know that leading lady is my daughter!' 'Let me finish!' says the agent.

The laughter floated me back to the Lyceum Theatre where a tea party was being prepared for an American family who had bid several hundred pounds on the night of Comic Relief to have tea with the cast. We had all worn red noses for the walk down that night and I'd sent Hugh out into the audience to auction his body (I was prepared to go up to seven million myself) and Shuler to wrestle anyone to the ground for a given sum. We collected £2,000. Now it was pay-up time and we took the kids backstage and beneath stage and answered their questions and generally shmoozed and kibbitzed until it was show time again.

On the Wednesday, we had two shows and a farewell party on a boat until 2.00am. On Thursday night after the show, I drove to a Cambridge hotel to meet Jack and Amy, for Friday was Adam's graduation ceremony from King's College, Cambridge at 9.00am. It was a beautiful Cambridge day. The service was, mercifully, imposing but brief and salmon and strawberries on the lawns was gloriously surreal. We stood with groups of warm, relieved parents whilst our offspring hugged each other, wrote down numbers and mopped each other's tears. It felt so like Jack's play, *Cold Enough For Snow*. So momentous, so fragile, so transient. I was so proud of Adam. Afterwards, we all went up to his room. When I saw the state of it, I had to be forcibly restrained from throttling the life blood out of him.

Back in London, Friday night's show was the best show ever. Ever. It could not have been bettered. It was light; it was easy; it required no effort. I wished I could have seen it.

Saturday's matinée was traditionally a disgrace and I'd like to apologise publicly for having the most outrageously wonderful time. News filtered through that Trevor Nunn was in, but the die was cast (which was probably more than any of us would be in future productions).

At one point Aunt Eller presented dungaree-clad Laurey with

an organza dress, wrapped in a box, for the party that night, on account, 'You ain't got nothin' to wear 'cept yer mother's ol' weddin' dress.' She opened the box and it contained another pair of dungarees.

There was a moment in 'The Farmer And The Cowman...' when Eller takes the hands of the little children and softly sings the verse:

I'd like to teach y'all a little saying
And learn these words by heart the way ye should,
I don't say I'm no better than anybody else
But I'll be damned if I ain't just as good.

This day there were no children. Actors Jimmy Johnstone and Kevin Wainwright took my hands and led me forward and the whole cast did a barber shop chorus around me while I tried, red-faced and shiny-eyed, to get through the words without popping my clogs.

This was the show where Nicola wore a false ear on her upstage side, the one where dancer Shaun Henson offered young Ben Garner a sweet which turned his mouth blue just before the auction scene where he had his one line – 'I'll give you ten dollars.' It never got a better reaction than when said by a man who had no idea he had cornflower-blue teeth. It can't remember much else, except that there were two rabbits in the trial scene and a woman seemingly levitating in the prompt side of the wings – but I'm sure you get the general picture of a highly professional woman with 32 years in the theatre behind her. And I mean *behind* her.

It was a triumph of smile over content and it left us exhausted. The Saturday night audience seemed to be made up of 2,000 people who'd been before and loved what they'd seen. Hugh had built up a following of excitable groupies and the ovations throughout were like the last night of *Seinfeld*. There was a tiny scene after the death of Jud when Eller warns Laurey that she mustn't give in to self-pity.

'All sorts of things happen to folks – sickness and bein' poor and hungry and bein' old and afraid to die. Thas the way it is. Cradle to grave and you can stand it. They's just one way. Ye got to be hearty. You gotta be. You cain't deserve the sweet 'n' tender in life unless yer tough.'

It was never said more severely than the night of 26th June. Josefina and I were plumb about to lose it. Her eyes were so full of liquid she looked like she needed turning down to simmer. My voice was wobbling up and down like Sally Field accepting an award. It was snarl or die. I snarled, Josefina added terror to her tears and somehow we got through. The curtain calls went on for days. We brought on Trevor. I meant to thank him but words were out of the question. On this day we so missed being able to thank the dynamic 'Stro', stuck in the US, for making us so much more than we were. I clung on to Hugh, the best on-stage partner I'd known. I looked down into Row E on the best off-stage one, banging his hands together for the fifth time and the beam on the upturned mush of his daughter, and we just let the tears come. It would salt the stage for *The Lion King*. The familiar orchestra, the friendly stage crew, stage-door keepers, Wendy wigs, Anne Marie costume – we needed Sally Field after all, to do the honours.

Pack up six months into the car boot, fall into the last supper at Jo Allen's and sleep the sleep of the just, and if you think *that*, you haven't been paying attention. The next day the migraine just stood there in my brain saying, 'You asked for this,' and it was right. I was due at my friendly refloxologist Tony Porter's to cut a cake for the ten-year anniversary of his A.R.T. seminars in a London hotel. Amy and my neice Anastasia, who was acting as my dresser, held me up. Tony took one look at me and got his keynote speaker, a Dutch reflexologist and migraine specialist, down from the podium to the conference lobby where my shoes and socks were removed and my feet seriously pummelled. Waiters came in. The taxi driver brought back my mac. I didn't notice. A Chinese scientist emerged beaming and before you could say 'holistic' I was out there doing my third speech in seven days.

Just an average week at the end of an average year. By the law of averages, I'll never see its like again.

Can You Hear Me, Mother?

My friend, Ruby, had to reassure her friends that she hadn't died. Since she is the halest, heartiest 80 year old in the galaxy it took some inspired Miss Marpl'ing to find out from whence the rumour sprang.

Finally, it was tracked down to a phone call between two acquaintances. 'Oh, so and so's got the family over, so and so's back on her feet after the op and Ruby's in the South of France,' said one. This was somehow interpreted as 'Ruby's had a heart attack' and consequently spread a lot faster than mere holiday arrangements.

You can generally get an easy laugh with a joke about deafness.

'Tickle your arse with a feather?'

'I BEG your PARDON?'

'Typically nasty weather,' being one of the first to warrant a snigger in my childhood. Bellowing colonels and monstrous ladies with ear trumpets are the stuff of vintage comedy and few families manage to conceal their irritation with the relative whose most frequent comment is 'You what?' It would be regarded as unspeakable, except perhaps by Woody Allen or the Pythons, to make the same kind of comic mileage out of blindness.

Try asking the rhetorical question, 'Would you rather be deaf or blind?' and most people would opt, so to speak, for deafness. I wouldn't. It's the isolation I would fear, when, perhaps, fearing ridicule or irritation, one might miss chunks of conversation rather than ask for a repeat. I'd give up the telly for the radio or a sunset for a symphony, if push came to shove.

I notice my mother, left to her own devices, has the TV on at a level which makes my sinuses reverberate. I think this is less because she's hard of hearing than because she likes the company.

It makes the house feel full. When I turn down the volume with my customary subtlety ('For God's sake, you could hear this in Brittany!'), she can hear it as well as I can. Perhaps it's easier to concentrate when others are in the room.

Her father was, in his later years, hard of hearing. He once answered the phone in his son's office equipment firm.

'Can you tell Mr Pearlman we've got the metal chairs he wanted?' said the supplier.

'Yes,' replied Grandpa. 'You've got the little chairs he wanted.'

'Er . . . no. The metal chairs.'

'Yes. I've got that. The little chairs . . .'

The caller decided to spell it out.

'*Metal* chairs,' he enunciated. 'That's M for Mary, E for Ethel, T for Tommy . . .'

'T for what?' said Grandpa.

It's a sketch, isn't it? Or at least an advert for BT.

I've been blessed with excellent hearing, which is fortunate as my eyes are pathetic – as instruments of sight, that is. I mean, they look quite nice given a coat of mascara and some bag concealer but for looking through they're about as useful as a broderie anglaise loo-roll cover. Of touch, taste and smell, I have no complaints and my sixth sense is a work in progress.

My husband, on the other ear, would be the first to admit to a problem with sounds, particularly at parties when musak, glass clinking, small talk and theatrical shrieking can all penetrate at the same decibel level and drive him out on to the nice quiet London streets.

Once, in an effort to unblock his ears after a heavy cold, I applied Hopi Indian candles to his aural orifices. He lay on his side and I put a candle – no, don't laugh, we've done stranger things in the bedroom, I tidied it up once – in his uppermost ear, holding it in place with a circle of cardboard around the candle. Then I lit it.

To say the next five minutes were unusual is to minimalise. As the candle burned down, the pair of us shook with laughter at the thought of the window cleaner putting in an appearance. Still, it has to be said that the amount of wax in the hollow tube, after we'd snuffed the flame, was nothing short of lyrical.

Listening complications arose whilst holidaying with two friends in Switzerland. She has tinnitus and he has one good ear, one bad. Combined with Jack's affliction and my dog-like sharpness, it used to take us half an hour in car or café to get ourselves seated:

'So, if I have my back to the wall – and you go on the left – no, Jack'll have to be on the right of . . . Oh, sod it, let's have a take-away!'

Another chum suddenly developed terrible rushing, roaring noises in her ears that nearly drove her to the brink. In desperation, she went to a cranial osteopath and a Vietnamese acupuncturist and because of one of them (she has no idea which) mounds of stuff started pouring out of her nose. Granular stuff! Mounds of it. She actually had it analysed and it turned out to be plant fibre! 'Do you work with plants?' asked the chemist. 'Ye-e-es,' said my chum. 'Silk ones!'

One night, interpreter Wendy Ebsworth 'signed' a whole performance of *Oklahoma!* After the shock of seeing a beautiful young woman waving her hands very close to where I was churning my butter prior to 'Oh, What a Beautiful Morning', we all found her eloquence and dramatic skill gave the show new meaning. It made me want to learn this marvellous, expressive language.

Perhaps in the year 2000 we all should. Let's spare a thought for that when the Christmas bells start to ring, shall we?

All Clear

It was time for the dreaded annual scan. I was scared. My shoulder had been painful for some time during the *Oklahoma!* run. I had some physiotherapy and we replaced the heavy gun I fired on stage with a lighter model. The pain went, and came back again. I felt tired and couldn't sleep. I'd got it into my head that two years was the time it took for the tumour to return. I went to see Graham the faith healer.

'There's nothing there,' he told me. 'It's all in your head.'

'What is? A tumour?'

'No, *fear*, you crazy woman.'

I went for my scan. That same morning of my scan, I spoke to Aussie novelist Kathy Lette. She had agreed to speak at the Women Of The Year lunch and we discussed the theme of human rights. Kathy had seen *Oklahoma!* and, like all of us, had fallen hopelessly in love with Australian actor Hugh Jackman and his wild, wonderful wife, Deb.

'They're coming to dinner tonight. Why don't you come?'

'Not my best day, Kathy. Thanks, anyway.'

'Why?'

'Oh – I'll tell you sometime . . .'

Off to the scan, anchor in my heart, into the tube, heart hammering in unison with the mysterious knocking noise of the machine. After twenty minutes they took me out to inject dye into my arm. The radiologist said, 'I'll get the consultant down to give you the injection.'

I panicked again. Why did they need the consultant to give me an injection? By the time I was dyed, I'd be dying. Twenty minutes later they took me out again and there were tears in my clavicle.

'Come now, Maureen,' remonstrated the young doctor. 'You're

an actress. You ought to be able to do better than this.'

Now, just a week before, my daughter had arrived home with hair the colour of the fluorescent strips on a lollipop lady's coat. I'd wager the bottle probably said 'Satsuma and then some!' I'd been primed to expect the worse.

'I'm coming in to see you now,' she called up the stairs. And added, 'With my hair.'

It was twenty to one on an *Oklahoma!* show night and I was in bed, flossing, when she stuck her beacon round the door and came in.

'It's nice, darling,' I said through a big friendly grin. 'It's really nice . . . It suits you.' She was peering at me. 'Honestly it does,' I lied.

She continued to peer in a tipsily suspicious fashion and said, 'Mum, you *are* an actress, you know. You could at least pretend to like it.'

At the time I couldn't take it out on her, so I took it out on the radiologist. He copped for everything, poor chap. Afterwards I felt bad, but not bad enough to go back and apologise. I dressed and went up to see Mr Crockard, who passed me on his way down to see the X-rays. The five-minute wait was interminable. I'd given up on life and most of its expectancy when two thumbs appeared around the door, followed by a beaming face. The thumbs were up.

'You're clear,' he said. 'Completely clear – I'm so happy.' I hugged him for ages. Some dancing may have ensued.

Back in the hospital foyer, I phoned Jack to tell him, then Zelma, and strolled in a reprieved sort of manner, as you do, up Wellington Road towards St John's Wood. The sun was shining.

I'll have a cappuccino, I thought, and sit outside and read something preposterous like *The Stage*. Then – I swear the thought popped into my mind although I'd never been to her house nor had any idea where she lived – I'll probably bump into Kathy Lette and tell her I *will* come to her dinner party tonight now I've got something to celebrate. Which is exactly what happened. There she was, hurtling towards Richoux in pursuit of a cake for the dessert.

Well, we shared a moment there, and a coffee and, because she'd come out without her money, I *shtipped* her twenty quid for the cake. Later, many hoe-downs later, Hugh Jackman, Deb and

I had a delicious after-show dinner with Kathy and her husband, Geoff, and their guests, and at the end of the evening we entertained the company by chasing each other round the dining room, her trying to pin a £20 note on me, like at a Greek wedding, and me refusing it. The following night, on stage during the *Oklahoma!* auction scene, Curly the cowboy bid for Laurey's picnic basket with $30 and a Bank of England 1999 note to the value of £20 with a large 'Thank You' written on it from Ms K. Lette. I was too happy to protest.

New Year Revolution

My resolve for the penultimate year of the millennium had been to take life easy for, unlike most of my thespian contemporaries, I'm not getting any younger.

I was thinking back to the night the Queen Mother came round to meet the cast after seeing *Oklahoma!* on her 98th birthday. There she was, sprightly in floaty chiffon and three-inch heels, chatting to 45 burbling strangers in sweaty tights (and that was only the stagehands!) at twenty past eleven when a mere twelve hours earlier she'd been waving to the faithful from a balcony window. Ninety-eight years old! Made of Sheffield steel.

'A three-hour show, Ma'am! It's awfully brave of you after a day like you've had,' I heard myself prattle. 'You must be so looking forward to going to sleep.' 'Not at all,' she replied incredulously. 'We're going back to Clarence House now for a family supper.' And no doubt on to an acid house party, then bagels and a knees-up in the Mile End Road. I don't know what the great lady is on – but I'd sell my Equity Card for a thimbleful.

So, as all you readers welcome in dark strangers bearing lumps of coal and sing of 'auld acquaintance' being forgot, I find I don't want parties and punchbowls...I want peace and quiet. I just think this year I may have earned it.

My New Year spanned the last week of September and the first week of October – a fraughtnight that encompassed the Day of Atonement, seventeen back-to-back performances of *Oklahoma!*, a hip replacement, Bell's Palsy, a tooth abscess, 2,600 egg cups and a car crash. Shall I go on?

On the Jewish New Year, I appeared in the Chief Rabbi's TV broadcast, filmed in the Olivier Theatre. We talked about the feeling of pure joy which sometimes courses through you when audience and actor are at one. 'At-one-ment' if you like. I hoped that would help me through the omnipresent feeling that wherever I am, I should really be somewhere else.

The following Sunday I took my husband into hospital to be relieved of a bony hip in favour of a titanium one. We do not approach hospitalisation casually, my old man and I. Experience is a hard teacher and neither of us care much for the curriculum. 'It's nothing these days,' was his mother-in-law's comment. 'It's like having a tooth out.' Mother was down for the New Year and her rice pudding was already cooling on the draining-board. It would be followed over the next couple of weeks by the chicken soup, the courgette 'Kugel' (don't ask!), the salmon fishcakes and the complaints about my oven. This was war and provisions came in military fashion.

Meanwhile, the daughter came home with half her face in revolt. It's called Bell's Palsy and requires a combination of shock, virus and draught to really set in. It nearly always resolves itself but try telling that to a 24 year old with a Viva exam and job interviews to follow. We huddled together in bed, she clutching her pink and grey mouse, Anatole, and me hugging my lamb, Borghini. I'm almost sure some thumb-sucking took place.

The show, of course, must go on...and on it went, every night and twice on Wednesdays and Saturdays. I took to visiting the hospital afterwards, creeping in at ten past eleven, in the manner of Princess Diana. The operation had gone all right, but the aftermath was not good – culminating in a blood clot. I began to panic. Amy was having painful acupuncture and her brother was somewhere in Amsterdam on a pay-phone. Meanwhile, my mother gamely tried to roast a chicken in tin-foil in an oven she had never come to terms with. It came out steamed like tripe.

Sunday was my day off. Usually. This Sunday we recorded the whole of *Oklahoma!* on video. The cast was hysterical with fatigue and, with retakes, the show took five and a half hours. As I climbed back into my Act I costume at the end of Act II, I began to whimper audibly. No-one heard me – they were too busy whimpering themselves. Afterwards at the hospital, I forlornly ate Jack's fruit. He was slightly improving. I was getting worse.

Yom Kippur came and went. The theatre canteen provided me with an omelette and chips before the Tuesday night show and 24 hours later – after a weary, hungry matinée – I broke my fast on a banana and flapjack. My tongue was magnolia and my head just about rolled across the stage in 'Everything's Up To Date in Kansas City', but I'd done it. Sort of. If you don't count the Redoxon and the nibble of a prop apple in Act I, I was cleansed, forgiven and would never bitch again.

The next day my jaw swelled up with the noxious contents of debris in a root canal and I had to play the last two shows looking like Jimmy Hill in drag. We finished the seventeenth consecutive performance, without a day off, with a hoe-down in Rehearsal Room 3. Too knackered to enjoy it, I crawled into my car and smashed it sedately into a concrete pillar. Neither the car nor I registered any pain.

Back home I had an old friend Marilyn, staying – on her way to an egg cup convention in Oxford. She has a collection of 2,600 of them in her cottage in Inverness-shire. She was wearing a Tam o'Shanter topped with four tartan egg cups and a tartan Loch Ness Monster that played 'Scotland The Brave' on bagpipes. Out of the two of us, I knew for certain I was the mad one.

Part IV

Wife of One Writes Memoirs

Festive Hotting Up

I know – but it was all the travel agent had. The New Year's invitations were few on the ground so we reckoned we'd be better in the air. We would take Zelma with us because Florida is warm and balmy and – well – language couldn't encompass the phone call had we not. Besides, Zelma loves hotels. Adores them. She pretty well adores most things in life except walking. Oh, and one other thing. She defined it herself to costume designer Penny Rose one day: 'There's only one thing in life I can't stand,' she said, smiling, as we prepared to eat lunch in a Soho brasserie, 'and that's silence.'

And it's true. Recently we were staying in the Malmaison Hotel in Manchester. After a very chatty dinner and a discussion of the temperature in the lobby as compared to the lift, we walked the 55 yards to our adjoining rooms, after which Zelma concluded, 'Well, I think we must all be too tired to talk!' The oxymoron 'companiable silence' is a non-starter in my mother's vocabulary. As we prepared to get into a car to go on to another engagement, she confided in me, 'Ooh, I love doing one thing afer another with no space in between.'

So, Florida it was to be. Naples, Florida, to be exact. And a bloody enormous hotel, to be exacting. And it was fine. Fine. No – really... It was impersonal – but fine.

It just wasn't entirely the getaway from it all I'd had in mind. I'm sorry, I know I sound like a spoiled prat, but it was dodgy in Israel for tourists at that time and so an awful lot of people who'd been going there for Christmas had been relocated to Naples and here was I, like a piece of cheesecake in a display cabinet in a North London health farm. Zelma loved it.

Holidays are people and customs as much as places. Naples,

Florida, is richer by the square mile than anywhere else in America. People go there to bury their bones and their bonuses. The houses and malls are as fabulous as those of Beverly Hills. It's wide and white and spotlessly clean, and they take their Christmas very seriously.

The houses are decorated above and beyond the call of Nativity. White fairy lights define the delicate branches of every tree. Twinkling sleighs, sporting six pairs of reindeer and a fat-free Santa, decorate even the most modest of houses. Perfect lawns are carpeted in perfect shop snow and cherubim and seraphim nestle in the sun's relentless glare, outgrottoing F.W. Schwartz, Hamleys and Bethlehem all rolled into one.

From every chic boutique or brass-railed brasserie comes the sound of Andy Williams roasting his nuts on an open fire and Jack Frost continues to sell wet suits to surfers of all denominations down by the boardwalk. In the land of the free, business is booming.

'Happy Holidays!' cry all the shop assistants, afraid of offending any ethnic minority. 'And Seasonal Greetings,' always with the upward inflection, for added warmth. Christmas is a time when you really notice how hard people have to work. Normally I'd be one of them. More shows would be crammed into the Christmas period to enable poor producers to eat in the coming year. Presents would be exchanged – generally in the form of a communal grab-bag – and stairwell conversations would revolve around trains home to Scotland and night buses back from Cardiff to make the Boxing Day matinée in time.

Now here I was, footloose in Florida, wondering whether to eat turkey roast in the hotel or pull a wishbone with Colonel Sanders. The hotel restaurant could only fit us in for Christmas lunch at 12.00 noon. This was about the time I felt like rising, or at least knocking back my Florida pink grapefruit. The idea of plastic holly round the condiments and waiters in antlers made me feel a bit wan. I was already thrown by the sight of two professional elves in the lobby. I'd seen them around the pool, in pre-elf incarnation – two very small, very old troupers, who, it seemed, had toured for years with circus and summer stock shows, wherever it said 'little people required'. Now here they were, in the pre-Christmas build-up, welcoming all the overdressed and underwhelmed kiddies to sample fairy coke and cookies, dressed in identical Kelly green Lycra suits, complete with matching wings, matching bootees and pointy ears.

The Christmas lunch decision could no longer be avoided. We were having a quiet drink in the piano bar when a large, affably crumpled American stopped to say hello.

'Aren't you Marine Lipman?' he enquired in Brooklyn tones. 'I'm a great fan of your work.'

'But how on earth do you know me? Have you lived in England?'

Although he couldn't quite remember in *what* he'd actually admired me, he was funny and urbane and we soon asked him to join us in a drink. When his wife, returning from the restroom, saw that her husband had attached himself to a group of strangers, her face registered instant weariness. He must do this a lot, I thought.

Still, it was a pleasant evening. Angus and Erin lived locally, she being the manager of Barnes & Noble, our favourite bookstore, he, Zelig-like, seemingly having worked for Kennedy, Kinsey, Kissinger and probably, we thought later, the Kremlin. Angus was that New Yorker talker who immediately feels like my missing cousin, and Erin, when thawed, had a gentle Irish irony which made you want her to think the best of you. By the end of the evening we were friends.

The following morning, those friends rang to offer us Christmas dinner at their place with her sister and brother-in-law. Following family tradition, lunch was pancakes, eggs and fried-over potatoes. Zelma pronounced us mad to go to a perfect stranger's house. (The subtext being we'd be sold into slavery and end up lap dancing in Hong Kong, etc.) We demurred for as long as it was decent, then jumped at the idea, racing round for house presents so we shouldn't arrive empty-handed. Thus it was that we had the noisiest, jolliest, most unusual Christmas lunch we've ever had. Zelma loved the informality and high spirits and began dropping one-liners with the best of them. They thought she was a real cracker. Looking back, I suppose she was right to be cautious but I've always trusted my instincts about strangers and about 98 per cent of the time they let me up rather than down.

On New Year's Eve we did the Philharmonic thing in the imposing new Theatre Centre. We witnessed Florida new and old money giving a new meaning to dressing up. There were rocks on ears which could have hypnotised Rasputin and more beads and sequins than frail osteoporitic shoulders could shoulder. The atmosphere was charged – as were we all – and the concert was merely a prelude to the real business of the day, the buffet.

'Isn't it fabulous?' cried Zelma, as balloons showered down from the ceiling during 'The Thunder And Lightning Polka'. 'I say – if my friends could see me now!'

It *was* a fun do. But the best was still to come. 'Watch the aristocracy at the buffet,' Angus had warned us. 'It's an eye-opener.'

Except you had to keep your eyes closed – or risk having an elbow in them. As the waiters bore down with vast silver tureens towards the rectangle of trestle tables, the scene changed instantaneously from *The Bostonians* to *National Lampoon's Animal House* as the exquisitely dressed matrons and their consorts kicked hell out of each other to fill their plates first.

The joke was that everything on one side of the tables was replicated on the other, so the slow shuffle around in search of variety was unnecessary.

Yet still the cognoscenti made an invincible wall around the table's perimeter and anyone attempting entry would find a face, either caked with Estée Lauder or lifted so wide the owner appeared to have been caught in a wind tunnel, turning full round, exorcism-style, and snarling: 'Get in line, will ya! This is a line – doncha know!'

Now we Taureans don't take kindly to red rags and I'm afraid that's just what was being waved in my face and I found myself behaving disgracefully. Particularly for a rank outsider.

I forced my way under a tuxedoed arm as it stretched across a vat of coleslaw. 'Hey!' shouted his chiffoned companion, who was blobbing on the potato salad. 'We were here already, young lady!' (I liked that bit.) 'You get back in line.'

'Quite right, sir, and of course you were, madame. I only want the plates, just the plates – nothing but the plates,' I said. 'Tha-a-nk you!'

I grabbed eight or nine plates and bobbed back under the arm, leaving my lower half and leg glued to the side of the table. Then I started handing out plates to other rank outsiders, or as I like to think of them, considerate human beings.

'Here's your plate, sir. Now, would you like salmon or

casserole? Casserole. Right you are, sir, coming up now.' I passed him the casserole in one hand and the veg in the other. 'Just help yourself, sir, and Happy New Year to you . . . '

I suppose I served a dozen people that night – all of them quite discombobulated by my behaviour. Still, that didn't matter. Pretty soon the area around the tables was empty and all the food had been replaced with seconds of the same. There was enough food left to feed every alligator in the Everglades.

We ate our strawberries and ice cream standing with a distinguished couple in a white tuxedo and cerise taffeta (work it out for yourselves, will you). Where I find these people I'll never know. After five minutes of courteous olde worlde charm, the kindly gentleman came out with a remark so homophobic that it practically winded me. Faggots and nancy boys were mentioned through dazzling white teeth only slightly spinach speckled. Time to head off home, I thought, before new acquaintance be forgot.

Mum spent much of the holiday in search of the perfect beach dress. She'd exhausted the hotel shops and most of the malls in search of a black dress with strappy top and flared skirt to cover her bathing suit. The bathing suit which would remain perfectly dry for the duration.

Now, I'd never seen my mother in water. Never. Not ever. I've seen her in a bathing costume when she was younger, but it has always been a dry one. I think 'the water' occupies a similar spot in her heart to silence – but 'the water' is not to be sampled, let alone endured. Mum is a fire sign and water just puts her right out – she doesn't even like to drink it. To swim in it is dangerous, unnecessary and probably obscene.

There was a small jacuzzi by the pool, in which folk would sit for a few minutes to discuss business back home. One day I suggested to Mum that she might like it:

'It'll be really good for your bad back,' I told her, 'and it's really warm and effervescent – like a bath.'

'Oooh, no,' she demurred. 'I wouldn't like that.'

'You would,' I assured her. 'It's not deep – it's no more than two feet high.'

'I'll be petrified.'

'You wouldn't.'

'Frightened to death. I couldn't.'

It took me a further hour of hints and promises to convince her but I did it. Together we walked to the pool and shed our wraps. 'I'll go in first,' I said, 'and hold your hands while you . . .' I stepped down the one step and stood there, submerged to the waist with my hands holding hers. Violently she snatched hers away.

'Oooh, nooo! No. I can't. It's, ooh – no, I'll do it later. I don't like it . . . Ooh, no – let go of me.' Her voice rose a couple of octaves and she began to giggle in a sobbing kind of way. It was make or break. Gently I pulled her forward. To say she came gingerly is an understatement. Somehow she managed to take one step forward whilst leaving most of her body elsewhere.

'That's great!' I overacted. 'That's brilliant. Now, just one more step and you can sit . . .'

'I don't like it. I'm too frightened to sit down.' She sat down like someone testing a land mine. 'Oooh – oh,' her shoulders went down, just a centimetre. 'It's not so bad, really, is it?' she looked around. 'Don't let go of me, though.' A slight smile. 'It's quite warm, isn't it? I don't mind it now I'm sitting down . . .' She turned her radiant smile on to an amazed spectator sitting two feet away from her. 'I don't usually go in water. Do I?' She looked to me for corroboration. I gave it. 'Do you like it?' She nodded dumbly. 'It's quite nice, really, isn't it?' Pause. 'Shall I get out now?'

By the time I got her back to the pool lounger she was exhilarated and I was exhausted. I felt very proud of her. I felt something significant had happened which perhaps would move her on to greater freedom. I guess I felt as she must have felt when I took my first tottering steps.

'Congratulations, Zel,' said Jack. 'You did it.'

'I know!' she said, beaming as she settled herself back on the lounger. 'But I didn't like it.' From that day forth, she never went near the pool again.

Later that day, at the poolside restaurant, a sealed envelope arrived by waiter. It was a fax from the management. It said, 'Congratulations, Mrs Lipman, on going in the pool for the first time.'

She was completely amazed.

'How did they know?' she said. Jack looked blank. I was blank.

Later that day we took a stroll along the beach. It was late afternoon, not too body-strewn, and we decided to hire some loungers and have a doze. A young man disappeared and reappeared with the beach stuff. As he unfolded Zelma's chaise and spread a towel over it, he said, 'By the way, Mrs Lipman, congratulations on going in the water today.' Zelma just stared, open jawed, at him. So did I. Jack looked blank.

Over the course of the next few days, shopkeepers would hand over receipts and congratulate her for going in the water and maitre d's in quayside restaurants would send felicitations on behalf of the staff. Chambermaids, cinema usherettes and bank tellers were all in on the act. It didn't take John Thaw to work out that the blank expression on Jack's face was there because, without it, he'd be grinning all over it. He was having the best fun, priming total strangers to congratulate a woman on doing something she would never do again in her whole life. Even in the shop where Mum finally found her little black dress, there was a comment from the assistant about how she could put the dress on after she'd had her daily dip.

It culminated on the flight home. The cabin wasn't particularly full and we were able to stretch out, cover our legs with blankets and watch my mother as she moved charily from seat to seat in search of a draught-free zone. I think she tried out six seats and adjusted six air-conditioned vents and each time the stewardess, one of those lovely middle-aged ones employed so successfully by American Airlines, would come up to see if she could help.

'I keep pressing the thing for the warm air, but it doesn't seem to stop the draught, you see,' said Zelma, beaming her enchanting beam.

'Actually, you are pressing the bell for the stewardess each time,' said the hostess gently.

'I'm not, am I?' said Zelma.

'Well, you are, actually, but don't worry, that's quite OK. It's the black button right here . . . '

Zelma stared at her. 'Is that how you knew to keep coming?' she asked. The hostess nodded as Zelma began to laugh helplessly. 'I wondered why you just kept popping up every time I moved. I thought you must be a genie!'

The stewardess and the draught dodger leaned up against each other, helpless with laughter for a good five minutes, and every time she passed Mum's seat, they started it all over.

About halfway across the Atlantic, the pilot gave us our altitude, expected time of arrival and the weather conditions we could expect in London. 'Thank you for flying American Airlines,' he concluded, then added 'and congratulations on behalf of the captain and crew to Mrs Zelma Lipman on going in the water for the first time.'

They thought it was all over. It was now.

The Right to be Wrong

'Give all those "request" letters dates in the diary after the show closes,' I said to Jacquie, my assistant, who was hovering around my breakfast with a vast pile of correspondence.

'Are you sure?' Her emphasis was heavy. She managed to imply in three words that a) when the time came I'd kick myself for being at a ribbon cutting in Kentish Town instead of a health farm in leafy Surrey and b) hell hath no fury like an organiser let down by a celeb at the last minute.

'The thing is,' I always explain, 'I'd be happy to speak and I do share your concern for getting the right sort of sanctuary for your donkeys but November 1999 is a long way ahead and...'

'Oh, I know that but we'd sell heaps of tickets if your name was – '

'Yes, and I'd be thrilled to...'

'So can I go ahead and – '

'Yes, but you must understand that if Martin Scorsese suddenly decides he really needs *me* to balance the acting styles of De Niro and Paltrow – well... you know, I'd really find it hard to commute from Hawaii to Horsham, so if...'

'Oh, don't worry. Fingers crossed. Thank you soooo much!'

And of course it isn't quite Scorsese, it's BBC Wales or *The Des O'Connor Show* – but does the donkey lady understand? (Is Slobodan Milosevic hoping his daughter marries an Albanian?)

Her response builds to gale force: 'But, but... she *promised*! The tickets are printed! How could she be so selfish? Who does she think she is? The stuck up... just wait till I tell the press. My husband used to be a mercenary – tell her to look after her kneecaps!'

Trouble is, I tend to be on their side. It is awful to be stuck without a figurehead for your function, which is why I've often stood in for others who have dropped out at the last minute. It was the wonderful Les Dawson who reported being introduced as follows: 'Let's have a big hand for Mr Les Dawson, who has kindly agreed to open the fete. I'm extremely grateful to him, because none of the big stars could do it.'

Yesterday, I pitched up at a church in Piccadilly to open a day of prose and poetry for a small charity, of which I'm a patron, called Home In My Mind. The church was a calm oasis in the miasma of West End London, with a Bechstein grand piano and massed lilies on plinths. The small market in the courtyard outside was buzzing with shoppers and browsers. Inside the church, however, were a desultory ten or eleven folk, easily outnumbered by the occasion's organisers. A couple of winos hugged the side radiators, one of them clearly annoyed by the use of the microphone to shatter his peaceful somnambulance.

Well, I said my bit about Aids-related dementia. Then Janet Suzman and Timothy West read their poems and Anthony Gray played superbly, despite the fact that the Bechstein kept sliding across the church floor. I wanted to scream, 'We need a barker here, not actors! We need to be outside, throwing civility to the wind and shouting through a megaphone, "Wonderful things are happening inside! Don't waste your time buying sweatshirts with Kool Brit emblazoned on them or queuing for Picasso – would he queue for you? Get in here and help the blinkin' needy!"'

But I didn't. Instead I launched into my Joyce Grenfell monologue for the devoted few, while the recumbent dosser shouted 'Oh, shit, shit, shit, shit, shit' as a rather startling accompaniment. As the day wore on, the audience filled up and a fair amount was raised, but those first couple of hours will leave a hollow feeling in my guts for ever.

The previous night I'd been double booked for the opening of a percussive dance ensemble at the Cockpit Theatre and a fashion show in aid of the JNF at Madame Tussauds. I was to show my face for the first half of *Footworks*, which promised 'Southern Appalachian Flatfoot, African Boot Dancing and Irish Clogging', at 9.00pm I was to appear at the catwalk alongside Cherie Blair and Esther Rantzen for dinner amongst the waxworks and Ronit Zilkha's winter/spring collection. It was a combo dreamed up by the Marx Brothers.

I was filmed in the theatre lobby alongside dear old Cynthia Payne by – wait for it – Manchester United TV. 'So why are you at the launch of a clog-dancing display, Maureen?' was their first question. It floored me. 'It *said* it in the diary,' I replied.

An hour later I knew why. On a bare stage, in costumes which looked hand-sewn some years ago, with three musicians in half-light, five women and one man tapped, clapped, beat and hollered their way into my heart. It was *Riverdance* with history and soul. In the cold theatre, a handful of guests and punters were on their feet screaming for more. I never wanted it to end – and I had to leave for a fashion show! I noted from my programme that the company had arrived that morning from America and were doing eighteen one-night stands including Sundays in arts centres all over England. Sometimes you feel very small and very spoilt.

Never more so than at the fashion show, where Esther was revealing details of her colonic irrigation to an understandably enthralled dinner table, and where the tickets cost £250 a head. Zilkha's clothes were divine combinations of frothy lace, panné velvet and faux fur and, as ever, the models looked like they'd been deprived of vegetables for their formative years and needed an osteopath.

Then there was Burma. Recently, in the pouring rain, the stalwarts of PEN and I held placards protesting about human rights abuses in Burma to a less than interested phalanx of photographers and the tops of passers-by's umbrellas. Later, inside the House of Commons, we heard heart-stopping stories of torture and imprisonment and the testimonies of dissidents read by Harold Pinter and Salman Rushdie and Miriam Karlin and other great fighters for freedom. It scarcely made a single column in the next morning's papers. Ethical foreign policy, indeed.

Afterwards, it was gridlock day in London. A combination of rain, half-term and roadworks. I took a cab to the BBC in Acton, where I had a wig fitting. It took an hour so I decided to Tube it back to Tottenham Court Road and home. A young actor said 'hello' at the BBC gate. He was down from Wales for an audition with his eight-year-old daughter and we chatted all the way on to the train and for several stops about the difficulties for actors living outside London. It was only when the countryside emerged that we realised we were at the end of the line on the wrong train going in the opposite direction. West Ruislip in the rain. I keep trying to make progress. Why do I keep ending up in the sidings?

Heaven Scent

As I tried unsuccessfully to waft the smell of fried fish from the kitchen without opening the back door to let in the coldest day of the year, I got to thinking about olfactory issues. What was the smell of fish actually like, aside from being 'fishy'? Although it was so completely recognisable, I had no words in my vocabulary to describe it. When I left the house I would no longer be aware of it, and when I returned it would have transmogrified into the smell of fried fish 'in the past'. Fish mixed with curtains and carpets and, later on, my clothes when I removed them; later still, it would linger in the hair of the fryer as he snuggled lovingly up in bed beside me.

Recent studies suggest that our sense of smell is one of the most undiscovered and immediate routes to recovered memory. Certainly the smell of fried fish was an all-pervading one in my parents' house, and although my mother, now in her new cosy flat and fashionably aware of her cholesterol level, seldom fries anything, I still smell fried fish when I go there. It's all in my nose, I knows that.

Certainly the scent of monkey nuts makes me feel slightly faint and I trace this back to the first 'funny turn' I ever had. I must have been about seven and was sitting on the beige, mottled tiled surround of a fireplace in the lounge of one of those sets of aunts and uncles which permeated our young lives and who, in fact, were neither. As I recall, the nuts were warm from the fire and the uncle was cracking them and handing them round. Lord knows why I felt a consciousness retreat at that point – I was always a bit of a drama queen – but I've never smelled a monkey nut since without feeling vaguely 'Uncle Dick' – though it was Uncle Leslie who was handing them out. Oh – and coriander. Same effect but totally inexplicable as the existence of fresh coriander in Hull in the fifties of my childhood is about as likely as finding a threepenny bit in a millennium Christmas pudding. And once again I can't describe those smells – which is infuriating to me. Every house in Hull had its own familiar, not unpleasant, smell, which I can almost conjure up with major concentration and much visualisation of cardigans and teacups.

The most familiar popular smells are probably fresh coffee, newly mown grass, hyacinths and freshly baked bread. Certainly it's a long-known estate agents' trick of the trade to have percolating coffee and a 'heat 'n' serve' crusty roll in the oven of any house seller when the prospective buyer calls to view. In fact, coffee is one of those rare ingredients, in my opinion, which actually smells better than it tastes. But what does it smell *like*? Bitter? Roasted? Nutty? (Help me! I don't have the connections between the parts of my brain which reproduce fragrance and the parts which provide adjectives.)

OK. Unpopular smells, then. Petrol? Ugh! Metallic, acrid, sour? (Mmm . . . some improvement.) Old-fashioned dentists. Hairdressers, full of hot air and 'setting lotion'. Freshly painted anything. Pubs and parties the morning after. Elderly food. 'Is this milk "on"?' my son used to shout after a short lifetime of watching his parents sniff bottles and say, 'I think this milk's off.' Oh, and inevitably other people's wind – note the 'other', because your own is always perfectly acceptable. Well, almost always – let he who has never eaten three-bean salad cast the first moan. Men's urinals, old BT phoneboxes and houses with more than one cat. Acid, sulphurous, slightly sweet? (Five out of ten – could do better.)

Conversely, I love the smell of the side of a matchbox. Love it. Have spent whole minutes of my life in serious sniffing mode. AND . . . And! . . . I adore the sort of white sauvignon which smells of cat's pee. Fruity – acidy – grassy – elderberryish? (Pathetic, Lipman. See me after school.) Wine waiters regard me with barely suppressed hauteur when I mention the feline thing, although I know I'm not alone in appearing to be an expert on collating the scent of the contents of a cat's bladder into my aromatic index. In fact, my local Oddbins once amazed and delighted me by providing a wine which was actually labelled 'Cat's Pee on a Goosberry Bush'. I couldn't believe it! It was like suddenly 'coming out'. Realising there were other people in the world experiencing my own aberration. Then finding there's a support group! Unfortunately, the next time I popped into Oddbins, it had been withdrawn. Or maybe I dreamt it.

When I first moved into my dressing room at the Lyceum, it gave off a heady fragrance of drains and whitebait. Every time I came off stage, I was regaled by it all over again. I burnt coconut and lime candles, I filled the place with freesias, I sprayed and pot-pourried and looked in vain for one of those sinister wicks which my mother used to produce from a dark green bottle before guests arrived. Finally, one day, it went. Well, it was superseded by a stronger smell in the aromatic evolutionary survival chain. Carpet! A new carpet was laid by invisible carpet layers who came and went in the daylight hours when thespians sleep and dream of Olivier Awards. And you can't top that smell – the sweet, dry, rubbery, wet, woolly smell of fresh underlay. It soaked up the opposition in a single sitting. Or laying. Whatever.

Old books, orange peel, small boys' napes, almond oil, fresh vanilla, clean sheets. Look, it's all subjective, isn't it? And mysterious. I can't help thinking when they finally isolate, source and recreate scents we may be in for another sexual revolution. In the meantime, my advice is to read or reread *Perfume* by Patrick Susskind. It's a work of literary genius and a lexicon of the most secretive and sensual of all our senses.

Some time in the late fifties, the impresario Mike Todd, creator of Todd A.O., who lived to become Liz Taylor's fourth husband and died prematurely in a plane crash, produced a new technique for movies called, I think, 'Smell-O-Vision'. The cinemas would be adapted to produce the relevant odours to complement the films. The first experimental film was called *Scent of Mystery* and may have starred Orson Welles. Thank the Lord it was also the last. Otherwise, just imagine what we would have had to smell during *Pulp Fiction* and *There's Something About Mary* and *The Blues Brothers*, for Heaven's sakes! 'Two seats for the 7.40 programme, a tub of popcorn and some nose clips, please.' Phew!

Shopping and Trucking

The roads are getting narrower. I'm not just getting the hump about fast-propagating speed bumps, or the sudden arbitrary appearance of small islands to block previously negotiable roads. Nor is it the slow-moving tailback, which, when the reason finally becomes apparent, is nothing more than 22 cones and a striped hazard warning. No workmen, no drills, no freshly smoking tarmac. Just a blocked lane for 200 yards with one solitary figure, bum crack visible over trousers, talking lugubriously into a mobile phone.

No, the real reason why driving through the metropolis has become 'loiterus interruptus', is that nineties phenomenon, the four-wheel drive automobile, without which any self-respecting surburban dweller feels vehicularly challenged. They are the status symbol of the decade. Huge, mean and menacing, they allow their driver to perch high above the traffic and look down on the rest of us like Jeremy Paxman on a King's College, Cambridge, mascot. Protected by wrap-around steel bumpers to secure inmates against marauding herds of wildebeest, they brandish their rhino emblems on sturdy spare wheels to teach us that we, not they, are the endangered species. They lumber or thunder up the narrowest roads in London ferrying one slim blonde driver in designer shades from the East Finchley Leisure Centre to the Seattle Coffee House in St John's Wood where, with the arrogance of a refuse cart, they park, or preferably double park, wherever the hell they like. Get two of the buggers dropping off a couple of Ruperts and a Phoebe at the gates of St Annunciata's Preparatory School and any chance you ever had of hitting the dentist before fluoride went out of fashion fades into fantasy and you resign yourself to an entire tin of barley sugars and several hours of Jimmy Young.

I mean, I can just about see the usefulness on the wilds of

Dartmoor, with wellies rattling around the boot and six hairy lurchers baying in the back. And yes, if your work depends on carting massage tables from a seminar in Sydenham to a woman with sciatica in Stoke Poges, or you landscape gardens for the Duke of Devonshire or live in Belgium but sell concrete bird tables in Billericay. But no – the owners of these mobile road blocks live in Barnes or Bayswater and jump into them merely to buy a bottle of Badoit and a wilted rocket baguette for consumption after a Step 'n' Spin class at the club.

The only comfort is that there are now so many of them that they are just a smidgeon short of common. Knightsbridge must look like a trailer park. So it can't be long before couldn't-live-without turns into wouldn't-be-seen-dead-in and Rupert's dad reverts to post-colonial eye levels and buys a nice little Polo like the one that nice T'ai Chi teacher jumps into after a heavy evening of self-defence.

Let me not close this whinge without pointing the finger at that other fecund culprit in the traffic-snarling competition, the supermarket. It always puzzles me that millions of us need to restock our fridges and pantries every week in a way which entails hours of mesmerised wandering in charge of a lethal trolley up and down the seductive aisles of our local Tesways, Budgeburys or Marks and Wait. Involved in this time-saving exercise is queuing for the car park and finding change for the pay and display ticket which will fall from your window because of the condensation inside due to your heavy breathing on arrival.

Your blink rate will rise and you will spend at least £50 more than you expected to – £70 if knickers and tights are displayed by the cash register – and 40 per cent of what you overbuy will reveal 'Not suitable for home freezing' on the label. The sell-by dates will glower at you in the fridge and you'll throw away what you can't stomach and end up back in the trolley park only days later. The system doesn't work.

Yet it grows and it breeds. The beautiful, elegant art deco Hoover building on the A4 is a supermarket. It makes my heart go clunk. Supermarkets cover every highway and byway and eat any opposition. They create a need which we then propagate. How long did it take to buy fresh veg, a chicken breast or two and some fruit from your local shops?

Not as long as it did to trail your bleary toddler down 27 aisles, park, unpark, drive, negotiate traffic, unpack, separate – and you *still* didn't get the packet of cornflour you went for!

We could stop it, you know. We could support our local row of shops before they *all* turn into outlets for Colonel Sanders. Now I understand Sainsbury's and Tesco's have opened their own corner shops. First eat the opposition, then replace it with a genetically prettified version of what used to be both functional and tasty.

All right. I'm finished now and I feel better for letting it hang out. I'm off out to buy half a dozen free-range eggs and a soda bread from the organic butcher. Breakfast calls and I'm having a boiled egg and soldiers whilst reading a biased but well-written newspaper. Ah, the life of the middle-class, middle-aged ranting reactionary.

Royal Flush

It was a three Queen day. The first of its kind to my knowledge. Rumour ran rife round the company (i.e. company manager, Jools, tells me, 'On no account mention this to anyone else but...') Her Majesty and the Duke of Edinburgh had decided to have a whole day of theatre. This may not seem to be enough for one who is patently happier out in a high wind in a headscarf than stuck in a side box with a perfect view of the wings, but it's a start.

The Duke would visit *Chicago* first thing in the morning (chorus girls, black basques, chair straddling) and we *Oklahoman*s should all be ready in full costume and make-up at 10.30 in the morning, with orchestra, for the 'scheduled rehearsal' of 'The Farmer and The Cowman...' – you know, like you do after playing it eight times a week for six months.

Still. No-one minded really. Certainly no-one in the orchestra minded (because orchestras are paid by the nanosecond) and the rest of us just buckled down because it was a royal appointment and we wanted to keep it. *Oklahoma!*, the original 1947 production, was reputed to have been a favourite show of the then newly married royal couple and 'People Will Say We're In Love' was their song. When the company manager gingerly asked if this was the case, the Duke, true to form, retorted, 'Not as far as I know!'

So, after the theatre had been Mr Sheened from circle to pit and the minders had swept through doing what minders do, largely glancing from right to left rather rapidly, we got the word 'They're here!', the flymen raised the rudimentary barn, the orchestra struck up and we all went into overdrive. I separated battling factions, parted pounding fists and, finally, exasperatedly fired Curly's pistol in the air, pointed it at Pop Carnes and growled 'Sing it, Andrew!' to start the wildest, most athletic, muscle-demanding seven-minute barn dance you've ever seen.

At the end, instead of the ovation which at night sometimes seemed impossible to bring to an end, there was a smattering of polite applause as we held our final positions on taut, aching muscles. It had been a long time since the silence of a rehearsal room at the National and it was nostalgic to hear, once again, the sounds of collected heart attacks as 25 people under 30 and two codgers over 50 (myself and Sid Livingstone) fought to restart our breathing mechanisms. We could feel the vibrating hairs in our lungs.

As the royal party was brought round backstage, my thirst got the better of me. My tongue was stuck to the roof of my mouth...it had to be released before I faced a royal question, or she may take me for a red-neck. I raced towards the water dispenser in the ante-room to the wings, only to find Sir Cameron leading the royal party towards us. 'I need a – water – Sorry, Ma am, is that OK?' was my somewhat cryptic remark. Bless her she looked at me more in pity than in sorrow. 'It does look terribly energetic,' she said to the first sweating hand she shook. 'Yesheur esh, Ma'am;' wheezed the first recipient. People always ask what the royals actually say to you and of course you can never answer because your mind turns to polenta as soon as they speak to you. Which is why they have to endure such boring conversations. Actually, Americans and Australians with none of our rigid class distinctions tend to cut a swathe through aristocratic society. 'G'day, Yer Madge, yer lookin' bonsa today,' would be quite refreshing, I guess, after a line-up of, 'Yes, Ma'am, it is...very energetic,' and, 'Oh...you know...er...it's not so bad really ...Keeps the physiotherapist employed...heh, heh, heh!'

Afterwards, everybody peeled off their 'slap' and the dancers slipped back into their skinny bootlegs and cropped tops and contemplated which cappuccino bar to conglomerate in and which jazz dance class to attend.

As for me, it was corsets off, broken veins cleaned off, flat hair under wig pleaded with to rise and into my smartest suit for the next gig. One o'clock lunch at The Ivy with the monarch and other members of the theatre world.

The other members chosen amounted to about 50-odd

producers, directors and actors assembled in an upstairs room with one question on their lips: 'Why me?' Jonathan Miller was ASTOUNDED to be included. Braham Murray of the Manchester Royal Exchange Theatre 'had no idea' and Thelma Holt, a republican in wolf's clothing if ever I saw one, just grinned and dismissed the whole thing as spin for the people's monarchy.

The actors were there because our shows were the ones visited: Maria Friedman represented *Chicago* and David Suchet *Amadeus*. Before 'their' arrival, David and I compared fatigues. 'Eight a week, though,' he moaned. 'It's a killer, isn't it?' I rolled my tiny eyes.

'What are you on?' I asked him.

He stared. 'Pardon?'

'What are you on?' Still no reply. 'I mean, what are you taking?'

He was clearly flustered. I couldn't understand why. David and I went all the way back to LAMDA – he was a year younger than me . . . Probably still is.

'I can't believe you're asking me that . . .' he stammered.

'Well, why?' I insisted.

'Well, it's not something I tend to . . .'

'I mean, what? Ginseng? Royal jelly? Guerana? What are you laughing at? . . . What? Whaaat?'

It was suddenly clear that he'd thought I was asking how much money he was making – a thing actors never do. Writers, probably, but actors, never. All through lunch – we were at separate tables – David kept catching my eye and dissolving again. My table consisted of the Queen, flanked on either side by producer Michael Codron and director Jonathan Miller, Michael Frayn, me, Braham and then Sir Andrew Lloyd-Webber and Genista McIntosh of the National Theatre.

It was a lovely lunch. Dr Miller took up all Her Majesty's time, arms flailing, words bouncing around the roulade, and very occasionally she would turn to Michael for a few words. (I couldn't help but notice the next time I was in his office the placecard 'H.M. The Queen' sitting on his desk.) Apparently when Dinzey the rastafarian-locked waiter, tried to offer Her Majesty milk for her coffee, Dr Miller engaged her attention again. Hindered in his ability to pour, the waiter said to Michael, 'Does she take milk?'

'How the fuck do I know?' said Michael's entire expression.

Her Majesty is very dry. She has a sharp sense of humour and I although I couldn't say I felt relaxed, the atmosphere was very easy. At one point she mentioned that she understood I would be coming to the palace shortly (to pick up my New Year's Honour).

'If I can possibly find anything to wear, Ma'am,' I replied.

Several weeks later, as I was curtseying and she was pinning a medal to my grey and white coatdress, she twinkled up at me and said, 'I see you managed to find an outfit, then.'

I think that was flaming bonsa, don't you?

After lunch I went back to my dressing room at the Lyceum to sleep it off on the rickety put-u-up. It seemed like minutes before they were calling us down for the vocal warm-up and the minders and entourage were back sniffing out the areas around which the royals would sit that evening, for tonight they were to see the whole show and afterwards we would all line up again for polenta-time. I don't know for whom *Groundhog Day* would be more appropriate.

'Y'd shore feel like a queen sittin' up on that carriage' brought the house down as it never had in several hundred previous performances, but otherwise the show was as good as ever. And I finally had something to say when I shook her hand for the third time that day: 'I'm so glad you saw us from the front circle instead of your usual place, Ma'am. It must be so much easier on the neck.'

Funnily enough, when my mother saw the show from the box (her eighth visit), she pronounced it the best seat she'd ever had. 'It's fabulous,' she declared. 'You can see the whole audience all the way through.' I've tried every which way to make that into a compliment . . .

There is nothing like being in a hit. It's the headiest feeling, more so because of its rarity. I suppose this was the third time it had happened to me. The first time was in 1973 in a National Theatre production at the Old Vic called *The Front Page*. Written in the forties by Hecht and McArthur and directed by Michael Blakemore, it starred and made stars of Denis Quilley, Anna Cartaret, Alan McNaughton, Clive Merrison, Benjamin Whitrow and David Bauer and gave great lines to every good character actor in the building – including me as Molly Malloy, the tart with the heart. It was always Full House, the laughs were like cannon shots and I never met a soul who didn't love it, punter or pro. A cast of twenty-odd people and never a cross word.

The second was *Re-Joyce!* in 1980. Also a happy company. Just my accompanist, Denis King, and me. And now *Oklahoma!* 1998–99. Three in a 32-year span. I reckon that's a pretty good average.

The difference touches everything. So often the dressing-room door opens on an anxious face, split by an even more anxious smile, announcing, 'Hey! Wow! It's us. We said we'd come . . . Hey! Wow! You old fox . . . you look great . . . Love a drink, yeah. So . . . Gosh, nice dressing room – wow! Got your own sink and everything . . . Kids all right?' Then finally, 'What an interesting play . . . What do you think it's about?'

They love you, hate the play or they love the play but can't stand the leading man – or they hate the play and can't help thinking it would have been better without you. Or, best and most common of all, they never mention the last two and a half hours they've spent in your company, not once. Not during dinner or the drive home – not ever again for the rest of your (rapidly shortening) acquaintance.

So when the hit hits it's above the belt and the newsagent, the chiropodist and the rabbi's wife all tell you they loved it, and how they left the theatre singing, and how they hadn't wanted to go because they'd had post-viral syndrome but they forgot themselves from the first trumpet and have felt vaguely happy ever since. And the letters come and the TV clips are shot and the Royal Variety Show want an excerpt and the rumours fly about Robin Williams being in tonight and you're tired and exhilarated at the same time and your bones ache but your heart sings. Every night you take a curtain call to cheers and wreathed faces beam up at you and strangers hang about outside the stage door and ask you to sign their collection of heel grips, and it's incredible!

Actually it was HM The Queen Mother's 98th birthday treat to see our show. We were still at the National Theatre then, and I used to start the show 60 feet under the stage on the drum of the stage. At the beginning of the overture the drum would revolve and rise to become part of the gold-tinted prairie. On this particular night, during the inevitable delay, one of the most taciturn stagehands took it upon himself to attack Her Majesty in the 'What the fuck has she ever done for us?' mode or much worse. I got instant 'drum rage'. I know I'm heading for *Private Eye*, but the few minutes before a show begins are the time for good thoughts. Whether you're playing Lady Macbeth, Lucrezia Borgia or Eric Cartman's mother, it's important to think well of yourself. To take a quiet moment to look through the character's eyes, surrounded by the character's world and prepare to shape-shift for as long as it takes. Just to be able to look out front and see land not audience, hear cows not coughing, requires a bit of self-hypnosis. My encounter with the gorilla in the pit angered me not just because of the badmouthing but because of his rotten timing.

The language which came out of me could have aroused the ghost of Lenny Bruce. Worse, I was sprung to lunge at him as the drum began to rise, and, with it, the sun and the first strains of 'Oh, What A Beautiful Morning!' There were few good thoughts but it sure put a spark in the first scene.

After the curtain call we told the audience we had another song to sing, 'and it's not by Rodgers and Hammerstein' – and the whole audience joined in. I'm not actually sure who wrote 'Happy Birthday To You' but his back royalties must be phenomenal. We presented present-day royalty with an *Oklahoma!* cake, made by my friends, Judy Bastyra and Charles Bradley, which matched the T-shirt design Amy had done for our first night – an elephant, a large ear of corn and a measuring stick. The corn *was* as high as an elephant's eye that night. Rumour has it that staff whipped her cake away back at the party in favour of the one they'd made earlier, but she insisted it was brought back and that she had a slice. It may not be true but it's a good thought.

Listen, while I'm Queen-dropping, I'll finish off with the investiture and the canine speech at Clarence House and then I promise I'll get out of your hair. I'm often accused of trying to seem as though *everybody* shares my experiences about royal enclosures and press disclosures and first-night parties and back stage hearties. I can see their point. It's hard to define how my life continues to feel very ordinary and is, mostly, uneventful, so that these odd moments, caused by the nature of my job, are thrown into such extraordinary relief. Besides, it's such a lark to tell. 'Leave it out,' I hear. 'You're just showing off.' I can see that point too.

But how could I forbear to mention the night of the Home Farm Trust After-Dinner Speech at BAFTA, when Zelma gave me the best one-liner the Princess Royal could have heard that day?

It was during dinner that the build-up began. I'd done my speech and my stomach had undone enough to tackle some food. Princess Anne was on my right, host Richard Price on my left and on his left was my mother. At some point during the main course, she leaned across Richard and hissed, 'MAUreen...Maureen.' I excused myself and leaned into her. 'What is it?'

'My bridgework's come out in the lamb chop.'

It sounded like an end-of-the-pier song by Max Miller. I had to ask her to repeat it. Sure enough, 'My bridgework. The three teeth on a bridge. They're on the plate.'

I took a deep breath, turned back to the Princess and said, 'Would you excuse us a moment, Ma'am?' Smiling, I turned regally to Zelma and said, 'Get the teeth.' We headed off for the cloakroom. There, by climbing underneath her jaw, I located the hole in the bridge and, glasses and reading glasses both perched on nose, screwed the appliance back in. Let's face it, I was never going to have my own surgery in Knightsbridge specialising in orthodontics and labial collagen injections – but my mother would be saved from having a mouth like a desecrated village. It wasn't perfect but it would save further embarrassment.

'Now, don't eat and don't talk,' I told her, knowing as I spoke that this was like saying 'Don't burble' to Richard Whiteley.

'Sorry about that,' I told producer and Princess, and we picked up what was left of the conversation. Five minutes later the dreaded hiss came again. 'MAUreen... Maureen.' This time I looked at the plate before I looked at my mum.

'Would you excuse me again, Ma'am. I'm awfully sorry...but it's a bit of an emerg...'This time I had an easier time getting it back in but my warning to avoid the chop was veering on the ferocious.

'I won't. I'm not even hungry any more.'

We both adjusted our lipstick. As we returned to the room I swear she said, 'I'll just have my dessert, that's all.'

This time when I took my seat, I felt some sort of explanation was due. The Princess was smiling at me whimsically. 'Ma'am,' I said as I sat down wearily beside her. 'I bet you all the rice in Chinatown that I've just done something for my mother that

YOU'VE never done for yours.'

OK. Which brings me back to her grandmother and what I like to call my canine speech. I was invited by Dame Frances Campbell Preston (Reggie Grenfell's half sister and lived with him in Elm Park Avenue when she wasn't in service as lady-in-waiting to the Queen Mother), at St James's Palace, to address the Queen Mary's Clothing Guild AGM. Frances is now over 80 but her energy and wit are like those of a woman half her age. I've always felt very at home with her. I'd made a policy decision not to do any daytime shticks (not a word that I'd bandy with any royalty, save Ed Wessex) while the show was on, but when the request came in to go to St James's Palace, preceded by lunch with the Queen Mother next door at Clarence House, I cashed in my policy.

Look. I understand the Republican argument. Royalty is an outmoded mode. Palaces and diamonds as big as ostrich eggs and tiaras and Rollers and glasses and handbags. I know. Anachronisms. I know. And overdrafts . . . It's just a) that the work they do is backbreaking, mentally and physically. OH YES IT IS!

Does anyone have any conception of how bone-grindingly tedious a few days of 'Oh, really, and does that flacket fit straight into that plonge or does the flumpascope have to truncate in its own whimsicroft? How very interesting' can be?

To be charming, well disposed and well informed with hundreds of strangers every day of every week of every year would drive those of us, untrained-for-the-job, mortals insane. One could only survive it if one were removed from emotion like a soldier at war or a surgeon at work. We may not feel close to our royal family, but we can admire and respect what they do. We may not love Princess Anne or Prince Charles, but a glance at their diaries and the constant quality of their performances, at close quarters, should quell the chunters of 'all' altogether for all time. And somebody has to hand out the prizes and the medals and open the renal units and cut the ribbons, and Lord, wouldn't you rather have a professional who's spent a lifetime doing it beautifully than, say, Robin Cook? Or Grant Mitchell? Or Baby Spice? Or me?

They've been doling out compassion long before the late Princess Diana invented it. Right through five years of the Blitz and 'Fight them on the beaches' and austerity and rationing and

'You've never had it so good' and *That Was the Week That Was* and 'Rejoice, rejoice' and 'We are a grandmother' and the one with his underpants on the outside and Blair's Babes and Fergie's toes and Kara Noble's bank account and there they are, still doing the endless work with endless patience and good humour. And b) Well, who the hell needs b) after that lot!

So out came the grey coatdress and Jack's equally grey bird's eye and awf we trolled for drinks before lunch. It was deliciously grand, with about twelve or fourteen guests, and as we glanced at the place list, Jack went ashen. 'I'm on her left,' he hissed, his eyes so round they looked like Harry Potter's facing Quiddich. 'What will I talk about?' 'You'll be fine. You'll talk about all sorts. Tell her about Eric.' This was a reference to Jack's rediscovered hobby – sculpting Manchester United players in clay and having them cast in bronze. He's awfully good.

Everyone else in the class is working on a reclining female nude. Listen, the main thing is, he's happy.

So, it was a first-rate lunch in jolly company – Mr Rosenthal talking ten to the dozen, Queen Mum showing no eye-white. Apparently she turned to him and said, 'I'm so delighted to be sitting next to you today.' To which Jack replied, 'See if you still think that in half an hour, Ma'am.'

Afterwards we repaired through to the second palace, admiring a single throne in the small ballroom (well, relatively small. Hell, what do I know about sizes of ballrooms?) salivating over the artwork and thinking, I shouldn't have had that second glass of white – I can feel it in my ankles.

There were about 200 women and a few men lunch guests present and some assorted staff – St John's Ambulance, etc. There was a podium at the end and there I was seated to nod and smile at the audience until Her Majesty arrived. She had changed outfits! Swapped green for lilac. She sat with us on the podium and the chairman delivered her annual report. Afterwards, I stood up to do my stuff. It's a relief when the audience laughs early on. The whole task is so much easier when the resistance is low, when they're on your side and not thinking, as they used to say in Hull, 'If she's that bloody good, what's she doin' here?'

Joyce Grenfell had been a speaker there. I told them how I'd recently performed one of the nursery school sketches at a North

London kindergarten. Afterwards my letter from the headmaster read: 'Your nursery school teacher sketch was hilarious. One of the girls laughed so much she wet herself, and that was the geography teacher.' As I launched into 'Gather round, children, because we're going to do our lovely moving to music...' there was a slight diversion at the back of the room and two sharp-featured latecomers bounded into the room, their bellies preposterously near the ground. I carried on: 'Now, Miss Boulting is going to play her piano and we're all going to be lovely flowers growing and dancing in the grass.'

'Arf! Arf!' came an unexpected sound as the two latecomers approached the microphone, put two of their four paws on the podium on either side of me and cocked their ears. 'Arf! Arf!'

'Let's make a nice wide circle, shall we? Wider. Wider, Sidney. Let go of Rosemary... No, she doesn't like it, Sidney – '

'Arf! Arf! Arf! Arf!' said the short heckler on the left.

'Well, because flowers don't hold hands, do they, Sidney?'

'Arf! Arf! Arf!' yelped the tubular heckler on the right.

The place was in uproar. Every time I spoke, they barked. The audience laughed every time they barked. It was chaos. It must have been something about that tone of voice – they recognised it. Or maybe they remembered Joyce. Or maybe they saw something the rest of us didn't...

Finally I turned to the Queen Mother and said, 'What are their names, Ma'am?' 'Minnie and Rush,' she replied through helpless giggles.

'Minnie,' I insinuated, Joyce-style. 'Don't do that!'

Minnie responded at once with her most pugnacious bark yet. 'Arf!'

'Now, Minnie,' I said. 'What did I tell you NOT to do?'

'Arf! Arf!' ('Search *me*' was the rough translation.)

'Well, don't *do* it.'

No animal trainer could have taught those dogs the kind of timing. It was genius. By comparison 'Eddie' in *Frasier* is dog meat.

Afterwards, Jack and I had afternoon tea while Her Majesty stood, greeting every member of the charity individually.

Afterwards she stood at the door and waved us off through the garden entrance. Then Jack went back to Eric's stubble at the Institute and I went back to an iron-grey wig and broken-veins to

play 53-year-old Aunt Eller. The 98 year old probably had another
gin and Dubonnet and hit the town.

The grey coatdress I mentioned was by Tomasz Starzewski. I
bought it to be 'commandered' in March 1999. White crêpe
blouse, knee-length grey skirt and slim coat with white pique
collar and white track stitches down the sleeves. I saw a picture of
Jane Asher in the same suit at a romantic fiction judging evening.
She hadn't stretched to the white-lined grey picture hat and kid
gloves but she didn't have Zelma for a mother, so she probably
has less emotional need to accessorise. I dropped her a note
enclosing a picture of Jack and me at the palace: 'If I ever see
Gerald Scarfe wearing this red tie, you will be hearing from my
solicitors.' Little bobby dazzler that she is, she wrote back:

Dear Ms Lippmmann
I was very distressed to receive your note of May 4th. As I
opened it I was in the process of changing into my elegant,
recently purchased Tomasz Starzewski grey suit to attend a
Brighton Literary Luncheon where I was to be the keynote
speaker to an extremely important group of elderly ladies.

The threatening tone of your letter caused me extreme
distress and quite threw my concentration and confidence,
resulting in my speech being very lightweight and full of
anecdotes about cakes – far removed from the thought-
proving, politically astute lecture I had planned on the way
forward for the Conservative Party.

I am surprised that a performer such as yourself lacks the
kind of sensitivity that so many members of the artistic
community pride themselves on possessing, and I trust you
will ensure that more tact is employed in future should you
wish to criticise my wardrobe.

Never let it be said, however, that I have no sense of humour,
and I did much enjoy the picture of you in the funny hat that
you had put on to amuse your husband.

Yours sincerely,
Jane Scarfe

The night before the ceremony I took a cab from Muswell Hill to Sloane Street, and had it wait while I picked up the newly altered outfit then take me on to the Lyceum and the show. The assistant could find everything but the blouse. The minutes ticked on by. Phone calls were made. No-one knew its whereabouts. Downstairs we frantically went through rack after rack, fighting crazier and crazier battles with the wretched plastic covers. Finally I heard myself say a sentence which afterwards the cast of *Oklahoma!* never let me forget. 'You know – honestly! – this is frightfully *bad form.*' It was an alien who spoke, obviously. 'Frightfully?' 'Bad form?' Moi? She found the blouse in the end, unmarked on a rail of blouses. In that twenty minutes I'd lost all the joy of the thing.

The shoes had been a great source of glee. The assistant's suggestion that I pop along to Manolo Blahnik? Jimmy Choo? for two-tone grey and white courts costing £350 left me over-enthusiastically beaming in a glazed fashion. 'Yeee-s, I'll er...I will, I'll go right there ... Great suggestion.' Sunday morning saw me in Kate Kuba, Muswell Hill's best-kept podiatic secret, where I found, on the sale rail, in my size, the perfect match. The only thing which put me off was the price. Bit beyond my budget at...£29! And Debenhams had the matching bag. Fine. *Parfait.* 'Purrrrfect shoes!' cooed the assistant back in Sloane Street. 'Where *did* you find them?'

The morning of the ceremony found me with my head in the loo at 6.10am. One of those migraines which starts halfway through the night, so the only respite is the strongest painkiller which can't be taken on an empty stomach, so a banana gets rammed down your mouth before you're awake. By 10.00am I was fit, fine and ready to go, if a little spacey. Jack was in his suit, Amy in hers and Mum was resplendent in dog's tooth and large black hat. The hat looked great but it shadowed her face entirely on the one spot on the video in which she appeared. I reckon that hat's in for an early grave.

The equerry's address to the honour recipients is a collector's piece. He gave a great, sweeping theatrical and hugely patronising performance and one day I shall steal it and use it shamelessly. Her Majesty was friendly, and as I've commented earlier, brilliant at remembering our last conversation, and before you could say 'Why me?' again, it was over and we were being seamlessly transported back to where we came from.

'I hate stairs with no banisters,' said Zelma as she came down the majestic front steps, and, 'Fancy – they don't even give you a cup of tea . . . My mouth's as dry as a bone.'

'We had the jolliest of lunches, at The Ivy, where dryness was relieved and appetites whetted with dear friends and family, then I set off to walk to the theatre to lay my head down before the evening show. I cut a bit of a swathe in Covent Garden, I can tell you, with my huge picture hat and my gloves and pearls and my bargain shoes, but I was beginning to feel my years. All this hob-nobbing was doin' my 'ead in, as they say in the New Vic.

Just before I turned into the stage door, I passed Charles Fox, the theatre make-up shop. It hit me that I'd promised Amy a week ago that I'd go in there to buy her some fake blood for a production of *Zoo Story* being done by her student friends at Birmingham University. As I hovered, undeterminedly, priorities battling with self-pity, I felt a hand on Mr Starzewski's beautifully cut, fine wool shoulder. I turned round to face two of the most inebriated Scots dossers I've ever seen outside *The Stanley Baxter Show*. They were regulars in the area and they smelled like Yates's Wine Lodge on Blackpool Pier.

'Aww, Morreen, yer lookin' grand. 'Ave yew bint' Ascot now, Morreen? Does she not look a cracker?' He turned to his friend, who put a finger through his balaclava to poke his ear out. 'Grand, she looks grand. Can yer give us a little something now, Morreen. We're near starving and . . .'

'Look, fellas,' I groaned, 'we've been through this. If I give you money you'll drink it and . . .'

'NOOOO! Noooo! We won't, we won't, I promise – look, just give us the price of an egg,' he breathed, 'and we'll get outya hair.'

It was an inventive one . . . I was kayboshed by it. I needed to think. I blurted and babbled something and neatly slipped into the make-up shop.

They followed me in. It was quiet in there and the sight of an actress dressed up so high she could only come down with a bump, accompanied by two steaming derelicts in stained trousers, string round their shoes, clinking bottles of ginger wine and swaying, was one for the bar after work.

The assistants stared. The Holy Triumverate stared back.

Finally I spoke. 'Er . . . do you, by any chance, have such a thing as a bottle of blood?' I petered out. '. . . It's for my daughter. . .'

That night I wore my tracksuit with my CBE medal for the warm-up. Just as it should be, no-one noticed.

Service With a Smirk

SERVICE: To perform the duties or do the work connected with: to attend or assist: to supply: to furnish with materials. Thus speaks the *Chambers English Dictionary*. Furthermore, it goes on to mention religious ceremonies, tennis, cars, the army and, with relation to the male animal, the act of copulation. A serviceable word, in fact.

The reason I sought out the services of the English dictionary was to find out if it mentioned anywhere that service was a dirty word in this sceptred isle of ours. It didn't, but by God it should quickly get it in the revised edition.

Here's the scenario. Feel a whinge coming on? You are 100 per cent right. We took our daughter and her fella to a well-known restaurant chain for her birthday dinner, phoning in advance to ask for a small cake for four plus a candle, for dessert, from the downstairs patisserie. 'Any message on the cake?' asked the assistant. 'Erm, well, yes, OK,' I said. '"Happy Birthday, Amy" will be fine.'

On the night we had a decent enough meal in the pretentious, piled-up fashion of the day.

The cake which followed was dry and almondy, the candle a fizzling sparkler, and we consumed it in four gulps.

Which was half the number of gulps I gave when I got the bill for the meal. Scouring it for unordered truffles and caviar, I saw that the eight-inch cake had cost £25.

'Don't start, Mom!' warned my daughter darkly. She'd eaten with me before and wanted to be embarrassed in public in front of her boyfriend like I wanted necrotising fasciitis.

'Excuse me. love,' I called the waiter over. 'Is this a mistake? Are you seriously suggesting I pay twenty-five pounds for this enlarged bun?'

He looked sheepish. 'Yeah, I'm sorry about that,' he muttered 'but it's thirteen pounds for the cake, two pounds for the sparkler and five pounds for the written placard...' He petered out, as well he might.

'Leaving five pounds by my reckoning,' I prompted.

'Er...that's five pounds for eating it here, I'm afraid.' He almost ducked as I repeated in bleak tones, 'Five pounds for eating it here?' He nodded. (Later, when I repeated this conversation to my friend, Valerie, she immediately snapped, 'Did you ask him how much it would cost to shove it up his tochas?')

I didn't. Instead I said evenly 'Where would you like me to have eaten it?'

He looked at his shoes and mumbled something about cakes eaten on the premises and cakes taken away being subject to different price rates. I stopped him. 'I'll pay this bill,' I said dangerously, 'but I will never eat here again.' He went off to confer with management and I was offered a £7 reduction on sparkler and cover charge. But it irritates the hell out of me that anyone has to be subjected to this avarice,' I said, and departed, never to return. Service was included, I noted from the bill.

Fade out and in again some months later to a small coffee house in Headrow, Leeds, where I'd retired to eat breakfast whilst the crew of a live video, which I was to record that night at Leeds City Varieties Music Hall, crawled over the ceiling and set up their lights.

I'd been too nervous to eat breakfast in the hotel and it was now 10.30am and I was starving. Tim, my director, ordered two cappuccinos and I asked for a fried egg on toast.

'...and would you mind awfully,' I requested, 'if I have a piece of my own pumpernickel bread which I've got here with me because I can't eat wheat bread.'

The young woman stared at me as though I'd asked for at least a slice of marinated marsupial and the jawbone of an ass. In aspic.

'Allavtoaskmeboss,' she chuntered. Her boss being a surly middle-aged man at a nearby table in an otherwise almost empty café.

I smiled, I hoped, winningly. 'It's just that I can't eat ordinary bread because off...er...allergies...and...I...' He was puffing up like Barney the Bashful Bullfrog. 'I'll pay for the whole thing. I just need a plate for my bread.'

He hit the table with one flat palm and his forehead with the other, then changed hands. The routine had a flamenco feel to it. 'Thirty-two years!' he hollered. 'Thirty-two years in dis business and neverr inna my life has *anyone* asked to bringa der own bread! Dis is a RESTAURANT, neh? Next ting you will be wantin' to bringa your own eggs!' It was an Anthony Quinn performance and had real violence in it. I pondered pouring the cappuccinos on the floor and sweeping out but figured he might just shoot me in the foot.

I've nearly finished frothing now. I mean, don't think that I'm confusing service with servility. I don't want Uriah Heep or even, 'Hi, I'm Jason, and if there's anything I can do short of licking your face and purring, I'll be only too happy to oblige...' It's just that the concept of doing the job pleasantly has all but disappeared in a cloud of café rage. It's getting so I daren't go into a garage for petrol any more... for fear of what I'll get. After all, it's a service station, isn't it?

Old Foodie

Jack feels even more passionately than I do that food faddiness is out of control. 'Ciabatta and circuses.' 'The winner of the cookery thing – wait till I show you, love, you won't believe it. If I tell you . . . It was unbelievable! I was helpless! You'll never believe . . . I mean, the only way I can explain it is to show you . . .'

My husband was excited to Ben Eltonesque proportions as he began to unload the fridge for a 'Here's one I made earlier' type demonstration.

It was 12.10am and I'd just arrived home from the theatre with Anastasia. Our places were laid at the table for our special post performance platter – that night's fare being baked potatoes à la Delia Smith (she's revolutionised the baked potato, hasn't she, bless her) – but they sat plaintively baking to death while the chef positively exploded culinary curmudgeon.

It was a funny old life for the *Oklahoma!* widower. He said the only voices he heard after we left for work at 5.15pm (12.15pm on Wednesdays and Saturdays) were his own and Desmond Lynam's – oh, and mine when I rang, once in the interval to say, 'Hi, what ya doin'?', and once from the cab at 11.15pm to say, 'Russell Square, heavy traffic, see you at 12.00.'

Of course, he wrote a bit and pottered a bit and twice a week he goes to his sculpture class at the Institute. On this particular night, however, his excitement was to do with sculpture of the edible variety. 'The man that won . . .' he spluttered. 'The man that won made a tall, narrow meal. His first course was a layer of leaves – ' Here he plastered a couple of napkins on to the plate 'With a slice of whatsit – aubergine – on top.' Here he added an inverted saucer. 'And on top of that a slice of toasted goats cheese!' Here he placed an egg slicer on top of the saucer. 'And,

AND, on top of *that*, a beetroot and celery rosti!' This he illustrated by adding his wallet to the pile. 'Topped with – hang on – topped with beef tomato, toasted bacon and deep-fried avocado.' He was running out of props now, so he just popped a notepad, a banana and a tin of tuna on the teetering heap. 'Then he dribbled a load of red stuff all over the edge of the plate, the buzzer went off and he won! The meal was seven foot high! You'd have needed a tennis umpire's chair to eat it! Or Fred Dibner. That's not food, that's the Leaning Tower of Pizza!' Plainly the programme had made an impression on him.

I often wonder how I would fare on *Masterchef*; being as I can't eat 50 per cent of what gets served up. 'Gosh, that looks lovely, Lloyd, but I can't actually eat the prawn bit – or the ham. Sorry. Er . . . gosh, fantastic spread but er . . . is it cheese? It's just that I'm a martyr to migraine, so I'll just try the mousse – Aagh! was that chocolate? Eh! Bleughgh! Oh, sorry about your floor, Lloyd.'

The preponderance of foodie programmes on TV is well chronicled. A Martian landing on earth would assume from our TV and our high streets that we are a civilisation of people who watch other people cook then buy pre-cooked food from M&S or eat out. In the good old days Fanny and Johnny Craddock held court as TV cooks – now every lunatic with swirling eyeballs, surly manners and his own set of stainless-steel skillets can have half an hour a week on Channel 4 and make a fortune afterwards in the dumpbins of W. H. Smith.

One thing is eternal. In the same way that if you talk well, you can probably write well, if you love to eat, you can probably cook. Given time, Radio 4 and an empty kitchen, I can turn out about six things which don't occur in recipe books but will bring a beam to your face and a breadth to your beam. My soups are messes of pottage and my braised lamb chops with pot barley and prunes have had men slavering for more and women for less. Jack loves my cooking but I suspect that's because he so rarely gets it. Also, I've noticed most husbands have grown so used to their wife's cooking that they've lost any objective judgement on it. And, of course, men are now free to cook without being regarded as sissies or Frenchmen. Jack's post-theatre suppers were positively extravagant. Sometimes, when I'd had pasta take-away and a café latte between matinée and evening show, I longed for just a piece of toast and a cuppa. Faced with baked fish, mashed potatoes, three veg, a salad and a rice pudding at midnight, though, what's a woman who loves food to do? Exactly. And that's what I did. And that's also why, after leaping around the stage for hours like a hyperactive ibex for months, I didn't lose a kilo.

One evening we arrived home to find a note pinned to the front door. 'CHIPS!' it screamed. 'Anastasia's CHIPS now being perfectly cooked on the premises.' He wasn't having us on, either. At the time that most men are glued to Channel Porn, slavering over some Ulrika substitute, our man in Muswell Hill was blanching, drying and salting his precisely planed potatoes, ready to dip them in sizzling sunflower oil, just as our car-phone rang his kitchen mobile. God, they were good. Crisp on the outside, soft and melting on the inside. Salmon patties sat casually in their Pyrex homestead, just challenging you not to wolf them down as accompaniment. Pickled cucumbers and beetroot and horse-radish sauce topped the bill. All at 'Chez Jacques'. And service included. 'They broke the mould,' sighed Zelma, the mother-in-law, wistfully dabbing her lips with a napkin. They did.

Man goes into restaurant: 'I want a full English breakfast, please. But I want both eggs broken and the yolks overcooked. I want the bacon limp and greasy. I want the mushrooms swimming in fat and the fried bread soggy and white. And I'd like a cup of stewed tea with it – lukewarm.'

The restaurateur gawps in amazement. 'But, sir!' he protests. 'I can't possibly serve you a meal like that!'

'Why not?' says the customer. 'You did yesterday.'

Leek and Barley Soup

Last year I found myself making two films. This is two films more than I've made in several years. The fact that they could best be described as 'art' films, i.e. a small, select section of the public list them as two of fifteen of the most interesting films of the past seventeen months, is neither here nor there.

One of them was *Captain Jack,* shot on location in Whitby, and the other wasn't. The other was *Solomon & Gaenor* by Paul Morrison, shot entirely on location in South Wales, in two versions, for £2millon. (Roughly what Roy Keane expects Manchester United to pay him a year.) And, wait for it – one version of the film was in Welsh and Yiddish. The other, Welsh, Yiddish and English. It was worth every sheckel.

It was a turn-of-the-century Welsh/Jewish *Romeo and Juliet* starring Ioan Gruffudd and Nia Roberts. My part as Ioan's mother, scraping a living and a life in the valleys, against the backdrop of 1911 anti-Semitic riots, was downbeat enough to make Aunt Eller look like an 'IT' girl.

It was an interesting gig. I met the writer/director and the producer, Sheryl Crown, in the laboratory in our local leisure centre and they offered me the part of 'Rezl'. The thought of another headscarf over the unmade-up face and all those grey and brown layers of clothes didn't make my CV sparkle, I'll admit, but the idea of speaking a whole role in Yiddish did.

Yiddish, at home in Hull, meant anything they didn't want the kids to hear. Preceded by '*Schweig – nisht* in front of the *kinder,*' it meant pricking up your ears immediately – someone was about to be trashed. 'Shall I *shtipp?*' was my dad asking my mother whether the porter or waiter merited half a crown. 'Go *pamelach,*' was automatically muttered every time one of us went outside or

211

upstairs or anywhere – go carefully, slowly. A *shloff* was a sleep, a *fresser* one whose eyes were bigger than his belly, a situation soon reversed in any of the houses of my childhood.

It was a language of the oppressed, a heady mixture of German, Polish and pidgin, coined to be colourful and ambiguous.

There used to be an enormous number of Yiddish plays, books and films and the language travelled into the diaspora for at least two generations. Grandparents spoke it to parents, parents occasionally to children; children learned only the slang and the swear words, which were onomatopoeic and expressive. A typical Yiddish curse would be, 'May a rich pig open a shop in your spleen and prosper.' The opening of the shop in a person's spleen is not enough, you understand – the pig must be there for ever!

I phoned the producer. 'I can't do it. It's too much. I'm sorry...I just...I mean, I had no idea how difficult...I can't.'

She was calm personified. 'Now you mustn't worry. You've got lots of time – and listen, if you really can't do it we can put some of it into broken English, or we can even CUT some of it...'

This is what we in the ego business call 'brilliant tactics'. Suddenly the lines began to learn themselves. Within a few days I could say them backwards. David Horovitch, who played my husband and had been raised in a totally assimilated home, was an even quicker student. As for our son, the talented Ioan Gruffudd, whose Yiddishkite was as profound as my Welshkite, he had the whole *schtik* off to perfection. Youth, dammit!

We all met in Cardiff for a readthrough. It was a strange one. To our surprise, I think, we all found the music and rhythm both natural and familiar. It felt like a living language and one that I'd spoken before. It made the timbre of my voice sweeter, gentler, the cadences more lyrical. I found it comforting and comfortable. I expected to feel like an idiot (for which there are eighteen different Yiddish words); instead, I felt like a very old soul.

Because there was little money, we all shivered together during filming in one small caravan. Cyril Shaps, that splendid and irrepressible character actor, David Horovitch and me.

Fingers mittened, faces besmirched, shawls clutched around hunched shoulders, we scurried to the welcoming pub in Nant Moel to stoke up energy for the next take. The set, under Paul

Morrison's direction, was a very serious place, no room or time for the usual thespian tomfoolery. We saved that for the pub and the caravan. In fact, the more gruelling the scene, the more sublimely silly we were 'off'.

One of the bleakest, coldest set-ups was for a funeral scene on the sharp edge of a hillside cemetery. The family was burying their (only?) son, Solomon. The wind was biting, and sleet blew into our faces and stung our eyes during take after take after take.

When we finally made it back to the tiny changing cubicles, lit by Calor gas stoves, I had lost all feeling and mobility in my right thumb. It was like a pom-pom suspended from a woolly hat. I could feel it but had no control over it. Back at the location base I swallowed hard and rang home. 'Book me another scan,' I told Jacquie grimly. 'I'm in trouble.'

Weirdly, fifeen minutes later, my thumb was thumblike again and it's never bothered me in the same way since. The scene was cut from the film, so I would have been bloody cross to lose what distinguishes me from my cousin, the ape, for something which ended up in a waste-paper basket on a cutting-room floor.

Perhaps, because the film was so unrelieved, I tended to be dismissive of its power. When I saw it for the first time, in a Cardiff cinema complex, I found it overwhelming. Beautiful to look at in a palette of subtle sepia colours, the photography by Scandinavian Nina Kellgren, who'd done such a great job with Jack's *Cold Enough For Snow*, contributed hugely to the period flavour. It was moving, stark and very dramatic. The two languages really worked together: the two cultures clashed and complemented each other.

Later it went on to win 1st Prize at two European Film Festivals and have a respectable run in London. The Screen on the Hill in Hampstead was the only cinema ever to greet Nia Roberts and I with the billing in lights, 'Screen On The Hill Welcomes Maureen Lipman and Nia Roberts.' It wasn't quite searchlights but it was a glint.

It was a charity première and it took place shortly after the Oscars ceremony. I had decided to make my speech in the Gwyneth Paltrow mode and had asked our excellent Yiddish coach, Barry Davis, to translate her acceptance speech into Yiddishism for me – with a touch of Roberto Benigni.

'*Teiyerre freint*... (My friends, today I want to make love to a water melon, already!) *As ikh bin fardanken far alz tzv meine tayere tatte* (my dear father – sob) *meine tatte – mammceh* (sob) *meine leibste bubbe* (sob, sob) *unt meine bubbe-zeide* (wail) *foon beide tzoddim! Oon Tzooletzt – di machetoynim unti di machetaynistei – oy veys mir* (helpless, heaving sobs) *a schvrogers plimmenik oyf dem veibs tsod*...' And for those of you whose first language is not Yiddish, I was thanking 'my parents, their parents, their parents' parents, their in-laws, my husband's sister's husband with the funny eye, my agent, my travel agent, my podiatrist, my step aerobics teacher... etc.' It went down very well indeed with the charity audience. The reviews were an hors-d'oeuvres. Good for the kids. 'Lipman surprised with her shmaltz-free, stiff Yiddish momma,' said one critic. 'Sponsored by Channel 4, it would have been a wackily modern cultureclash comedy, but this is not the case with *Solomon & Gaenor*, EVEN THOUGH MAUREEN LIPMAN plays the mother' –

I keep thinking of Woody Allen in one of his marvellous middle-period movies, maybe *Stardust Memories*, overhearing someone saying, 'I liked him so much better in the early films when he was *funny*.'

Rifling through the *Solomon & Gaenor* file I came across a fax I must have sent to the cast and crew after I'd completed all my scenes and gone home:

Dir Cast unt Crew.

Danke. De flowers ver shein.

Es Tut mir Laeid dat I em shtuck in der hill of Muswell instead of fressing unt shickering in der hills foon Cardiff. Recording I am dis morgen der commentary foon de 'Reputations' about de Kenneth Williams (de late faigele already). Also I vas presenting de links for de 50 years simcha of Israel at Vembley. Mit Tom Conti, whobist ein Catholic. Till now.

Mazel in glick for de movie's success. 'A woman's movie,' said Oscar Levant, 'is one where the woman commits adultery all through the picture and at the end her husband begs her to forgive him.'

Mit der libbe unt der kushes.

M

I once heard a prominent lady author being interviewed on *Woman's Hour* about the sequel she was writing to some famous novel. It may even have been *Pride and Prejudice* – I mean, that famous – or Daphne Du Maurier's *Rebecca*. I forget. Did she not feel a little daunted by stepping into the great lady's shoes? Her reply gave me more genuine pleasure than Jonathan Aitkin's poem from prison gave Ian Hislop.

'Well,' she laughed, 'it is a challenge . . . Indeed, some might say I've got a bit of a *chutzpah* in taking on the task.' Except she didn't say *chutzpah* as in Peter Schmeichel, a Scottish lo*ch* or a Spanish Jochaim. She said it as in challenge or Chile or Champion the Wonder Horse. 'Tshutspar,' she said.

I love it that Yiddish has imbued itself into our colloquial speech, so that the very people who would have regarded those immigrants, with nothing to declare but their former professions, as inferior species, now *schlepp* down the shops for their bagels. Just as the new Asian humour is becoming mainstream – (innit?) with criticism from their old guard and all the old fears of putting heads over parapets – coming out of the community. Words continue to be dangerous tools of progress until, finally, familiarly, they are assimilated into the everyday. Lenny Bruce knew that 40 years ago. In the end, that knowledge killed him. Yiddish, which began so subversively, has ended up quaint and collectable. It feels good to *schlepp nachas*, to take pride in it once again.

I now have a Yiddish version of *The Pirates of Penzance* and can sing *Oklahoma!* in Yiddish. Maybe *Solomon & Gaenor* could use more fun to offset the tragedy but it's an awfully good film, a damn sight more honest than *Life is Beautiful* and you can catch it at any Welsh/Yiddish cinema of your choice.

Bosom Buddies

I'm really not too bothered by the age thing. Yet. I mean, I don't like seeing myself on camera in close-up, but then I never did. The first time I ever saw the daily rushes of the film I was making back in the heady sixties, I ran out of the viewing room, howling, with my fist in my mouth, and had to be prised out of the ladies' toilet by the sympathetic male director.

While I don't much like the sinking physiognomy and the simmering root canals, the thing I'd never bargained for is a sort of general non-reversible 'thickening'. I know I look thin to you but that's because I've got a thin *head* and thin ankles. It's the bits in between that are bearing the brunt of age and my love of the farinaceous.

Some time ago it was the mammography. A card came asking me and my breasts to put in an appearance at the car park of my local hospital for a breast X-ray, which seemed to give a whole new meaning to the term 'Pay and Display'. Sure enough, tucked into the side of the hospital parking area was a mobile home with a receptionist, fourteen assorted breasts in a kiosk-sized waiting room and one copy of *Hello!* I tried to disappear behind *The Queen of Whale Cay*, which just happened to be my current book, about a flamboyant, cross-dressing lesbian, but to no avail.

'You are Beattie still?' my neighbour opposite said. 'Er . . . yes,' I admitted.

'I knew that I knew her,' crowed the lady.

'I knew too,' retorted the lady on my right in unison with her neighbour. 'I already told my cousin you was Beattie.'

I held my breath and counted to five. It usually takes about five:

'So why don't we ever see you on the telly any more?' This is marginally preferable to the more innocuous-sounding alternative

– 'They must have used a lot of stage make-up on you for Beattie' – because whereas the former leads to a discussion of the awfulness of television today, the latter requires the sad revelation that very little make-up was used other than a pair of glasses and a wig. At 45 I just *looked* like that. They had much to discuss after my departure into the X-ray room.

'Take off your clothes to the waist,' said the radiologist. I did, and looked around for a gown, a towel or two saucepans. Having never been to ballet or boarding school, I'm a bit shy about letting it all hang out before strangers, so I crossed my arms over my bosoms, which had the effect of hoisting the whole caboodle on to a sort of ledge. It was anything but casual and the radiologist and I both knew it. 'When did you last have a mammogram?' 'Have you noticed any unusual puckering?' 'Have you felt any changes in consistency?' Even if I had I would have answered, 'No', just so I wouldn't have to expand on my answer whilst standing there looking like a naked woman selling rugby balls.

Out of the corner of my eye I caught sight of a notice warning you that 'the breast had to be compressed to see inside it and that any pain or bruising was uncomfortable, but temporary'.

It was then that I remembered why my last mammography was years ago. It's a bit like childbirth. You know, when you think, Well, thank God that's over with because I'm sure as hell never going through that again. Then you completely forget about the pain until *just* after the gynaecologist has confirmed your second pregnancy.

Actually, the X-ray is really not that bad at all. I mean, if you like having your breast picked up by a stranger like a pound and a half of sourdough and flattened, you'll love it! I have this inability to enjoy my pear-shaped bits being made into perfect rhomboids – it's a weakness, I know.

Still, it only lasted a few minutes and I scampered back into my bra and baggy clothing before you could say 'sex goddess'. As I passed through the waiting room I gave what I hoped was the sort of grin which said, 'Well, that was nothing to get ruffed up about', but they were all too busy discussing the Bob Hoskins campaign compared to mine to notice.

Since my trip to Florida where liver spots are proud to call themselves freckles and osteoporosis makes everyone appear to be permanently shrugging, I have come back feeling like a spring chick, albeit a slightly spatchcock one.

Yesterday I bought a gorgeous trouser suit. It looks adorable but for two small 'crinkles' between the lapels and the shoulder pads, which somehow made me think of Florida and shrugging.

I called over the smart and snooty shop assistant to ask why such a pricey outfit sported such 'crinkles'. She faffed around a bit, reminding me of mammaries and car parks, then said, 'It could be taken in but, frankly, it would hang much better if your breasts were higher up.'

Remember the recent news story about the man in Houston, Texas, who'd had a remote control device fitted to his penis to deal with his impotence, then found that he had an erection every time his neighbour opened or closed the garage doors? Well, this has nothing to do with the story I've just told you except that I think I know how he felt.

To Win or Toulouse

It's a mere two-hour flight from Toulouse Airport to Heathrow and we were feeling relaxed and cheerful after a farmhouse week with David and Kate and the two-and-a-half-year-old twins. Joseph is my godchild but it's impossible to love one more than the other, especially when each bedtime involved a rowdy rendition of 'The Farmer and the Cowman Should Be Friends' (I couldn't believe I was still singing that song every night at 7.30pm.)

In the departure lounge I was ogling and earwigging as usual. There was a delightful watchable family: a good-looking Frenchman, bonny English wife in shorts and downy-haired baby on hip and at least two other youngsters running around. How do people have the energy to deal with more than two kids? The paraphernalia – books and nappies and wet wipes and smelly-feely blankets and 'Where's Brown Ted? I thought *you* had him.'

On the narrow plane, Jack helped this family to put stuff in the overhead hold alongside ours. The five of them were squashed into two rows and there was some cheerful swapping of roles as parents do what they do best at given times, i.e. feeding or colouring in. After a while old fluffy head began flirting with me over the side of the seat and I began responding in a way which, had she been present, would have infuriated my daughter, although 24 years ago she found it bone-rattlingly funny.

As we taxied into Terminal 2, bags were lowered down, buggies folded and unfolded and tired little limbs unstretched. Standing on the courtesy bus I watched their last-minute dash to catch the folding doors with relief. I mean, there are Teacher Awards, there's probably Welder of the Year – where's the Mum of the Millennium, eh?

Georg, a friendly German minicab driver, was there to pick us up. Contrary to racial stereotypes, Georg has a sense of humour. It's more ironic – well, let's face it, he put the chasm in sarcasm. On the journey home I glanced casually through the duty-free bags and was surprised to find that one contained Madame Rochas perfume. This is not my perfume. It crossed my mind to ask my husband for whom he'd bought the perfume but perhaps not with Georg in front to say, 'But, of course, it is for his mistress, Maureen. You must be sophisticated about these things...'

Once home and pre-cooked chicken on the slicing board, I remembered the perfume in the white plastic bag. 'Madame Rochas, then, eh?' I said smirking. 'Since when do you splash out on Madame Rochas, then?' The face that framed the word 'Pardon?' at me was the face of the late great Eric Morecambe.

'You what?'

I repeated my statement.

'*I* never bought perfume – I didn't even go into duty free. It's not even duty free any more.'

'Well, who do you suppose did go in, then?' I said, slapping the plastic bag down. 'Look, perfume, two rolls of film and two...'

My words froze on my lips. 'Two... passports. Mrs Emily Berolini, Benjamin and two children. Oh my God.'

It was 8.30pm – an hour and a half after we'd landed. That poor couple would be stuck at immigration with two kids and a baby and the kids would be hungry and crying and she'd be distraught and her husband would be pacing the floor and saying he'd never wanted to come anyway and immigration would be searching their luggage, or worse... and they'd be kept in a cell all night and deported back to France and France wouldn't let them in without a passport and...

The chicken returned to its former frozen state. I picked up the telephone and from 8.45 till 11.50 I stayed on it. Air France (they passed me on), Immigration (they told me to ring the police), the contact number in the back of Emily's passport (unobtainable), the police (they said call Air France). Finally I managed to ascertain that they'd all been allowed into the country because they had a 'carte' – don't ask me – just thank God they'd got one and were on their way to Bath. At 11.30 Air France gave me the number of the house in Bath. Emily's mother answered the phone.

'They've just this minute got in. Hold on...' It was now ten to twelve. I was mortified. How could we have put their bag into ours without so much as a single check?

Emily sounded remarkably sanguine and cheerful for someone who'd just spent nine hours travelling. 'Oh, thanks so much for ringing,' she said. 'My husband was convinced I'd left them in Toulouse. That's such a relief. Thanks so much.'

The next day I packed up her belongings and added abject apologies, chocolates and everything but my current account. She was thrilled and insisted we pop in on them next time we were in Toulouse. Might take her up on it. I could do with a holiday.

Prying Tonight

I don't know exactly how the press have got total access to my ex-directory number, but they have. It gives them free reign to ask me how I feel about important issues of the day like Steffi and André or whether GMTV means Genetically Modified Viewing. They almost always choose early Sunday morning or late Monday to Friday night and Jack generally removes me manually from the handset in order to spare me the embarrassment of reading the subsequent misquote.

The day before Derek Nimmo's memorial service, a young woman from a tabloid newspaper rang me at home to ask me for private information about one of his children. Before replacing the receiver I asked her if she was happy in her work. She seemed perplexed by the question. I had to remind myself that she was somebody's daughter.

'No reporter ever lit up when confronted with evidence that the person he was interviewing was happy,' wrote Aldous Huxley. On the contrary, the need for some kind of privacy bill is the natural outcome of the baying for celebrity blood which currently passes for investigative journalism.

After Princess Diana's death and Lord Althorp's oratorial condemnation, I guess we all thought the climate would change and certainly the paparazzi had a thin time of it for ... ooh ... several minutes. Then it was business (malpractice) as usual.

It appears that the words 'The public deserves to know' are synonymous with 'That rich layabout deserves to be cut down to size'.

Was it fair game to destroy Will Carling's credibility and career after he transformed the sport and brought it into the twentieth century? He had a bad track record as a 'love-rat' but did he bring his profession into disrepute?

What would be the tabloid verdict on Mozart? 'Sex, drugs and piano rolls?' 'Should Tourette's Syndrome suspect be allowed at court?' 'The world loves him but is his music safe for its children?' 'Is this punk musician a good role model?'

What in heaven's name is a role model? What it ain't and never has been is what parents expect it to be. The pressure on young achievers to opine on everything from their favourite brasserie to their favourite brassiere is immense. Most of the poor souls are famous for doing one thing well. If it's dance, film or sport then they probably spent their teenage years training for six hours a day or on film sets with a tutor and a scrambled egg bap. They never had the time or the freedom to think for themselves. Their thoughts and their intellectual opinions could be contained in a ping-pong ball. Suddenly, they're 21, famous, free, rich as Croesus, courted by both sexes, surrounded by mindless minders and basically as lonely as a lighthouse keeper. How easy to unburden your confusion on to a total stranger who emanates compassion and, possibly, passion to go with it.

One thing is certain, in the same way as we get the leaders we deserve, we also get the press coverage we deserve. Most people, myself included, turn to the showbiz gossip section before we scour the editorial. Reading *HellO.K!* is as addictive as watching TV soaps or eating stacking crisps. It requires nothing but suspension of disbelief, no imagination or effort and it leaves you thirsty.

Watching the fall of Hugh Grant made men and women gloat equally and separately. Women felt elated that the unachievable perfection so easily achieved by Liz Hurley was no guarantee of fidelity and men felt better for confirmation that the floppy-haired public swoonboy would probably fancy ''er indoors' or possibly ''er outdoors' rather more than the face of Estée Lauder.

It's no coincidence that celebrity interviews and modern criticism reveals more about the interviewer than the interviewee. It's meant to. Careers have been built on the demolition of careers. Lynn Barber, known as the Demon Barber of Fleet Street, decimated celebs by the poundage.

I've never forgotten her critique of Richard Harris playing pocket billiards through his tracksuit. I don't suppose he has either. We are sitting ducks, lambs to the slaughter, hapless and helpless, and we never have the last word. Damned if we try to please... ('Would you like a cup of tea?' translating seamlessly into 'She fussed around her two-tone kitchen arranging shopbought biscuits on two-tone plates'), damned if we don't... ('I've no idea what makes my marriage work' becoming 'She seemed strangely shifty on the subject of her marriage.'

In 1995 I gave the Baggs Lecture on 'Happiness' at Birmingham University to a thousand students and masters. I had great difficulty compiling it because I kept wanting to write, instead, about unhappiness.

Not that I'm unhappy – and if I am, I'm not unhappy about it. It's just that melancholy is so much more interesting and accessible. Just like villains are more fun to play and savage criticism more enjoyable to write. I delivered the talk and it was well received on the day. It was very personal and very jokey and the serious issues which the subject threw my way were touched on lightly. Four years later, four of the lectures were selected by producer Lynette Quinlan for broadcast on Radio 4. David Attenborough, Richard Wilson and John Mortimer were to be my fellow lecturers broadcasting on four successive Saturday evenings.

On Sunday morning, casually cruising the papers, I was stopped mid-bagel. The *Sunday Telegraph* radio reviewer, David Sexton, had torn me to shreds. 'It was,' he said 'a travesty, coming after Attenborough's.' He mocked my construction, compared me unfavourably to the great anthropologist, laughed at my familial sagas, my political thoughts, my humour and finished – frothing by now all over his AppleMac – by accusing me of 'a grovelling cliché' in ending with the happiness I found in my radio.

Against my better judgement, I wrote to remind him that the lecture was given to students, so any 'grovelling' to radio would have been wasted on a live audience. I could have excised it for the broadcast, which would have been another form of grovelling. This time I sent the letter. Did they print it? Guess...

Writing this book has made me look through reviews of old shows. It's an odd experience. They're always slightly better than one remembers them. I suppose because at the time, the bad bits stick in your brain cells. 'Don't let Mo read *The Times* today,' hissed Julia McKenzie down the phone at Jack after I opened in

The Rivals at the Manchester Royal Exchange. 'Too late,' he told her. 'We've already had the early morning *kvetch*.'

Georgina Brown in the *Telegraph*, who had visited the play *Birdy* in the same week as *Live and Kicking*, complained that it kept coming back to her in an absurd parodied form . . . Ms Lipman's vague resemblance to a chicken (full bosomed, scrawny necked)' – Thanks, Georgie, and cluck off – didn't help matters.

Well, you can do a Jo Brand or Hylda Baker and make yourself look so unappealing that you pre-empt that kind of physical criticism, which only ever comes from a woman critic, or you can do the best with what God and your own taste gave you. In the nineties, the greatest sin you can commit to an audience is that of appearing anxious to please. 'She appeals ingratiatingly to every section of the audience,' wrote Ms Brown. Slickness is a sickness.

'It's vital to be unpredictable and slightly moody in interviews,' I, who have spent my life being utterly accommodating, would tell young wannabe actors. 'Throw the question back at them, viz: "Why did you ask me that question?" Take a tape recorder to the interview and turn it on simultaneously with theirs.' Scary Spice will always give better copy than Baby Spice, Jack Nicholson than Tom Cruise, Chris Evans than Cliff Richard, because the interviewer is the one who's anxious to please rather than the other way round. 'For better or worse, the sneer goes down better than the smile.'

One of the reasons why awards ceremonies always seem to get decisions so wrong is because actors rarely appear on judging panels. They're deemed too partisan, too prone to petty jealousies. The actors who are 'actors' actors', those beloved by their peers, are quite different from those admired by the media cognoscenti, because actors tend to know what goes into a performance as well as what comes out. We also know the roles which make the great look so great. The Tom Cruise role in *Rainman* is infinitely more taxing than the Dustin Hoffman one, requiring huge restraint and generosity. A disabled role, be it deafness, blindness, autism or physical handicap, particularly when combined with death (a slow one is good) is Oscar and Bafta material almost without exception. *Forest effing Gump* couldn't f-f-fail.

But nobody chooses to look at how difficult or easy a role is. Playing a king or queen is a piece of gateau because everyone else on stage does the work for you – you know, bowing and scraping and er-hum, my liege-ing – and audiences are so impressed with the actor's uncanny ability to make a monarch have human qualities.

One of the best and most unsung film performances of last year was Laura Linney's, who played the wife in that superb film, *The Truman Show*. If Jim Carey was a lesson in comedy playing, she was the entire curriculum. Bear in mind she was playlng on three levels at once: to the TV audience, the husband, slowly realising his whole life was a TV sit-com, and the puppeteer management behind the scenes. No! Four, if you count the audience in the cinema. There is a scene in a car when she is trying, for the sake of the cameras, to bring him back in line and trying to save her own life at the same time, which is about as good as anything I've ever seen in movie acting. She makes it look easy. Her collapse on the TV set, in the face of his changing the rules of the soap, when she screams, 'It's – It's so unprofessional!', is a definitive moment in a film so stuffed with irony that the Academy Awards panels ironically looked right past it and her.

The *Oklahoma!* reviews were marvellous and Hugh Jackman, who played Curly, was universally praised. But mostly for one thing. His GOOD LOOKS. He is good-looking. He is as good looking as anyone I've ever churned butter on stage next to, but his looks were the second to last thing that mattered in his portrayal of Curly, the curly-headed cowboy. Curly is the definitive workhouse donkey role in a musical. Never off stage, biggest songs, ballet number, fight number, a knackering, occasionally thankless role. 'He was,' said Julia McKenzie, who knows a thing or two about musicals, 'quite simply the best leading man I've ever seen on stage.'

It's not just talent. Everyone in the show had more than they needed in that department. It's talent. Plus. Plus what? Dunno. Joy, maybe – or soul. If I did know, I'd take a contract out on his life, have it bottled and sell it at every centre for media studies in the land.

It's odd how often the word *schadenfreude* is used to describe the predominant feeling of the *zeitgeist*. It's as though the English don't quite have the words to describe cultural unkindness. I will never see a more perfect fusion of actor and part than Peter O'Toole playing the alcoholic journalist Jeffrey Bernard – for once the critics and the public recognised the truth. The night I went, Kevin Spacey was watching it for the fifth time 'It's a masterclass on acting,' he said afterwards. In felt, quite literally, drunk and slightly ill, when I left. I identified so much with the old rogue. Only the great Paul Schofield has ever affected me in that way. 'This is better than any old King Lear,' I said, hugging the fine towering origami figure that was O'Toole. 'Oh fuck King Lear!' bellowed Peter and lit a Camel. It was a life affirming evening about a man slowly killing himself. A roaring battle cry to individual choice and unredeemed eccentricity. His technique was so formidable – speaking in endless subjunctive clauses and parenthesis, seemingly in one breath, whilst lighting and smoking and drinking and refilling and ironing. Dangerously on his toes – unstintingly generous to other actors, vocally varied, filling the glorious Old Vic to the last tier – like Mr Spacey, I'll be back next week for more. And how very sweet that he should triumph so in the scene of his critical crucifixion for Macbeth. Sometimes we fail, sometimes we succeed. It's just a bump, a hiccup, part of a whole life. Just a play. Or just a job? Bring back the word artisan and we'll never be 'luvvies' again.

It Doesn't Add Up

So let me get this right. Winter white is the new grey, gardening is the new cookery and poetry is the new rock 'n' roll. Hope I've got that right. Wouldn't want to be uncool. (I'm delighted that the huge and deserved success of Ted Hughes's *Birthday Letters* and Seamus Heaney's *The Spirit Level* have helped to turn what was often a dessert course into a *plat du jour*.)

There was always something 'nancyish' about liking poetry, even at school, and yet large tracts of it remain lodged in my brain. I can remember almost anything which once made me cry. 'Lord, dismiss us with thy blessing, thanks for all who'll meet no more' had me in shreds at the end of every school term. In my hand was clutched the sealed envelope which, once again, would reveal to my parents that their progeny would do well if she paid as much attention to lessons as she did to doing impersonations of the people giving them.

Still, the mournful sound of 'Those in peril o-o-on the sea' could send me and the rest of my hardened gang into a sentimental slump which lasted right through prayers, locker clearing and trashing of the school bike sheds.

Remedial maths is what I need. Because I'm just beginning to be fascinated by numbers as my days of them dwindle. Sometimes, when I can't drop off to sleep, I make myself do simple sums in my head. It works better than sheep because sheep have faces and you can start giving them personalities and storylines. (The other possibility is getting Jack to tell me about his computer. 'I switch the computer on and put it into Word Perfect by pressing Enter. Then I press Shift F10 to call up my...' Zzzzzz, I'm in Nod.)

But now I'm in maths mode and making exciting discoveries.

228

Like the wonder of the number nine. Can I bore you for a moment? So, I'm doing my nine times table and I get to two times are eighteen when I idly notice that one and eight together equals... nine. And to my naive joy realise that it works right through the tables, i.e. 36, 45, 54, 63, 72, 81, 90, 99, 108, 207, etc. (give and take that 99 is just 9 ... sort of twice. I'm not being too technological for you, am I?)

By now I'm wide awake and believing myself to be the reincarnation of Einstein – because the first five multiples turn out to be the same as the second five BACKWARDS! WOW! 9, 18, 27, 36, 45, yes? Then 54, 63, 72, 81, 90. I'm now wondering if we call 999 for help because it's an easy number to remember or because we are summoning the police by magic. I feel nostalgia for the poetry of my youth and tenderness towards the literature. I feel forlorn about the geography and respectful of the history. About anything scientific or mathematical I feel nothing but shame. It's as if I had an undeclared disability, like chronic incontinence or savage halitosis. At one time I thought it was cute to be the artistic one, the creative one, yes, even the ditsy – 'you add it up, darling, it hurts my little brain' – one, but at 53, it's a problem that's not cute, it's acute.

I am numerically dyslexic. Numbers bounce off my eyes like disco lighting. The left side of my brain is overdeveloped in comparison to the right, compounded by which, I am so bad at not being good at things that I bury my failure in defensive mirth. I roared with laughter at my maths mock O-level result of eight per cent. What the hell was a per cent, anyway? (I've finally learned through 'Service Not Included'.)

There are risible gaps in my times tables around the seven eights and six nines areas and diagrams were like diaphragms – just something a nice girl would never need. And as for 'If a man digs a seven-foot hole in one and a half hours, how long would it take seven men to dig the same hole if they stopped for tea and Bourbon biscuits for fifteen minutes in every hour?' – well, my dears, what in heaven's name was he digging the bloody hole FOR in the first place and couldn't they get a drill? Then I remember the article on Nostradamus, where the ninth minute of the ninth hour of the ninth day of the ninth month of 1999 turns out to be end of life as we know it. Armageddon.

Readers, friends (for, as someone once said, what are friends but God's apology for relatives?) I could have about 30 seconds left to learn perfect French, to get a flat stomach, to say sorry to those poor schoolteachers I tormented, and solve the computer bug. Phew – what a relief! Back to the drawing board, Nostradamus, and back to Paris, Paco Rabanne, who was so convinced the Mir spacecentre would fall on Paris, on that date, that he moved his shoe factories and all his staff to the south of France in preparation. I wonder what shoes one might select for walking back into an abandoned factory, covered in oeuf?

Last Writes

Once a month moon madness descends and I'm driven by deadline to write my article for *Good Housekeeping*. Various editors have been and gone since I took up my position on the back page, and unfailingly they've allowed me freedom of content and style. I write very quickly, often fuelled by some supposed slight or social injustice, and often, after twelve years of column writing, desperate for a topic which will bore the reader slightly less than it bores me. I read the first draft out to Jack, disagree with any suggestions and incorporate most. Hearing it out loud informs me what's wrong more than any editor. I always overwrite and cutting improves any piece immeasurably – well, measurably, however loathe I am to do it.

Meanwhile, I still daydream of writing something that has never happened to me, with characters I've never met. The reality is that although I pretend to have no time to write I'm actually too scared to try. Last Christmas I was due to appear in a Cliff Richard Special and I wrote myself a *Talking Head* about a waitress called Dinah who is an obsessively chatty Cliff Richard fan. Unbeknown to her she is serving tea to Alan Bennett each day and wonders where he gets his ideas from.

I was popping my vest with pride when producer Lisa Clarke accepted it for the show. As it turned out, the only thing special about this particular Special was that Cliff's throat cut out and the show was cancelled. Never mind, one giant step forward, one sort of Cliff-hanger back.

My 'speech drawer' is overflowing with numbered postcards covered with cryptic mnemonics, which are unfathomable to me only days after I've made the speech. 'Know your audience' is my advice to would-be speech givers. Ask the organisers about *who* they are made up of, what their shared interests are – are they Radio 2 or 3 listeners or *Sun* readers? It will make all the difference. Too many times I've turned up accompanied by a tote bag of Jewish jokes and twelve Zelma stories, only to find myself facing 200 people who have come together to decipher the Dead Sea Scrolls and play the clavichord.

One of my folders contains memorial speeches and glancing through it makes me mourn my friends all over again. In fact it reminds me that they're gone because it's so easy to believe they're still around and we just haven't seen them for a while. In a sense, of course they are. Derek Nimmo is hovering somewhere overseeing a production of *How The Other Half Lives* in Jakarta, Michael Denison is pouring a drink for Dulcie somewhere on tour near Bath and Benny Green is telling George and Ira stories in that deli-diner under the Edison Hotel in New York. After speaking at their memorial services, I had a sensational letter from Miriam Karlin, the gist of which was, 'It occurred to me after seeing you on Friday – can I book you for my funeral? I realise your services are much sought after, hence my making what I consider to be a very advanced booking.'

I replied in kind. 'Dear Miss Karlin, Thank you for your enquiry which my secretary has duly noted... Unfortunately I am totally booked until the year 2016. If you can wait till then, which would give us all great pleasure, then I will happily oblige.'

Her reply was a masterstroke... 'I'm afraid I can't hang around even for your first available date. However, should a window of opportunity arise for me to leap through, due to unexpected demise or complete recovery of any of your clients, I do hope you will contact me again. If I do not hear from you within six months, I shall have to seek the alternative services of Claire Raynor or Vanessa Feltz.'

'Just think', she added. 'You won't have to write anything – you can just read out this correspondence.'

Michael Denison died a gentleman's death. He poured his beloved wife a drink, sat down and said, 'You know I love you very much indeed,' then closed his eyes and died. Dulcie Gray has been formidably brave and embarked on an eighteen-week tour of *The Lady Vanishes*. I went to see her give a platform interview at the National Theatre. She was interviewed by Sheridan Morley.

Aged 80, she was sprightly, sharp, humorous and entirely without self-pity. Her life reads like that of a twentieth-century adventuress which is what she is. Sent to boarding school in England from Malaysia, aged four and a half, she next saw her mother when she was fourteen, and spent every holiday as the only girl left behind at school. Back in Malaysia, aged sixteen, she tied the sheets together, *Lettice of the 4th*-style, and escaped to the jungle where she taught native children English. It gets even better on the journey from English governess to international movie star, lepidopterist and distinguished crime writer.

(Afterwards I wrote to *Omnibus* and *The South Bank Show* telling them how superbly she had spoken and how fascinating her life was. Both wrote back thanking me but regretting that there was, unfortunately, no slot for a programme of this kind in their future scheduling. I think of this often when I watch their tributes to Boyzone or Damien Hirst.)

Benny Green died after an impossible struggle against cancer. We had shared his table, his stories and his bonhomie for some years and his death leaves a giant hole in our hearts and particularly in our radio on Sundays, which ever since have felt, without his voice, strangely hollow. Making Benny smile made me prouder than making anyone else laugh, although the only time I ever saw him *cry* with laughter was when Jack played the violin. A few months after he died we sat with his marvellous family and friends in the garden of his St Albans home and watched his son standing beneath the 'chuppah' with his bride, Maya. Like all aspects of our faith, it was bittersweet. I tried to put his qualities down for a memorial concert.

It wasn't just the stories
That were an inspiration,
What Benny really valued
Was the Art of Conversation.

Encyclopaedic knowledge
The mind of an enquirer,
Everything you ever want to know
'Bout George and Ira.

He hated plugs and cars and planes,

He couldn't send a fax,
He loved his kids, adored his wife
Revered his Tenor Sax.

We miss him round the table,
And in his favourite chair,
Especially on a Sunday,
When it's empty on the air.

Still we're rest assured he's smiling
In his place in Happy Valley,
Bending the Almighty's ears
With tales of Tin Pan Alley.

Then Derek Nimmo had his fatal accident, falling down the cellar steps of his Kensington home, slowly regaining consciousness, only to slip away suddenly, leaving a permanent void. Pat, his loving, loyal wife, had been in my dressing room two days before, her only outing after months of day and night care – she came with Geoffrey Palmer and his wife. She was frail and worn but full of hope, and said that for those three hours she had forgotten all her anxiety for the first time. At his memorial, one tiny grandson sang a 'ho-ho' laughing song and another recited a poem which prayed for lots of dinner parties in heaven for 'Gumpy'. Geoffrey Palmer made a superb speech which had the audience laughing tears of recognition.

'I first met Derek forty years ago when we worked together on a BBC children's series. I was a village bobby and Derek was a chimpanzee. He was the least convincing chimpanzee I've ever seen. He went on to star in several TV series and innumerable West End hits.' Long pause. 'Which just goes to show there's no justice in this business.'

I sang 'I Love Life' in a shaky falsetto and everyone repaired to his favourite watering hole, the (still all-male bastion) Garrick Club, to toast the dear old toff on his way. The Actors' Church, St Paul's Covent Garden, was packed inside and out with friends who loved him. It was a brilliant summer's day in the middle of London and everyone was beautifully dressed. The phrase on most people's lips was, 'Damn good turn out – he'd have *loved* it.'

Perhaps the most shattering loss, though, was that of my rabbi and friend, Hugo Gryn. When we heard the news we were at sea – both literally and metaphysically – somewhere between New York harbour and the Caribbean, on our holiday cruise with the Morrows. The last time we'd seen Hugo was when he officiated at his son David's wedding. We knew he was fighting cancer, we knew he'd been through powerful radiotherapy. We knew he was battling and we just assumed, because he was Hugo, that he'd win.

If there was a personal icon, then for me it was Hugo. He'd lived through the Holocaust, been imprisoned in two concentration camps, lost most of his family and arrived in England after the war as a young man. How he began to train for the rabbinate and how he learned his humanity after such a searing start in life is a story which will one day be told. When I met him he was already the rabbi of the leading reform synagogue of England, the West London Reform Shul, and a frequently in-demand speaker and broadcaster, perhaps best known for *The Moral Maze* on Radio 4. He dealt with doubters, dissenters, bigots and Dr David Starkey with the same compassion, humour and kindness with which he dealt with his parishioners.

Hugo contacted me after a zealot *meshuggener* screamed 'blasphemer!' at me during a performance of Martin Sherman's *Messiah* at the Hampstead Theatre Club. 'You'll burn in hell,' he yelled, before being kindly escorted out from the theatre. It was quite a frightening experience. Hugo happened to be in the theatre that night. We had lunch and he comforted me. Lunch with a rabbi? Unheard of. A human being who talked of this and that, (I was worried about my Hull-based dad's ill health at the time and I remember drawing a plan of my house on a napkin and Hugo enthusiastically amending the garage and living room area to become a separate flat.) My husband and I began to attend synagogue more regularly. His sermons were inspirational. The West London ambience was holy. Our kids loved going there. As Jews in a secular world, we did what we *could* to comply with the strictness of Judaism. If I had to light candles in my dressing room on a Friday night then so it was. 'Let us practise tolerance, cherish humanity and celebrate our differences,' said Hugo, and what he preached, he practised.

His sermons were all one-offs. It was like hearing a great orator, great comedian and a great guru all in one. They were always provocatively topical and relevantly ancient. My kids couldn't wait to discuss what he'd been getting at. My parents (cool about the Reform set-up) basked in the warmth of his friendship. For Jack and me he was faith personified and a friend in need. I know he was flawed – I liked him all the more for that – and I miss him.

What bound all these losses together for me was the love and longevity of each relationship and the courage and the beauty in resilience of all those widows. They each had love, interdependence and loyalty. If I ever have to face that moment, I hope to heaven that some kind of plastic bubble descends and gives me inner strength, because I so dread being a sobbing, fainting, buckling woman, unable to participate or register others' empathy. My past record is hardly promising. Any folk remedies for developing a tough outer membrane will be grovellingly received. I'd like it to be similar to the one I read for arthritis, which involved soaking sultanas in gin and eating nine a day. Nine exactly, mind you. I could get great happiness from a cure like that.

Cornwall Eclipsed

We returned to Cornwall a week before the eclipse. There was something warming about being the only people going against the traffic there and back, as indigenous Cornishmen headed out as we headed in, and the rest of the world headed in as we left for home.

We borrowed a house this time. It was on two levels with glass between us and the sea and that was all. White walls, white painted floorboards, wicker and wood, oil paintings reflecting the view and the four of us together for the first time in years.

I bought watercolours and we did the equivalent of Watercolour Challenge, each of us vying to decry our own miserable efforts and praise everyone else's. We played loud games of 'Jenga', pulling rectangles of wood out of a carefully erected pile, Jack losing every game because we made him shake with laughter every time it was his go.

I cooked and loved it. They had a gas stove – it was a gas! We walked into the sea fully clothed – or three of us did – and trekked over the cliffs – or two of us did – and read and wrote lots around the big pine table. We scarcely left the house or Mawgan Porth except to dine regally at Rick Stein's restaurants in Padstow, which were totally worth both the trips and the bills, and once to buy wind chimes in a delightful Japanese Bonsai garden 'customers note this Tea House does not serve tea'. We stopped for a cream tea at the St Mawgan post office and pondered out loud over the notice for 'Horrace', a missing silver tabby who was apparently 'newted'. (Sounds like a perfect pet for Ken Livingstone.) The days were endless and I've never wanted to leave a place less. At the end of a week we left wanting more and made a pact, The Four Just Men, to return every year or face the consequences. We shook hands and headed off – us for home, Amy for Manchester and Adam for Prague.

Still as my mother might, and frequently does, say – if you get the weather, England knocks Fuengirola into a cocked hat.

Back in london I'd forgotten, in spite of 20,000 words a day for the preceding three months, that it was Eclipse Day, and had arranged for a curtain maker to pop round. Five minutes before the event, we were admiring swatches in Adam's bedroom and discussing the impossibility of having a pole and rings in a bay window.

'It's on in five minutes,' yelled Jack up the stairs. 'Hurry up.' I left Mr Pinkus to measure up and went to sit by the TV with Jacquie and Carmela. Jack had made each of us two pieces of cardboard with a hole in one. He tried to explain the workings of this sophisticated astronomical equipment, and I tried really hard to understand him.

'You turn your back to the sun and hold – no, NOT up to your eye – hold it away and look at the shadow on the . . .'

The curtain man was preparing to leave. 'Come and watch the eclipse,' I told him. 'Have my card – I'm watching the telly.'

We watched Michael Buerk being amused, Patrick Moore being gutted and lots of Cornish revellers trying to get their spectacles on the box. Outside Jack called, 'It's getting darker,' before running in to see the TV getting darker too. 'Well, that was the most terrific experience,' said a reveller, wiping his eyes as the thick cloud began to re-emerge. I realised it was over.

Later on, watching the news at six o'clock, I was flummoxed to see that hundreds of people had gone to Alexandra Palace to watch it. 'We should have gone and watched it at Ally Pally,' I groaned. Four thousand people were waxing lyrical about what they'd observed only four minutes from our house.

Later still I realised the daftest thing of all. In our garden we have, courtesy of Adam's youthful obsession with astronomy, an observatory. A working observatory! It has an eight-inch Newtonian reflector in it! Can you believe it? Admittedly, we'd probably all have been somewhat blinded if we'd used it and the trees and clouds have, over the years, made us realise we're never going to see much through it but trees and clouds anyway – but to be sitting indoors, hunched round Michael Buerk when we could have been sharing a once-in-a-lifetime experience is just so typically Rosenthal that I could plug a book on the strength of it. Great moments in history and how I was choosing swags and ties during them.

So it's Madagascar in 2001 for me, I've decided. Book now for fear of disappointment. I can see it now: thousands of tourists with black plastic goggles, TV crews of every nationality, Patrick Moore with a black monocle and I'll be indoors somewhere, fiddling with a very remote remote control, totally lost in a subtitled Bogart/Bacall movie, my astronomical bent totally eclipsed by my need to see her purse her lips and whistle just one more time. In a sense, I'll be lip reading.

Dessert

I hope this book has given you a few inward smiles. I hope it's made one or two of you honk out loud on the District Line. If you've reached this point without a single amused moment then I'm losing my touch, or you're reading the Norwegian version.

Before you consign me to the virtual dumpbin of your local W. H. Watersmiths, remember there are other uses for this book without lasting side effects, viz:

1. It is an excellent width for placing beneath your head whilst lying on the floor to alleviate back pain. Place your feet flat on the floor, knees up, book between neck and skull and try to relax the small of your back into the floor. This is relax, as in sink, let go, drop, rather than jerk, press or crack vertebraes. Your hand, if placed 'twixt floor and lower back should fit neatly in, rather than slide out or be pressed into the shape of a skate in black butter sauce.

2. It can be a doorstop, paperweight, wobbly table leveller or missile for errant adolescent. When recipes say place a weight on a plate to press moisture out of eggplant – this is your man. Or you can stand on it to reach the yoghurt culture you left to grow in the late seventies, beyond your fingertips, in the airing cupboard.

3. If you are in Her Majesty's prison you can remove the inside pages entirely, following the Tim Robbins character in *The Shawshank Redemption* – excellent movie, terrible title, close second to another great film *The Hudsucker Proxy*, and keep your burrowing tools in its interior. If the warder asks why you've been reading the same book for months, tell him you're learning an important new sign language and you are planning a workshop on it later in the year.

Finally, and to sum up and in conclusion, may I assure all ecologically minded readers that this book has been printed using biodegradable, reusable, recycled pulp from man-made, third-generation saplings using non-genetically modified vegetarian organic fertiliser only. This will bring you the purest, most non-invasive low-tar fragrance-free product currently available. This produce contains neither peanuts nor E-additives. It will not damage your health, although it may temporarily imbalance your mind. Neither has it been tested on animals. Only family.

The cover is from an idea from the author's left brain hemisphere, entirely based on Dali's genius and executed by the fine photographer, Richard Horton, in an Islington warehouse. The design was by Andy Wadsworth, whose small son did his Godzilla impersonation through the entire three-hour session. The clothes were hastily culled from Charli of Muswell Hill and are by Sara Sturgeon who does not agree with Zelma that linen is 'disgusting – and it crushes like a rag', and the fruity shoes are from Kate Kuba, also of Muswell Hill and well worth checking out.

My make-up was extraordinarily done by Angela even though I kept telling her the foundation was the wrong colour and saying, 'You can't possibly *still* be painting my lip – they're only two inches across and half an inch down!' And don't worry Ange – the blobby nail polish came out real well!

Otherwise the usual martyrs to the cause are my beloved Zelma and *Good Housekeeping* for allowing me to resuscitate all their best lines, Jacquie Granditer, my assistant, for deciphering, typing, sorting and heading off posses at the pass. And Lorna Russell who took over the editor's job on this book on her first day at Robson's, went very thin very quickly, did a terrific job and still speaks to me.

Before *Lip Reading* this book was going to be called *Bonne Mo's*, before that it was *Anything In The Pipeline?* – a title derived from a) Zelma's inevitable question in the last week of every job I've ever had in 32 years and b) the intoxicating honour, last year, of having a 236-tonne tunnelling machine, a sewage device, in Hull named after me. The local kids apparently picked 'Maureen' 'cos it rhymes with 'boring.'

Then, I looked up 'lip reading' in the dictionary and it said 'gathering what a person says by watching the movement of the lips', which didn't really describe what I had in mind. Of course if you add lippy (slang), 'insolence, impudent talk' and lippein (Scots), 'to trust, rely, depend,' (adj.) unguarded, and lippitude, 'soreness of the eyes' and lippie, 'an old Scottish dry measure, the fourth part of a peck', and lipography, 'a writing from which something is omitted', and lipoid, 'a fat like substance', and biting one's lips to show annoyance or disappointment, and lip-service 'to show professed respect', Lippies loop, 'to travel in loops' – 'Lipshtick' which is more or less what I do I reckon, we've got it in eleven.

I leave you, inevitably, with a joke which is almost clean. Billy is going to his first day at big school. His mother tells him that he is a big boy now and shouldn't use baby words any more. 'We don't say moo cows or toothy peg or eggy peg, darling. We call them cows and teeth and eggs, don't we? 'cos we're a big boy now.'

Billy comes home happily from his first day at school and his proud mother asks him how it went.

'It was good,' says Billy.

'And what did you do at school?'

'The teacher said we could choose any book we did want from the bookcase.'

'And what book did you choose, darling?'

'I did choose *Winnie the Shit.*'